THE LOST
OLYMPIAN
OF THE
SOMME

THE FORGOTTEN STORY OF FREDERICK KELLY
AND THE HOOD BATTALION

THE LOST OLYMPIAN OF THE SOMME

EDITED BY JON COOKSEY
AND GRAHAM MCKECHNIE

BLINK

bringing you closer

Published by Blink Publishing
3.25 The Plaza,
535 King's Road,
Chelsea Harbour,
London, SW10 0SZ

www.blinkpublishing.co.uk

facebook.com/blinkpublishing
twitter.com/blinkpublishing

978-1-910536-70-4

Design by www.envydesign.co.uk

Printed and bound by Clays Ltd, St Ives Plc

1 3 5 7 9 10 8 6 4 2

Text copyright © Jon Cooksey and Graham McKechnie, 2015
Text © Frederick Septimus Kelly

First published as Kelly's War by Blink Publishing in 2015

Paperback edition published by Blink Publishing in 2016

Papers used by Blink Publishing are natural, recyclable products made from wood grown in sustainable forests. The manufacturing processes conform to the environmental regulations of the country of origin.

Every reasonable effort has been made to trace copyright holders of material reproduced in this book, but if any have been inadvertently overlooked the publishers would be glad to hear from them.

Blink Publishing is an imprint of the Bonnier Publishing Group
www.bonnierpublishing.co.uk

CONTENTS

SOMME

FOREWORD

BY STEVE WILLIAMS

Double Olympic Rowing Gold Medallist
Athens (2004) and Beijing (2008)

I have always tried to show the utmost respect for those that have died fighting for our country. I am sure, just like you, I have always worn my poppy proudly and watched the ceremonies at the Cenotaph with reverence. When I was part of the British Olympic Rowing Team, training stopped for nothing; nothing that is apart from one minute every year in November. At 11.00am on Remembrance Sunday, halfway through our second session, the cox would call the crew to 'Easy', then 'Drop' as eight oars fell to the water as one. For a moment we paused our relentless pace, the boat drifting in the river, our chests heaving and our backs steaming into the cold air, and made our own act of tribute.

At those times, I always felt the best way I could pay my respects was to imagine what it must have been like for the men and women who bravely stepped up to their country's call. What would it be like to row the boat to the dock right now, leave home, forego family and give up everything I loved in life to go and fight, even die, for my country? However hard I tried to imagine what that would be like, I never felt I could come close. Should I be feeling injustice, tragedy, honour, or all of these?

When I was asked to be involved in a BBC radio documentary following the diaries of Frederick Kelly, or Cleg to his friends [after Samuel Rutherford Crockett's 1896 novel, *Cleg Kelly: Arab of the City*], I had mixed feelings. I had always been fascinated by history, World War history in particular: I remember at school listening in disbelief to stories of young men storming recruitment offices and squeezing on to packed trains heading for the front line in the early frenzy for adventure. I have always been transfixed by the black and white wartime photos, as I stare into the drawn faces and sunken eyes of the men, marching across muddy moonscapes or sitting in those bleak trenches.

To follow Kelly's diaries and to visit the battlefields, accompanied by the editors of this book, Jon Cooksey and Graham McKechnie, was undoubtedly a privileged opportunity to find out more about the war and one of its great heroes. The roles were made very clear from the outset: Jon and Graham were there for the dates and facts, I was there to bring all of this to life for the listener through my own emotional journey. I didn't like to say to Jon and Graham that they were unlikely to get much emotion out of me. As Olympic rowers, we are drilled to overcome a lot of the emotional side of performing in the biggest race of our lives, in order to be able to think clearly and execute excellently. I was to be the conduit into Kelly's story for the listener, but what if I couldn't find, or simply didn't have the emotion to do it justice? What if I let everyone down: Jon, Graham, the listeners, but most importantly Cleg Kelly?

In fact, Kelly's and my life had already been closely linked for many years, for not only is Cleg a war hero, he is also a hero of the rowing world. I had joined Leander Club in Henley-on-Thames, the most successful rowing club in the world, at the beginning of my international rowing career, just as Cleg had done, and from that moment I had always looked up to the names of our Olympic legends on the honours board in the clubhouse. Would I have what it takes to have my name up there? The name of 'F S Kelly' is up there in gold letters forever, having won at the 1908 Olympics; Cleg's name, his rank, his honours and unit (LT. CMDR. F S Kelly DSC RNVR) are also on the memorial board to those Leander members lost in the two World Wars; and it is also on the trophy of the Stewards' Challenge Cup that we both won at Henley Royal Regatta, precisely 100 years apart.

I had also spent much of my rowing life right next door to Cleg's home, Bisham Grange, at the English Institute of Sport's High Performance Centre based at Bisham Abbey. Immediately as you drive out of Bisham, there is a tall cross on a grassy fork in the road. I must have driven past that cross over a thousand times, always curious but, I'm ashamed to say, never stopping to take a closer look at it – there always seemed to be a rush on to get back to Henley for the next rowing session. I eventually did stop at the cross, when Graham and I visited Bisham Grange, and I discovered the cross had been put up by Cleg's family in honour of him and his fellow fallen comrades.

Cleg and I trained from the same club, raced on the same water, won the same trophies and now both of us had our names in gold on the Leander honours board; but as close as our two lives had been, until I was introduced to Cleg's diaries, I hadn't fully recognised it. There was no reason why the name F S Kelly should stand out any more than the other names on the trophies and clubhouse boards.

All that started to change from the moment Graham took me to the River and Rowing Museum in Henley and I held a 1908 Olympic Gold Medal. There was no way of telling if this one was Cleg's and, next to my modern-day Olympic medals from Athens and Beijing, it was tiny, but none of this mattered; all of a sudden, 100 years disappeared and I knew Cleg because we had dreamed about, been driven by and pushed ourselves to the same goal.

I need not have worried about feeling emotionally connected to Cleg's story. In Gallipoli, my stomach turned as I faced the impregnable cliffs that Cleg was sent up against. In northern France, I was shaken by the frightening closeness of the two opposing trench lines and the impossible higher ground that Cleg had to attack. Through Cleg's diaries I discovered an exceptionally talented young man – Kelly was also a concert pianist, but here the similarities between us end – and felt his pain as he was cheated out of his dreams. I came to admire a proud and courageous man who was battered by the unrelenting horrors of war, but never beaten.

Retracing Cleg's steps across his final battlefield – which we could do chillingly accurately through other accounts and the still remaining scars in the land where the German trench lines had been – more than anything left me numb, with some self-searching questions. In rowing, we come to believe that at the Olympics the stakes are life and death; of course they are not, they can only ever be the most important thing in life. For Cleg it was life and death.

Ultimately the emotion of it struck me later in the day at the war cemetery where Kelly is buried. Graham and Jon had gone on to find Kelly's grave and left me in the car listening to Cleg's Piano Sonata. Kelly, ever the perfectionist and perpetually self-critical, is finally writing something he is proud of; I am sure he is outpouring the torture of war, the keys of the piano are being thrashed, it is a sweltering day but I have all the doors and windows shut to hear the full intensity of the music as it crescendos – it is stiflingly hot but I am totally absorbed in the music.

Then all of a sudden the notes stop coming. I start fumbling with the stereo controls thinking something has broken, probably overheated: I suddenly realise it is unbearably hot in here. I manage to rewind a little way and begin to replay again, but the same thing is happening.

And then it hits me. Cleg has been writing his sonata almost up to the morning of his final battle, in a moment of rare respite away from the front line. The notes stop. And so does Cleg.

I have to get out of the car. I walk into the cemetery but not to find Jon and Graham, I need some time by myself. I stand in the shade of a tall tree and am faced by rows and rows of sand-coloured headstones. I do not remember the last time I cried, probably falling over as a kid. I did not cry that day but my eyes welled up, my knees went weak, the cemetery began to spin and the sweat on my back and arms turned to ice.

I have always been fascinated by the war stories: the dates, the statistics, the black and white photos, the grainy, staccato footage of men marching and going over the top, but it is only through getting so close to one personal story do I start to fathom the enormity of the loss – it is crushing. Every single one of these graves – and hundreds of thousands more – stands for a personal story like Cleg's.

Cleg Kelly's diary tells a phenomenal story; it is a story of tragedy, of wasted life and talent, but above all it is a story of courage and honour.

INTRODUCTION

BY JON COOKSEY AND
GRAHAM MCKECHNIE

There were many ways in which men sought to escape the grim realities of the First World War, but few did it as spectacularly as Frederick Septimus Kelly. This most remarkable of men staged a performance of Tchaikovsky's *1812 Overture* in a wood not far from the front line in France. The audience of soldiers heard the famous climax to the stirring music as Tchaikovsky intended it: 'all guns firing like hell'.

The roar of the cannon was real, provided by the 18-pounders of a British artillery battery, raining down a deadly bombardment on the nearby German trenches. The military band performed with gusto rather than expertise. At its centre the conductor, in full military uniform complete with gloved hands and sporting a thick, black beard was fulfilling a long-held ambition. And what a spectacle it must have been for those who saw and heard this extraordinary concert. Tchaikovsky's cannons are fired in celebration of Russia's victory over Napoleon but in this wood on the Western Front it was a defiant proclamation of the victory of art over reality; of one man's spirit that refused to be crushed despite all that he had suffered over the past 18 months. The conductor was Frederick Kelly, a man who was not going to be beaten.

This is the war diary of a very unusual but very likeable man. Who else would have the audacity to stage such a concert? Kelly was the sort of man who would also use the songs of Wagner to entice German soldiers to surrender; who could sit in a trench and find the inspiration to compose beautiful melodies and phrases; who could be harsh to the men in those trenches, while taking excessive care of stray cats found on the battlefield. And he was the sort of man who inspired the respect of those who served with him, and the love and devotion of his many friends. Eccentric, defiant, rebellious, haughty and brilliant: there are many words which spring to mind when you read the diary of Frederick Kelly, and you cannot help but like him.

This is a war diary, but not written by a professional soldier, far from it. It is written by a man who had already achieved a great deal by the time he came to that wood. In a characteristically modest entry on his 35th birthday in May 1916, Kelly gloomily compares his accomplishments to those of Beethoven's at the same age. But Kelly had already led an extraordinary life in different fields: in music as a concert pianist and composer, in sport as an Olympic champion, and in his friendships with people of power and influence.

Yet it is Kelly as an observer of some of the twentieth century's most significant events and the characters who shaped them which makes his diary such an illuminating read. Kelly fought in two of the twentieth century's most appalling military campaigns: Gallipoli and the Somme. He is a reliable witness – factual, accurate, critical and sensitive. He rarely shows us his feelings. When he does and the emotional straightjacket is cast aside, you feel privileged to have been allowed to see the depth of his emotion. At other times he cuts a rather comic figure; out of time and baffled by the world around him. This is first and foremost a war diary, but it is so much more than that in coming from the pen of an endlessly fascinating, eccentric and enigmatic man. As such it is unique.

INTRODUCTION

Frederick Kelly was born in Australia on 29 May 1881, the seventh child (hence 'Septimus') and fourth son of an Irish immigrant, Thomas Hussey Kelly, who had made his fortune in wool and in mining gold and copper. Sydney was his home for the early years of his life. In what must have been a comfortable childhood in a city still in its infancy, the young Kelly showed signs of musical talent – it was said he could play Mozart sonatas from memory at the age of five – which began to flourish while attending Sydney Grammar School from the age of ten. Australia may have been the land of his birth, but the Kelly family were, in their outlook and attitude, impeccably of the British Empire and in 1893 they sailed back to the mother country for Kelly – known as Sep to his family – to be educated in the ancient halls of Eton College.

Kelly's musical education continued at Eton but with the ethos of muscular Christianity at the heart of a public school education in late-Victorian England, it was there that sport became a dominant force in his life. He enjoyed tennis, fives (hand tennis) and football, but it was not on the famous playing fields where he excelled. Kelly was a 'wet bob', rowing for the Eton eight in 1897. At the Henley Royal Regatta the following year he sat in the stroke seat (the most important position in the boat) as the Eton crew won the Ladies' Challenge Plate – a competition open to crews from academic institutions. This was the first of Kelly's many triumphs at the world's most important regatta. Kelly saw no conflict between the pursuit of excellence in sport as opposed to art, telling 'The Sportsman' for a volume on British rowers and yachtsman prior to 1914 that 'a love of outdoor sport, vigorous games, or of travel is by no means a hindrance to the more purely intellectual or artistic pursuits'. For the next ten years rowing and music would vie for Kelly's attention.

From Eton Kelly took the well-trodden path to Oxford University, winning a musical scholarship to Balliol College. A fourth-class degree in Modern History is an indication that his academic work lost the battle for his attention to music and rowing. He gained his Blue in 1903, rowing for Oxford in the Boat Race in the crew that lost by six lengths to Cambridge, but it was in the solitary discipline of sculling that he particularly excelled. Kelly won the prestigious Diamond Challenge Sculls at the Regatta three times, in 1902, 1903 and in 1905 with a course-record time that stood for 33 years. There were other successes at Henley too – three consecutive Grand Challenge Cups from 1903 with the Leander Club Eight and a Stewards' Cup in a four in 1906. But as a contemporary recalled, Kelly was no 'pot-hunter' – a gentleman of the time was hardly concerned with such trivialities as trophies.

The manner of the race was what mattered – the same observer noting that 'his style cannot ever be surpassed'; the *Eton College School Register* prosaically talks of his boat being 'a live thing under him' such was his poise and rhythm, while the *Manchester Guardian* observed: 'Kelly did not bang his slide back like a professional and finish with an ugly independent heave of the body. His swinging and sliding were perfect in unison and symmetry...the grace with which his hands left the body at the finish of the stroke, was like the downward beat of a swallow's wing. The whole thing was so astonishingly easy that at first sight it was impossible to believe in the pace of the boat. His bodily appearance and his impassive ways also deceived you as to the bodily strength. He seemed so pale and delicate, and his movements were so quiet and facile, that it was only when you had seen his leg drive that you appreciated the weight and wiry strength and boniness of the man. Altogether he was a fit subject for legend in his surprises.'

Victories at Henley Royal Regatta mattered a great deal, but it was Olympic titles that elevated rowing to a higher level of sporting consciousness, as it does today. Kelly had spent five years furthering his musical studies at the Dr Hoch *Konservatorium* in Frankfurt but it was the chance of settling an old rowing score which drew him back to England. He noticed in *The Times* that the Canadian sculler L F Scholes would be competing at the 1908 Olympic Games in London. Scholes had beaten Kelly after he reportedly set off too fast and was 'rowed out' – almost coming to standstill – in the Diamond Sculls in 1904. His 'fighting spirit' was rekindled and with just over two months to prepare for the Games, he set about the task with his customary single-mindedness. The rematch with Scholes never came about. Kelly ultimately accepted an invitation to row in a veteran Leander Eight (known as 'The Old Crocks') who were representing Great Britain.

Despite a great deal of customary anxiety from Kelly, the Olympic Regatta of 1908 – held on the stretch of water at Henley that he knew so well – proved to be his greatest sporting achievement. The Belgian crew was well beaten in the final by two lengths. Amid much rejoicing, even Kelly broke his teetotalism for the evening, although while most people celebrated at a dance in Henley Town Hall, it was all too much for Kelly who instead went back to the clubhouse to write a letter. That 1908 Olympic Final proved to be Kelly's last competitive race. He was an Olympic champion. That goal had been achieved. Now it was time to concentrate on his music once more.

Kelly's diaries from 1908 to 1914 cover his progress as a musical scholar, performer and composer in great detail and have been edited skilfully by the Australian musicologist Dr Thérèse Radic. The present diaries are about his war service, yet it is important to reflect on his musical development by the time he went to war. He threw himself back into music after the London Olympics and spent three years refining his technique and temperament as a concert pianist. As an amateur Kelly performed at countless concerts at country houses, parties and festivals working towards his professional debut. He took the big step in the country of his birth in 1911, performing Beethoven's Piano Concerto No. 4 at Sydney Town Hall. It was the first of a series of concerts Kelly gave in Australia which were generally well received. This was a satisfactory start for a young professional pianist but greater challenges lay ahead when he returned to face the English musical press in 1912.

It is fair to say that by the time war broke out, Kelly was showing potential as a concert pianist. There were reviews which could at best be described as lukewarm. 'There is every reason to hope', said *The Times*, 'that Mr Kelly's evident powers of expression will expand with increased experience'. Others were less kind and a pattern was set which was to last through his short professional career. A low-point came in September 1912, when Kelly froze during a concert at The Queen's Hall, London, in the annual Proms series of performances, a public disaster which surpassed his calamity in the 1904 Diamond Sculls. It is a wonder that such an anxious, highly-sensitive man ever managed to perform again but he did, sporadically, for the next two years before the events of the summer of 1914 brought his professional career to an abrupt halt.

While Kelly's focus in the years leading up to the outbreak of the First World War was on performance, he continued to compose music throughout the period. The body of work which we have from this period, like his career as a concert pianist, can best be described as showing his unfulfilled potential by the outbreak of war. He left vocal and instrumental pieces, largely for the piano but also some for strings. It is for more learned music scholars to judge the quality of his composition, but contemporaries again spoke of what might have been, how there was 'charm and delicate inspiration' but that he was a man still trying to find his own distinct voice. As with so many artists of his generation, it would be what he experienced at war which would send his music soaring above anything he had previously written. In December 1907, Kelly had written in his diary that it was his intention to become a 'great player and a great composer'. By the outbreak of war, he was yet to be either – the area of his life in which greatness had truly been achieved was in rowing.

What also makes Kelly such a remarkable diarist is the world he inhabited, both before and during the First World War. He was extraordinarily well-connected, sitting comfortably within the upper echelons of society. When war was declared in August 1914, how many other young men could head to 10 Downing Street to seek advice about which corps they should join? Kelly did just that, with the Prime Minister, Herbert Asquith, and his Secretary of State for War, Lord Kitchener, both in the next room.

Kelly was also a wealthy man, something which apparently troubled him, living a very comfortable life at Bisham on the banks of the Thames and on Queen Anne Street in London. He was a proud man of the British Empire, born in Australia but undoubtedly shaped by England and its great institutions, its culture, its society in which he moved, and its geography – the rivers and countryside he loved so much. Yet there is a sense that he was also an outsider – a colonial whose Irish father had made the fortune which enabled Kelly to glide through Edwardian society. Like a character in a novel, Kelly stands on the sidelines, observing some of the century's most significant events and people at close quarters. He had friends who were more brilliant scholars, performers, composers and soldiers, but they took to him and accepted him as a loyal and trusted friend.

It is the friendships which form, develop and die which are some of the great features of Kelly's diary. Within the Royal Naval Division (RND), and in particular the Hood Battalion, was a very unusual collection of brilliant men – intellectuals, artists, sportsmen – all thrown together to take part in what seemed to them in 1914 as a tremendously exciting adventure. Kelly and his friends within the Hood became known as the 'Latin Club' – a reflection of the high-mindedness that they were not ashamed to flaunt. Of the group, the three of greatest interest to Kelly's story are Arthur Asquith – always known to Kelly as 'Ock' – the third son of the Prime Minister; a remarkable fellow-colonial Bernard Freyberg from New Zealand and Rupert Brooke, the emerging superstar of English poetry, loved and adored by many, including Kelly. The diary is punctuated by reference to these intense friendships and others which Kelly made during the war, and when they are broken Kelly's reserve gives way to moments of great emotional lucidity and outpourings of grief.

Therein lies one of the contradictions of Kelly's personality: the conflict between the Edwardian reserve and the artistic temperament. Despite the conformity of many aspects of his life, Kelly has the capacity to surprise. He is at times a man of great warmth and compassion, but at others – particularly when writing of men under his command or of officers he considers to be shirkers – he can appear harsh in his judgements. The enormous self-discipline and drive which he harnessed to become an Olympic champion and a concert pianist meant that Kelly, according to Asquith, could be 'too austere to be generally palatable to his subordinates'. He can seem baffled by the behaviour of the rank and file, at other times disapproving of their tastes.

Two incidents illustrate the relationship between Kelly and his men: one tragic, one comic. In June 1915, when Kelly writes of his annoyance with the men who, under heavy Turkish fire, refused to leave the trench and charge towards the deadly guns, there is an absence of compassion or understanding. Six months later he notes the surprise of his men at Christmas when he gathers them round to pass on his 'expressions of goodwill': they had been expecting another dressing down for 'some breach of discipline or absence of gear'.

Kelly's relationship with those who served under him was clearly complex. Any respect he acquired as a military leader of men was earned by the example he set on the battlefield. He was, according to Arthur Asquith, 'as brave as a lion, aware and utterly contemptuous of all risks, he commanded the confidence and respect of all under his command'. Asquith also observed that soldiering did not come naturally to him, but that he set about it with the same single-mindedness he had shown in the other aspects of his life and he met with similar success.

Yet there is a vulnerability to Kelly which is not only expressed in his grief at the loss of men such as Brooke. Given his earlier treatment at the hands of the music critics, it is unsurprising to find him almost craving the approval of his peers for his music when home on leave. Friends considered him to be highly-strung and argumentative. As a pianist he was aware that he had to work on mastering his nerves, seeking help to overcome a twitch in the muscles of his jaw as well as a sense of weakness in his arms. To strangers he could appear blunt to the point of rudeness and his waspishness is evident in his diary. Others talk of his warmth and his absolute loyalty. But what his diary also reveals is Kelly's enormous sense of fun. It was perhaps something he felt the need to conceal to maintain the image of a serious intellectual and musician, but be it go-kart racing or blowing up unexploded shells for the unadulterated fun and sheer excitement of it all, there is an endearing boyishness to Kelly even when his surroundings were bleak.

Throughout his time in the trenches Kelly is able to cling on to elements of his past life to help him endure the misery. At Gallipoli he takes every opportunity to bathe in the Aegean – 'swimmers into cleanness leaping' as he says, quoting Brooke. He reads prolifically: Moliere, Shakespeare, Racine – all are his companions. He revels in the natural world even when on leave on the Greek islands, noting birdsong in the trenches. Above all else though, it is his music that continually frees him from the drudgery and the misery. Kelly seeks out the opportunity to play a piano whenever and wherever he can; he and his comrades sing together; to his delight he conducts the regimental band. He lives by Rudyard Kipling's mantra of 'Melody for the mind and rhythm for the body'. And despite the deep sorrow and unimagined horror around him, he is inspired to compose his greatest work, the *Elegy for Strings*, 'In Memoriam Rupert Brooke'. In one of the most evocative entries in October 1916 Kelly visits Thiepval Wood, walking through the appalling desolation of 'mangled' corpses and 'glazed eyes'. He muses on the conflict between art and reality and despite describing himself as callous, is haunted by the tragic scene. Yet the next day he is writing the ethereal harp part for his *Elegy* for Rupert Brooke, partly to escape the war, partly because it was his uncomfortable inspiration. Whichever is the case, it is an astonishing achievement.

Nevertheless as friends and comrades are picked off one-by-one, the diary takes on an increasingly despondent tone. One of the saddest passages sees Kelly reflecting on his lack of emotion when seeing a dead man and the ease with which he returned to his lunch. Kelly increasingly shows signs of what today might be diagnosed as obsessive compulsive disorder, brushing his teeth 12 times a day, wearing white gloves as he dislikes getting his hands dirty and developing a comic fascination with cats and kittens which he carries around with him in sandbags.

There is a great deal to enjoy and admire about Frederick Septimus

Kelly. He was a brilliant man who would surely have gone on to reach the heights to which he aspired as a composer, perhaps even surpassing the achievements of other Great War soldier/composers such George Butterworth, who has received posthumous critical acclaim. Unlike so many of his contemporaries, however, it is his all-round achievements which make him such a singular man – Olympic champion, composer, pianist, intellectual, leader of men and diarist. His story is a tale of daring, courage, tragedy and lost potential. 'He was a man of extraordinary vitality and physique, and of great powers which had only begun to mature and to find their unison and harmony', according to his first editor, Arthur Asquith, in the *Balliol College War Memorial Book*: 'Time alone was wanting.'

Jon Cooksey and Graham McKechnie
Stratford-upon-Avon and Whilton
April 2015

WAR AND THE ROYAL NAVAL DIVISION

AUGUST 1914–FEBRUARY 1915

'Has anybody here seen Kelly?'

*L*ike thousands of other men after Britain's declaration of war on Germany on 4 August 1914, Frederick Kelly was determined to join up and do his bit. But his route to enlistment was anything but ordinary.

Rather than heading to the nearest recruitment office, Kelly set out from his house at Bisham on the banks of the Thames and went to 10 Downing Street for advice from his friend Maurice Bonham Carter – the prime minister's personal private secretary. So began a frustrating few weeks for Kelly as he tried to join the army. Firstly he was rejected by the Inns of Court Corps which only wanted men with some military experience, then by the prestigious Grenadier Guards. On 3 September Kelly was accepted by the newly-formed University and Public Schools Corps but his time with them was to be short-lived. Word reached Kelly that a new formation called the Naval Brigade was seeking men without experience for commissions. Less than a fortnight later he learned that his application to the RND had been successful.

The RND would suit Kelly very well indeed. It was one of Winston Churchill's more brilliant and innovative schemes; a unit without precedent in its formation and make-up. As First Lord of the Admiralty, he recognised *that there would be some 20– 30,000 sailors for whom there would be no room on any ship of war when the navy mobilised and he was instrumental in the decision to use these men as a fighting force on land. At the time Britain had a relatively small army of just six divisions, with two more being gathered up from the outposts of the empire.*

Secretary of State for War Lord Kitchener knew that a long war was inevitable and vast numbers of men would be required. He also knew that the tens of thousands of eager volunteer citizen soldiers who had answered his call to join Kitchener's New Army would not be ready for battle for many months. The offer of a large force of trained men in the first few weeks of the war – sailors fighting on land as soldiers – was seized upon with alacrity by the War Office.

'Winston's Little Army', as the RND became known, was made up of volunteers like Kelly and officers, men, stokers and sailors from the Royal Naval Volunteer Reserve (RNVR), Royal Fleet Reserve (RFR) and Royal Naval Reserve (RNR). Despite being land-based and closer to the army, it retained naval traditions such as the use of naval language and nautical terms, retained naval ranks and even allowed full beards, unlike their army counterparts who had to make do with moustaches.

In a stroke of creative ingenuity, which ensured the development of strong and lasting bonds and an enviable esprit de corps, each of the naval infantry battalions went by the name of a famous British admiral – Drake, Hawke, Benbow, Collingwood, Nelson, Howe, Hood and Anson – and each marine battalion by the name of its Depot port, Portsmouth Battalion being one example. Churchill procured the services of a sprinkling of regular officers, mostly from Guards regiments, to command or act as adjutants to these naval battalions. He also advertised for a number of officers aged from 25 to 35 years at a time when the War Office wanted no untrained officers who were over 30. Kelly certainly felt uneasy when he arrived at his training camp to be pitched amongst several professional officers. Several thousand recruits, largely Tyneside miners and men from Scotland who could not be absorbed by the New Armies, were later added to the fold of the RND.

As regards its officers, never before or since can such a stellar group of high-

achievers have been assembled in one cadre of the British military. The RND attracted many men of high social standing – the sons of peers, adventurers, artists and famous explorers – considered to be amongst the most brilliant of their generation. Of these the poet Rupert Brooke was the best-known – and would become enormously famous in the coming months – but there was also his close friend, the composer, pianist and critic William Denis Browne, the brilliant intellectual Patrick Shaw-Stewart, the prime minister's son Arthur Asquith, diplomat The Honourable Charles Lister and British-born New Zealander and warrior Bernard Freyberg. There was also a cousin of Churchill, the charismatic young American Johnny Dodge. These men were to become hugely significant figures in Kelly's life and their names frequently appear in his diary. Together with their men – the ratings – they would go on to blaze an illustrious trail in British military history as a hard-fighting, elite unit. 'By their conduct in the forefront of the battle, by their character, and by the feats of arms which they performed,' Winston Churchill noted in the official history of the RND, 'they raised themselves into that glorious company of the seven or eight most famous Divisions of the British Army in the Great War... and their contribution will be identified and recognized a hundred years hence'.

But all that lay ahead. Kelly's days as a civilian were over. For a man who had so far lived and breathed music it was now time for him to learn the art of war.

Wednesday, 16 September 1914 – 29 Queen Anne Street, London

I received a communication by the first post from the Admiralty, addressed to Sub Lieutenant F S Kelly, informing me I had been appointed to the '*Victory*' [the RND shore station at Crystal Palace not Nelson's famous ship] and telling me to hold myself ready to repair to my duties accordingly!! I called for The Hon Francis Robert Henley at 49, Montague Square at 10.00am and we went to the parade of the UPS Corps [University and Public Schools Brigade], behind Knightsbridge Barracks to inform the CO (Captain Henderson) of the fact that we had received commissions in the RNVR.

After doing so, I spent the morning at the Union Club reading *The Times*, in which there were the speeches of the Debate on the Home Rule Bill, during which the whole of the Opposition left the House. I ordered my uniform at Daniels in Bury Street and went on to tea at the Bath Club with Charles Francis Meade.

At 9.30pm I went to the Ship restaurant in Whitehall to meet Eddie Marsh and William Denis Browne with whom were Rupert Brooke and a man called Mallory, an admirer of Jelly d'Arányi. Eddie Marsh had to return to the Admiralty shortly, but I went on with the others to Oddenino's [on Regent Street] for a glass of beer. Denis Browne came on to 29 Queen Anne Street to see Golden, with whom he is arranging to take his place as organist at Guy's Hospital, while he is serving in the RNVR.

Classical scholar, translator and career civil servant, Edward Marsh served as secretary or assistant private secretary to such political heavyweights as Winston Churchill and Arthur Asquith's father Herbert Asquith when the latter served as prime minister until December 1916.

Thirty-seven-year-old The Honourable Francis Robert Henley was a Balliol College man like Kelly, albeit he had been at Oxford a few years earlier. Born the son of Anthony Henley, 3rd Baron Henley of Chardstock and Clare Campbell Lucy Jekyll, he had been educated at Harrow School before going up to Oxford in 1896. He graduated in 1900 with a Bachelor of Arts followed by a Master of Arts in 1904.

Like Kelly he fought as a sub lieutenant with the RND at Gallipoli, caught enteric fever, was Mentioned in Despatches but left in January 1916 to take up duties in the Ministry of Munitions. He succeeded to the title of 6th Baron Henley of Chardstock in Dorset in 1925 and that of 4th Baron Northington of Watford, Northampton in the same year. In December 1925 he changed his name to Francis Robert Eden. He died in April 1962 at the age of 85.

Charles Francis Meade was a mountaineer who had climbed in the Alps and Himalayas, went on to serve in the First World War and wrote several books on climbing in the 1940s and 1950s. The Mallory mentioned by Kelly was George Mallory another Alpine mountaineer. A contemporary of Rupert Brooke at Cambridge, Mallory was teaching at Charterhouse School and moving in Brooke's circle, which included the writer Lytton Strachey, artist Duncan Grant and other members of the Bloomsbury Group when Kelly met him in 1914. Mallory famously perished on the north-east ridge of Everest with his climbing partner Andrew 'Sandy' Irvine in 1924. They disappeared, some 800 vertical feet from the summit, during their attempt to make the first ascent of the mystical mountain. His body was not found until 1999.

Friday, 18 September 1914 – 29 Queen Anne Street, London

I travelled down to Walmer with Francis Henley, Denis Browne and Rupert Brooke by the 9.15am train from Victoria. On arrival there we separated as the two latter had been allotted to the 2nd Brigade of the RNVR at Betteshanger while Henley and I made our way to the camp overlooking the sea. We first saw Commodore [Wilfred] Henderson who directed us to Captain [Arthur Hope] Travers…and we had lunch with him in the mess. When it transpired that we had had no military training it didn't seem to me that we were very welcome new arrivals, however Travers gave us a list of things to get and we caught the 3.30pm train from Walmer after taking a walk in Deal.

It was a fresh windy day and the Channel was a wonderful mixture of colours; there were a good many sailing ships off Deal and a cruiser and a torpedo boat. The sight of the tents and the efficient life going on within made a very pleasing impression on me. There was a naval funeral going on in Deal and the strains of the 'Dead March' from *Saul* [by George Frideric Handel] of a band affected me a good deal.

Monday, 21 September 1914 — 29 Queen Anne Street, London

Rupert Brooke dined with me at the Union Club and we were joined for part of the evening by his younger brother and another King's man, Cook, an ardent young Liberal who struck me as being a little quicker at assuming decided points of view than in substantiating them.

Rupert Brooke is very nice, sensible and mature in all his views.

Tuesday, 22 September 1914 – Walmer Camp, Kent

I travelled down to Walmer with Francis Henley, and we drove a fly [horse-drawn carriage] he had ordered to the naval camp. We arrived at the officers' mess somewhat late for dinner. The adjutant kindly saw to our wants in our tent, which Henley and I share, and we started turning in at 10.00pm. To hear the bugles and sentries shouting out 'halt, hands up', gives one quite an air of being in a scene of one of Shakespeare's historical plays.

Wednesday, 23 September, 1914 – Drake Battalion, Naval Camp, Walmer

We spent a very cold night in our tent – the cold coming from underneath our camp bedsteads. It was a lovely warm day, however. A Marine sergeant was told off [instructed] to teach Henley and myself Musketry Drill, both in the morning and afternoon. We were up at 7.00am and watched the men doing exercises. We were off duty from 4.00pm and at 5.00pm we walked in to Lower Walmer and Deal to get a table, chair and other necessaries for our tent, I wrote some letters beforehand. I spent the evening with Henley, [Lieutenant Edwin Dennis Picton] Pinks and a naval commander or captain in the ante-room. This first day of our new life has left a very pleasant impression.

Edwin Pinks had been in the service since 1905. Promoted to lieutenant in the RNVR in August 1914, he had been posted to A Company of the Drake Battalion. He would go on to serve with the Drake in Gallipoli where, in June 1915, he would be promoted to lieutenant commander but would leave the RND in November of that year on his transfer to HMS Excellent *for 'sea service'.*

Friday, 25 September 1914 – Drake Battalion, Naval Camp, Walmer

In the afternoon we marched out and watched the Drake Battalion advance against an imaginary firing line. It was done to accustom the men to advance into the firing line in short rushes. This was very interesting but the manoeuvres were not very well carried out. After dinner I was prevailed upon to play on a wretched little upright piano in the officers' ante-room, the Brahms-Gluck 'Gavotte', Rachmaninoff's 'Prelude', Chopin's '17th Prelude', Mendelssohn's 'Scherzo a Capriccio' and Grieg's 'Morgenstimmung' from the Peer Gynt Suite. My playing created somewhat of a severe atmosphere.

Saturday, 26 September 1914 – Drake Battalion, Naval Camp, Walmer

It was rumoured in the morning that we are to be sent abroad in a month's time; in the evening notices were distributed with instructions as to what we are to do in case of Zeppelin or aeroplane raids. These two things brought the war closer.

Sunday, 27 September 1914 – Drake Battalion, Naval Camp, Walmer

Francis Henley and I much appreciated the long lie-in in the morning, as we didn't have to appear till breakfast at 8.00am. We paraded at 9.40am and had a service on the parade ground. Francis hired a motor in Lower Walmer and we went to Betteshanger where the 2nd Naval Brigade are encamped, to find Denis Browne and Rupert Brooke but they had not yet arrived.

We went on to Canterbury and lunched at the Country Hotel. We wandered round the cathedral and attended afternoon service at 3.00pm. The central tower of the cathedral impressed me enormously and the Norman east end was delightful. The west front seems to be spoilt by restoration. The interior did not seem to me as good as the exterior.

I read Belloc's article about the Battle of the Aisne before dinner [and] had an interesting talk with Pinks about the feeling of the metropolitan rowing clubs against Leander [at Henley-on-Thames].

The French-born poet and historian Hilaire Belloc was one of the most prolific and versatile writers of the early 20th century, slipping easily between humour and comment on the great issues of the day. He was another graduate of Balliol College, Oxford.

Tuesday, 29 September 1914 – Drake Battalion, Naval Camp, Walmer
By reason of our inoculation [against typhoid] yesterday Francis Henley, [Sub Lieutenant Percival] McGrath and I were excused physical drill from 7.00am to 8.00am so Henley and I walked about the parade ground watching the different companies drilling. At 7.45am the colonel (Travers) came up to us and gave us a decided snub for having our hands in our coat pockets and sent us off the ground! From 9.00am until 12 midday and from 1.30pm until 4.00pm we did squad drill etc. I went to sleep for two hours befor dinner. [Sub Lieutenant] Philip Kershaw turned up at 7.45pm and has apparently been put into Drake's.

Wednesday, 30 September 1914 -- Drake Battalion, Naval Camp, Walmer
It was a lovely day, sunny and a trifle sharp. Francis Henley, Philip Kershaw, McGrath and I did physical exercises with our squad of future section leaders from 7.00am till 8.00am ending up with games – 'snake and mongoose' and a section race. We did rifle drill from 9.00am–12 midday and platoon drill from 1.30pm till 4.00pm. Before going to bed the officers took to various tricks and trials of strength in the ante-room.

Friday, 2 October 1914 – Drake Battalion, Naval Camp, Walmer
The arms of the men in our squad who had been inoculated prevented them from taking part in any exercise requiring much movement and we spent an unsatisfactory day. Our sergeant took us down to the north corner of the camp before breakfast to give us points as to aiming with a rifle, but very little was done as McGrath took half-an-hour of our time by arguing with the sergeant. He is a singularly stupid little man and is always interrupting the sergeant by asking questions.

I dined with Mr and Mrs George Rowe at 2, The Beach, Walmer and was given some good wines for dinner. I played my 'Study in Trills', Op. 4, Nos. 1 and 4, and with Mrs Rowe Beethoven's Violin Sonata in D and the first two movements of Elgar's Violin Concerto. I was interested to make the acquaintance of the latter again. The slow is somewhat of a masterpiece and there are fine things in the first.

I spent a restless night troubling over details of drill and words of command. Being convinced I was ordered to make a right turn and give the order to others, I succeeded in rousing Francis Henley from his bed and we both stood up in the tent for a moment or two until he decided to get into bed again!

Saturday, 3 October 1914 – Drake Battalion, Naval Camp, Walmer
I was orderly officer for the day and had a number of duties to perform such as giving the buglers orders to sound off the various calls, inspecting the canteens, the kitchen of the mess tent and seeing the men's rations served out. I ended up the day by inspecting the sentries at 11.00pm.

I took advantage of my offices to introduce one important measure – the introduction of fly-papers in the officers' mess and the dry canteen, and by the evening there was a good crop of flies.

Sunday, 4 October 1914 – Drake Battalion, Naval Camp, Walmer
We were woken up at 6.00am by Lieutenant Sandford, RN and told to get up at once as the brigade had been ordered over to Dunkirk. As a matter of fact Francis Henley and I were left behind as we had not sufficient kit. Everything was at sixes and sevens all the morning and the camp was busy packing up. The four battalions left at 1.00pm leaving Colonel Travers, Francis Henley, Philip Kershaw, a subaltern named Webb out of Benbow [Battalion] and myself in charge of about 600 or more of Kitchener's recruits and with about one sergeant and one petty officer [PO] to help us!

Travers has been passed over and has spent the day in what appears to be a justifiable state of anger at the insult, but he was ill able to control his feelings and behaved in a very petty manner towards his four junior officers, running down the Admiralty, the camp and the military capabilities of the men who had been sent over.

Commodore Wilfred Henderson, commanding the 1st Naval Brigade, later recorded that Lieutenant (Acting Lieutenant Colonel) Travers had 'proved himself, in three weeks, to be so inefficient' that he obtained permission to replace him with Commander Victor Lindsay Arbuthnot Campbell to lead the Drake Battalion during the 1st Naval Brigade's first action in the defence of Antwerp.

Already a renowned naval officer and experienced polar explorer, Victor Campbell had served as First Officer on the Terra Nova *Expedition to the Antarctic in 1910, the final adventure of Robert Falcon Scott – Scott of the Antarctic. Known by the nickname of 'The Wicked Mate' he had been chosen to lead the party to explore King Edward VII Land. He assumed command of the entire expedition in its final weeks after learning of the death of Scott's Polar party.*

In spite of Travers's understandable frustration at being passed over in favour of Campbell to lead the Drake into action, his criticisms were uncomfortably near the mark. Rushed planning and preparation despatched what amounted to a 'scratch' force of the RND across the channel in an effort to shore up Belgian resistance in what was now a German siege of Antwerp.

After the German invasion of Belgium and the helter-skelter battles of late August and early September 1914 the Germans had pursued the French and British armies 250 miles south. They were finally checked on the River Marne and driven north. By mid-September there was stalemate and trench lines were being dug on the slopes above the River Aisne. With deadlock on the Aisne, German and Allied eyes looked north to the opportunities for mass manoeuvre offered by the 150 miles of almost unoccupied country which stretched from the Aisne to the North Sea coast. If an army could be rushed north before the enemy could respond, a flank might yet be turned and an operational victory might still be achieved. So began the passage of the war which is often erroneously called the 'Race to the Sea' – neither side in truth having the sea as its objective but rather attempting to turn the other's flank and gain a strategic advantage. But there were armies to the north. Attacking from the trenches and obsolete strongpoints of their 'national redoubt' of Antwerp on the coast, the Belgians had already tried and failed to break out in two 'sorties' in an attempt to menace the German rear and flanks to assist the Allied cause. They tried – and failed – once more on 27 September and then hunkered down as the Germans, now virtually unopposed, began a siege of the city, which if successful and the Belgians retreated, would open the road to the channel ports and threaten the ability of the British to supply its army in the field.

The day before Kelly's diary entry of 4 October it had been decided by Churchill amongst others, that a further force of the 1st and 2nd Naval Brigades of the RND would be sent to augment its 3rd Marine Brigade, already despatched across the channel and now shoring up the defence of Antwerp with their Belgian allies on the right bank of the River Nèthe.

As Kelly had noted, the four battalions of his brigade had left Walmer camp for Dover and before dawn the next day were anchored off Dunkirk. Many of the raw recruits and new officers – men like Kelly – had only rudimentary military training. There were not enough haversacks, greatcoats and water bottles to go round, medical supplies had to be begged or borrowed, there was no transport, no wagons and, crucially, no independent artillery support. Herded onto trains at Dunkirk, by 7.30am on 6 October the men of the RND, minus Frederick Kelly, chugged into Antwerp station ready to fight their first battle.

Wednesday, 7 October 1914 – Drake Battalion, Naval Camp, Walmer

I found [Sub Lieutenant Wilfred] Bolton, the subaltern I had left in charge as orderly officer in search of Colonel Travers for whom an important telegram had come, and I guessed orders had come to send the officers and men over, who ought to have gone with the brigade to Dunkirk last Sunday. It was true, orders had come for the men to go to Antwerp via Dunkirk, but at the time of writing it looks as though Travers won't let Francis Henley, Philip Kershaw or myself go. [Sub Lieutenant Harold] Edgar will be in command and I suggested to him we might be useful as interpreters. He is at present consulting the colonel about taking one of us. About half-a-dozen large ships which look as though they might be transports are lying off Deal. The colonel proved obdurate about our going, so we went to bed at least with the comforting reflection that we should not have to spend the night packing up for an early start at 3.00am.

Friday, 9 October 1914 – Drake Battalion, Naval Camp, Walmer
On arriving back (from dinner) I found a telegram had come from the colonel – 'Prepare Camp for the immediate return of the brigade'. In Deal I wrote a couple of letters at the Union Club and heard much talk going on of a reverse suffered by the Naval Brigade at Antwerp, and bitter criticism of Winston Churchill for sending out what was practically an untrained body of men. Of course it remains to be seen what has really occurred.

Sunday, 11 October 1914 – Drake Battalion, Naval Camp, Walmer
We were called up on parade at 6.30am to strike some 100 tents for the Royal Marines' use and after breakfast two of their officers came and explained they had intended their men to take up their quarters here! This is rather typical of the arrangements here during the last week. News of the fall of Antwerp was in the papers and an account of how 2,000 of the division had been cut off by the Germans and been obliged to cross the Dutch frontier. It looks as though Winston Churchill should be severely handled for the loss of these men, as the report says that it is entirely his doing that the force was sent over in its present untrained state. At 5.00pm Francis Henley, Philip Kershaw and I took a walk beyond Kingsdown; on the walk Kershaw sang me one of Bellois' tunes to which he sings some of the verses.

Monday, 12 October 1914 – Drake Battalion, Naval Camp, Walmer
The Marines were arriving from Antwerp and being cheered by the crowd. As I returned to the officers' mess at 7.30pm two officers arrived

who had escaped from Holland, where they had been driven by the Germans in their retreat from Antwerp. One of them gave us an excellent account of his experiences since leaving the camp yesterday week. The Belgians appear to be thoroughly disheartened and he says they made no real resistance to the Germans in the later days of the siege. The Naval Brigade had the misfortune to lose all its luggage through German shell fire, practically on arrival at Antwerp. During the couple of days his men were in trenches, they had practically nothing to eat or drink. The brigade left this camp in a hopelessly inadequate condition, as far as outfit was concerned – a whole battalion having about a dozen water bottles (so I understood him to say) between them. They hardly ever saw Germans other than snipers, and just had to occupy trenches over which German shells and shrapnel were bursting. The headquarters, owing to the German shell fire always finding them out almost at once, had to change their quarters three times a day, and the men scarcely ever knew where they were and got very few orders. The whole undertaking seems to have been of a very harum-scarum character – thought out on the spur of the moment by Winston Churchill, who is said to have escaped from Antwerp in an aeroplane.

Arthur Asquith, who had fought at Antwerp with the Anson Battalion, felt obliged to comment on Kelly's assertion that the RND had left camp 'in a hopelessly inadequate condition', when he came to read the diary entry above. Clearly wanting to set the record straight he conceded that although what Kelly had been told certainly had the ring of truth, it had not been 'the whole truth'. From what Asquith had seen and experienced at Antwerp, he was of the opinion that 'Deficiencies of essential rations and equipment such as water bottles, bully beef and greatcoats were made good on board the transport, at Dunkirk, and on the way up to the trenches' and that the RND at that time 'were not less-well fitted than the majority of the Belgian troops for holding entrenched positions' although they 'had received no training for offensive action and had no field guns and no regular transport'.

The RND had begun to fall back from Antwerp on the evening of 8 October after it was decided that the defence of the city was no longer possible. Most of the 2nd Naval Brigade escaped and were shipped back to the camps in England. Casualties – five killed and 64 wounded – according to Commodore Oliver Backhouse's figures – appeared relatively light. But almost 2,050 men were posted as missing, many of them men of the 1st Naval Brigade under Commodore Henderson who had crossed the border into neutral Holland after believing their escape route from Antwerp was blocked. Interned in camp in Groningen, their war was over.

Tuesday, 13 October 1914 – Drake Battalion, Naval Camp, Walmer

It was a dull day with a fair amount of rain. The [remnants of the] 1st Brigade returned from their week in Antwerp at 10.45am and a very dirty and unshaven lot they looked. They apparently sat in trenches for two or three days under heavy shell fire, without ever seeing any Germans and at the end of that time had to make a forced march of 32 miles to get away. They were very insufficiently fed and altogether the expedition seems to have been somewhat of a fiasco. The *Morning Post* came out this morning with an attack on Winston Churchill and it looks as though the matter may be pressed home against him. I was orderly officer and was kept busy at work the whole afternoon getting lists of those who had returned [and] in witnessing the payment of half of the men who had just returned and were going away on leave.

All those who returned from Antwerp were granted a week's leave and week's pay in advance to enable them to get home, but a good number of men wanted to get to Scotland for which two weeks' pay was quite inadequate. It seemed rather unjust, especially as some of them were owed three weeks' pay and couldn't get paid up to date. I lent two of the men £1 each and some other officers also advanced money.

Saturday, 17 October 1914 – Drake Battalion, Naval Camp, Walmer

We had the afternoon off for 'make and mend' and to wash clothes. I determined to make trial of the 'housewife' [sewing/mending kit] I bought a fortnight ago and spent altogether an hour on sewing on two buttons and putting my materials away. A large part of my time was spent in undoing a tangle into which I had got my thread.

An officer, named Fraser, who had recently got back from Antwerp, gave us an account after tea, of the train-load of refugees in which he and his men had found places. The train (possibly through the engine driver being a spy) was driven into a siding, whereupon Germans began firing on them and a tremendous panic ensued amongst the refugees. Luckily there were about 150 Marines in the train, who refused to surrender, and with them he and his men escaped in the dark.

Wednesday, 21 October 1914 – Drake Battalion, Naval Camp, Walmer

I have been given the command of the 3rd Platoon of A Company (Drake), with [Lieutenant Cecil] Dillon as my company commander, Sir John Hume Campbell as second-in-command and Pinks as a fellow platoon commander. A Company was duty company so I did not have much to do, except make a list of the names of my platoon. [Lieutenant Commander] Henry King, the adjutant, sent Pinks and me up on parade at 11.15am to help drill C Company, but the platoon PO resented my intrusion very much, and lost no opportunity of showing his annoyance. His men were terribly slovenly in all their movements, but the word has gone round from the new brigade major, Wilson, that more attention must be paid to smartness and precision in drill, so it is to be hoped that the present state of things will speedily come to an end.

Sir John Hume Purves Campbell of Purves Hall in Berwickshire, was the 8th Baronet to hold the Purves title which had been created in 1665. Eton educated, he had joined the army in 1899 and was a lieutenant in the 2nd Life Guards by 1900. He served in South Africa in 1902 and retired the following year but took up a temporary commission in the RND in September 1914. Already a veteran of the Antwerp expedition he was soon to be promoted to lieutenant commander on 28 October 1914, with his elevation to second-in-command of Drake Battalion. Mentioned in Despatches and wounded twice

*on the Gallipoli Peninsula – the second a serious bullet wound to the chest –
he would leave the RND in October 1915 on taking up a commission in the
Royal Field Artillery (RFA).*

*Lieutenant Commander Henry Douglas King, then 33 years old, had
served on sailing ships since the age of 14. Appointed to Drake Battalion,
he served with it at Antwerp and went with it to Gallipoli and the Western
Front, ending the war with a DSO and the French Croix de Guerre. He
became an MP for North Norfolk and Paddington South and died in tragic
circumstances off the Cornish coast when the* Islander, *a cutter he had
chartered from a member of the Royal Yacht Squadron, was driven on to
rocks in heavy seas three miles from Fowey on 20 August 1930. All six men
on board were drowned.*

Thursday, 22 October 1914 – Drake Battalion, Naval Camp, Walmer

I spent the morning and afternoon superintending my Platoon PO Ellis
drilling my platoon. I was told to correct anything wrong or slovenly.
I find I can discuss nothing with Ellis as he cuts up rusty at once. The
order has gone out that all drill must be according to *Infantry Training
1914,* but PO Ellis has taught the naval drill for 27 years and isn't going
to take up with any new-fangled ideas at his time of life!

Saturday, 24 October 1914 – Drake Battalion, Naval Camp, Walmer

We were disturbed at our 8.15am drill by the alert and as we lined the
boundaries of the camp we watched an army airship sail out to sea
over Deal. I spent the morning doing platoon drill with my platoon
and in the afternoon Pinks took the company in company drill. The
men were served out by platoons with new clothing – the first they
have had since joining.

At 7.00pm I met Arthur Asquith, [Sub Lieutenant Harold] Farrer,
Denis Browne and Rupert Brooke (from Betteshanger Camp), Francis
Henley, Philip Kershaw and Pinks at the Royal Hotel and we dined
together.

Harold Farrer was a friend of Kelly's at Balliol College. His father William, the Vicar of Bisham, was a close neighbour.

Monday, 26 October 1914 – Drake Battalion, Naval Camp, Walmer

The Admiralty telegraphed for all the RNVR men who had been to sea and we spent an hour at 3.45pm while they were all called out of the company and their names taken. The whole brigade will thus lose about a third of its numbers and another fresh start must be made. These interferences with the composition of the force make it a very disheartening business to try and work it up into efficiency and there is a wearisome prospect of joining up with the other units and making fresh lists of names.

Tuesday, 27 October 1914 – Drake Battalion, 1st Naval Brigade, Crystal Palace

The Reveille went at 5.00am and we had to set to work in preparing for our departure from Walmer at 9.00am. The whole brigade left, and before doing so, struck most of their tents. We reached Crystal Palace at about 12.30pm and spent the afternoon settling down. About 30 officers, among whom are Philip Kershaw, Francis Henley and myself, are being boarded out in a house to the north of the Palace, called Ashurst. I have never been inside the Crystal Palace before, and found it rather amusing looking around – especially at all the things which date from the period at which it was built.

Thursday, 29 October 1914 – Drake Battalion, 1st Naval Brigade, Crystal Palace

I was orderly officer for the day and as it was the first day of a new routine I had a good deal to do, instructing the guard in their duties. I spent a very tiresome afternoon from 2.15pm till 4.30pm in charge of a fatigue party (not my platoon) which had to clear gear out the polo stables and clean them. As soon as I had come in to tea I was given a chit by the brigade major to take six men from the duty platoon to fetch in some fodder that was due at the polo stables from 6.00pm till 6.30pm. I had great difficulty in collecting the men, who were at their tea, and when we got down to the stables I waited there till 7.00pm without any fodder arriving. On arriving back at 7.10pm another chit, from the adjutant, was handed to me to say fodder was waiting at the stables and that a PO and 12 men must be sent to get it in. No PO was to be found, so I had to collect the men and set off again. Of course nothing had arrived there, and I arrived back an hour late for dinner, not in the best of tempers.

At 9.30pm, the fire alarm sounded, but so many men had somehow got wind of it in advance that no-one was found unready – except some of the parties that should have been told off to work the fire hydrants. As orderly officer I was dropped on by everybody for whatever was amiss! The whole episode teamed with humorous situations. For instance our brigade major giving me a friendly hint that the fire alarm might go at 9.30pm – just to make sure that the thing would not be a complete fiasco. Of course the word spread in no time, and for 20 minutes beforehand a great many of the officers were admiring the statues – not far from their posts.

Friday, 30 October 1914 – Drake Battalion, 1st Naval Brigade, Crystal Palace

My platoon stood off duty until 2.00pm parade, having just come off guard. Thinking my presence on parade, after the stand-easy at 11.00am, was superfluous, I sat down to study the drill-book till lunch time, but after lunch-time I was dropped on by the 'Agitant' for a breach of discipline.

Sunday, 1 November 1914 – Ashurst, Crystal Palace

At 11.15am we paraded for inspection by the First Lord of the Admiralty [Winston Churchill], but at 12.30pm it was announced that he wouldn't come after all and we dispersed, not in the best of tempers, at having had our weekend leave stopped for no purpose.

Friday, 6 November 1914 – Ashurst, Crystal Palace
I dined next to Philip Kershaw and [Sub Lieutenant Patrick Houston] Shaw-Stewart, who arrived here yesterday.

While not as famous then or now as some of his close friends and fellow officers in what would become known as the Latin Club, Patrick Shaw-Stewart was in many ways the most outstanding of them all. A scholar of almost intimidating brilliance, he had also studied at Eton College and Balliol, and his academic career was unrivalled at both.

According to the Balliol College War Memorial Book, *Shaw-Stewart was 'possibly the most brilliant of all the Balliol men killed in the war'. At Oxford he won numerous scholarships, was awarded a double first in Classical Mods and Greats, and was elected to that most exclusive of academic institutions, All Souls College. He turned away from academia and by 1913, aged just 25, had become one of the youngest managing directors in the history of Barings Bank. He was killed by a shell whilst in acting command of the Hood Battalion on 30 December 1917.*

Wednesday, 11 November 1914 – Ashurst, Crystal Palace
After doing an hour's arms-drill with the officers' class the word came round that the Drake officers were to withdraw from it. Drake [Battalion] is to go to Berwick-on-Tweed next Saturday for musketry, and in the meanwhile the men and officers are to do nothing else than prepare for it. It is a pity we are to withdraw from the class where we are beginning to learn something, but we prevailed upon King, the adjutant, to allow us to attend the lectures if not the drill hours.

Saturday, 14 November 1914 – train on journey from Crystal Palace to Greenlaw
I had to march A Company to the public baths in the morning and see they washed. I packed in the early part of afternoon and at 5.15pm A Company fell in [with] their kit bags and we marched down to the High Level Station where a special train awaited us. We left at 6.30pm

or thereabouts – A Company and the machine-gun section under Sub Lieutenant [William] Ballantine, Sir John Campbell and the new adjutant, Major [Godfrey] Barker, had one carriage and the other six officers had another big coach. We got dinner baskets at King's Cross and I spent a comfortable night in my Wolseley valise [bed and bag combined] on the floor.

Sunday, 15 November 1914 – Town Hall, Greenlaw

We reached Greenlaw [Scottish borders town to the west of Berwick-on-Tweed] at 5.15am and marched off to our quarters in the town. We got breakfast on arrival, but had to wait an hour-and-a-half for our luggage. We fed at the Castle Inn and the junior officers (six of us) share a large room in the Town Hall. The petty officers are in a neighbouring room and two platoons are in the large hall. As the whole floor is covered with straw there seems reasonable probability that a fire may break out. It snowed heavily the whole morning. Sir John Campbell motored me off through the driving sleet with Commander Campbell and the adjutant, Major Barker, to Purves [Hall], his house, to lunch.

Monday, 16 November 1914 – Town Hall, Greenlaw

I had orders to march my platoon out to the butts [firing range], to be there ready for firing at 8.00am. The butts are placed in the most delicious little moorland valley. As we had to breakfast first and the butts are a mile-and-a-half away, I had to wake myself at 6.00am and very uncomfortable it was. There was no oil in the lamp in the washing room and I had to shave by electric torch. The adjutant, Major Barker, was to meet us out there, but he was 20 minutes behind time.

The key to the butts-storing cupboards had been forgotten, but, after some delay, we managed to break them open and so got at the targets. The men were very shaky about the orders of the various motions of loading and unloading and by the time the whole platoon had fired five rounds at 100 yards it was 11.00am and time for the next platoon to begin. The adjutant made me superintend the men's firing and pointed out some of the faults to me.

At a wooden hut, some 500 yards back from the range, we were told to find the means for boiling water to clean the rifles, but here again the key had been forgotten and when we got it, after three-quarters-of-an-hour's delay, we found the iron chimney that went up through a hole in the corrugated iron roof, quite stopped up with straw and what looked like the remains of old birds' nests. We only discovered this after starting a fire in the iron stove and in a very short time the hut was thick with smoke. The rest of the morning was spent in taking the chimney to pieces and clearing out the accumulation of straw with a broom-handle and sticks. Finally we discovered there was nothing in which to boil the water, so we arrived home with our rifles uncleaned. Some sleet fell in the morning while we were out on the butts and in the afternoon there was some rain.

In the afternoon I had trouble with one of my section leaders, PO Smart, who lagged behind in a short route march we did and when told to catch up, he said he couldn't double [march quickly]. I sent him home and brought him before the adjutant, Major Barker at 5.00pm. He got such a talking to that I think he would have preferred to be disrated on the spot. The adjutant gave the officers a lecture at 6.30pm on the importance of insisting on good discipline and making men stand to attention when speaking to an officer. There are no rooms in which to assemble the men in case of wet weather and in which one could lecture them.

I was ready to go into dinner when a note came to me from Commander Campbell from Purves to say he had accepted an invitation from Lady Nina Balfour for me to accompany him and Sir John Campbell to dinner there. I found a car waiting at the door and picked the Campbells up at Purves. It was about a ten-mile drive to [the Balfour's home] Newton Don and we found Captain [Charles] and Lady Nina alone. There was the usual excellent food and Lady Nina made us all laugh a good deal. They are apparently going to put up one of the Drake companies in their stables and before we started back Captain Balfour showed us round them. I didn't get to bed till 12 [midnight].

Captain Charles Barrington Balfour was the cousin of ex-British Prime Minister Arthur Balfour and had served in the Scots Guards. His wife, Lady Helena, was always known as 'Nina'.

Saturday, 21 November 1914 – Town Hall, Greenlaw

I was orderly officer for the day and from 3.00pm had a good deal to do, mostly clearing the public house of drunk men who had received their pay in the afternoon. At 9.00am I went out with the company to make an attack across the moor to the north of Greenlaw. We took our sandwiches with us and on our way back we fought a rearguard action, half a platoon being detailed to harry us in our retreat. An officer, [Sub Lieutenant Graham Goodenough] McHardy, is much worried by the state of the men's boots and clothes and the fact that they are not receiving their full pay. Certainly we are kept miserably short. The miserliness in dealing out our kit seems, however, to be due to lack of organisation, as we are equally short of pull-throughs, flannelette and oil for our rifles which are in danger of being ruined through the men's inability to clean them after firing.

Sunday, 22 November 1914 – Town Hall, Greenlaw

We had a church service at 10.00am in the hall where the men mess. There was no piano or organ and when the parson announced 'Onward Christian Soldiers' there was an awkward pause until Sir John Campbell nudged me and told me to begin. For the second hymn I gave them the pitch by humming the first four notes and conducted.

Monday, 23 November 1914 – Town Hall, Greenlaw

At 3.30pm we went for a route march along the road leading west across and alongside the railway. On the way back we judged the distance of a man on the road about 500 yards away and a good many of the men got it right. The platoon surprised me by a burst of song when I made a remark about its unmusical character. Apparently the men were under the impression I wouldn't allow singing on the march. One of their songs was 'Here we are, Here we are, Here we are again! Here we are, Here we are and here we are again!' I could discover no continuation of the tune or the text!

Tuesday, 24 November 1914 – Town Hall, Greenlaw

My platoon was at the range from 8.15am till 11.30am (in a heavy shower). I shot [five rounds] at 200 [yards] kneeling without a rest [scoring] 5,5,3,5,5 and at 300 kneeling with a rest when I missed the target in one shot but got some such total score as 13.

At 6.30pm I took my platoon out and spent a couple of hours making dispositions for the defence of the roads. At the end I marched a picket [temporary advanced post] across they gorse and tried to surprise one of the sentry groups. This the men thoroughly enjoyed. On the way back, among the snatches of song that the men were singing, I heard 'Has anyone here seen Kelly?'

Saturday, 28 November 1914 – Town Hall, Greenlaw

It was another day devoted to serving out clothing and making out lists. I inspected my men's bags in a room opposite the recreation room in the village and was once or twice disturbed by shouts from the other side of the room of the song 'Has anybody here seen Kelly?' which is evidently a joke among the men. I read Belloc's weekly article in *Land & Water* before dinner.

At dinner I was the senior officer, the others being McHardy, Farrer, [Sub Lieutenant Henry] Luckham and the doctor, Williamson. I had sent for half-a-dozen of the 1906 Vin d'Ay Brut, which I have bought from Randolph Payne and we had three bottles for dinner. The wine was new to me and was not unpleasing, better than the 1904 and not unlike the 1900 vintage, but not as good as the 1892. I taught the buglers some of the exercises I had set them at 9.30am and also the Drake bugle call I have written. One of the buglers is very untalented.

Randolph Payne and Sons, London wine merchants, supplied wines and spirits to Winston Churchill in the 1930s. Land & Water: The World's War was a popular magazine published by the County Gentleman Publishing Company, London and edited by Hilaire Belloc. The issue of 28 November 1914 also included maps of several theatre of war, including Flanders, Poland and Serbia.

Monday, 30 November 1914 – Town Hall, Greenlaw
It was a wet day and I was thus obliged to fill in the time by lecturing the men in their quarters. I chose the parts of the rifle and got on pretty well except for the dreadful moment when I was unable to put the magazine back!

Wednesday, 2 December 1914 – Greenlaw
We were at the range from 11.00 till 1.45pm and in addition to shooting with the rifle at 200 yards and 400 yards, I fired with a Webley [and] Scott automatic pistol under Luckham's guidance. It seemed to me an infernally dangerous implement. At 3.15pm I took my platoon marching and placed half-a-dozen men concealed by a road within 150 yards to see if they could detect them. It came on so dark that I could hardly see them myself.

I did a good deal of semaphore with Dr Wiliamson after tea. We had champagne at dinner and had a jolly evening. I received a letter from Henschel yesterday or the day before, in which he enclosed a sonnet he had written apropos of the war:

What music's this that floats in doleful chords
From friendly shores across the watery main?
It is the wail of innocent children slain,
Of women slaughtered by inhuman hordes.

Where is the tongue that can to deed lend words
As must for aye a nation's honour stain?
Deeds that e'en to repent now must be vain:
The doom is nearing – vengeance is the Lord's.

Oh land of song, how hast thou fallen low!
Was it not thou, e'en thou, that gavest birth
To Master music-makers of the Earth?
Degraded in the eye of friend and foe,
In shame now hide, O Germany, thy head,
Thou art unworthy of thy glorious Dead.

Kelly had given recitals of concertos by Beethoven, Schumann, Mozart and Brahms with the London Symphony Orchestra, then under the baton of Breslau-born baritone, composer and conductor Sir George – or Georg – Henschel, in 1912. Henschel was clearly giving Kelly a preview of a piece he intended for publication as it appeared in print – with several important revisions – a month later in the Musical Times *of 1 January 1915.*

Monday, 7 December 1914 – the Castle Inn, Greenlaw

I was orderly officer and had a busy day since, besides teaching the buglers calls from 2.45pm till 3.45pm I had to muster the company for pay. I fell foul of a great many people during the course of my duties and put the PO of the Guard into the Orderly Room report at 5.00pm. He completely disregarded some orders I gave him and if it had been Barker, the adjutant, before whom he was brought up, it would have gone ill with him, but Sir John Campbell is lenient to an extent of letting his officers down and the man got off with hardly a warning. I kept my record of falling foul of everyone by turning out the whole of the 3rd and 4th Platoons from their quarters after lights were out. This was in consequence of shouts and catcalls as I left the quarters.

There is a decided drawback in the conditions of training here and that is that there seems to be no method of punishing men, short of putting them in cells. One can give men what is called an hour's extra drill, but as it is dark as soon as parade hours are over no drill can be done. Chief Petty Officer (CPO) Jones says he puts the men on fatigue duties, but when I went at 6.15pm to see how they were getting on no-one had mustered and Jones himself had not turned up. The other platoon commanders feel the need of some backing up.

Arthur Asquith later reflected that Kelly 'combined something of the recluse's ignorance of the thoughts and feelings of all sorts and conditions of men with something of the artist's exacting austerity. He spared neither others nor himself in his efforts to avoid a single false note, and thus at this time – although, I think, in a diminishing degree throughout his career as a regimental officer – he was apt to ruffle the men under his command by rigid insistence upon the punctilious discharge of every detail of discipline and ritual. The NCOs (non-commissioned officers) were mostly still untrained and the men new to discipline, and perhaps at this stage the most that could usefully be aimed at was a rough harmony – to be achieved by insistence upon essentials and a blind eye to minutiae'.

After several days of inspections, map reading and mock attacks in the fields above Greenlaw jail, Drake's junior officers moved out of the Town Hall and took up residence in three rooms in what Kelly called a 'little house' over Veitch's, the grocer's shop. Kelly slept in the same room as McHardy and Harold Farrer.

Monday, 14 December 1914 – the house over Veitch's, Greenlaw
I was particularly restless during the night and told Farrer and McHardy to make their platoons line the two windows! I was also convinced the flickering of a lamp on the table which had not been properly turned down was Morse [code] signalling. After dinner I played Pinks my counterpoint to 'O God our Help in Ages Past' which on Sunday I invented during service and felt tempted to try when playing it for the men. I also played my studies in F Major and C Minor and at Pinkie's suggestion improvised him two pieces in B Minor and C Minor besides making up imitations of Mendelssohn

and Mozart. I was in good improvising form and the Mozart imitation was quite good.

Tuesday, 15 December 1914 – the house over Veitch's, Greenlaw

I was orderly officer but things went fairly easily and I spent an hour-and-a-half of the morning getting my Platoon Book – containing every conceivable piece of information about the men, from the number of socks they need to their religion – into order and from 3.45pm till 4.45pm I thought out a few points for a lecture on discipline.

Wednesday, 16 December 1914 – the house over Veitch's, Greenlaw

I had breakfast at 4.50am and started off at 5.10am. We reached Duns at 7.45am having had two stand-easies on the way. On one of them I asked some of the recruits to point out the Pole Star, which they had had explained to them on night operations a fortnight ago. They had, of course, all forgotten, but I was dumbfounded to find that having had the Pole Star pointed out to them, three men whom I told to point to the east, pointed respectively to the north-west, north-east and south.

The men now have a complete khaki outfit. I lunched at 3.00pm and soon after Pinks told me of a rumour that the Germans were landing a force at Newcastle and that we were to be ready to start at any moment. Instead of a much hoped for rest I spent a feverish afternoon preparing for a possible departure.

Friday, 18 December 1914 – the house over Veitch's, Greenlaw

The company went out for the day and was blessed with fine weather. We reached Greenlaw at 4.45pm after an unprofitable day, except for the exercise. Harold Farrer and I had the impression that [the company commander] started out without any clear idea as to a plan of attack and the result was we were given no clear orders and learned very little. It was, however, delightful out on the moor and at sunset the colours were soft and wonderful.

We were all somewhat peevish in the evening. On dismissing my men I gave them orders to go up by sections to the burn and wash their feet and owing to several of the men refusing to obey the orders of their section leader I sent three of them up to the Guard Room.

Sunday, 20 December 1914 – the house over Veitch's, Greenlaw

It was a lovely bright frosty day. The battalion parson came over from Duns to take service at 10.00am and we had it in the church at the back of the Town Hall. I had to play the organ – an organ with two manuals, pedals and about 12 stops – and I went to the church at 9.30am to feel my way about it. I improvised before the service on the manual without pedal and after the service I made a voluntary on 'Good King Wenceslas' – which weakened in the middle because I got cramp in my left leg and couldn't go on using the pedals.

McHardy and I lunched at Purves with Sir John Hume Campbell, Mrs Home Purves, Mrs Duplatt Taylor, Commander Victor Campbell and the adjutant, Major Barker. We had considerable fun afterwards racing around the lawn at the back of the house in the two children's go-carts. I pushed Commander Campbell in one of them against Sir John Campbell who pushed the adjutant in the other.

Monday, 21 December 1914 – the house over Veitch's, Greenlaw

I spent the morning inspecting my men's kit and attending their medical inspection in the sick bay. Some scandalmonger had passed the word that some of the 3rd Platoon were verminous, but all my men came triumphantly out of the inspection and the organisms in question were eventually detected on some 4th Platoon men!

Thursday, 24 December 1914 – the house over Veitch's, Greenlaw

It was a lovely bright, still and frosty day. The streets were all frosted over with a film of ice half-an-inch thick and the village boys were sliding down the Duns road into Greenlaw on improvised little toboggans. I had a slack time and in the morning read a pamphlet on Germany by

G K Chesterton, which I carried away from Newton Don the day before yesterday. It struck me as being extremely sound in its reasoning as well as witty.

Friday, 25 December 1914 – Xmas Day, the house over Veitch's, Greenlaw

The frost made any sports or football out of the question so that the men had nothing to do but eat and drink. We had a service at 9.00am in the church and I began by playing the Choral Prelude on 'Good King Wenceslas' and it all came to an end just as the parson had finished praying and was ready to begin the service. I didn't get on well with the hymns as I haven't any mastery over the pedals and cannot get the necessary support in the bars without them. I took the opportunity of finishing the E Minor piece I composed at Walmer. Pinks, Farrer, McGrath and I had a Xmas turkey and plum pudding for lunch and washed it down with some burgundy.

Saturday, 26 December 1914 – the house over Veitch's, Greenlaw

The thaw had set in overnight and the streets were wet with melting ice. I was orderly officer and had a strenuous afternoon looking after the scrubbing with Jeye's Fluid of the 3rd Platoon quarters, the storing of two loads of fresh straw which are to go in them and the transport of a grand piano from the station to the Castle Inn. The [piano] is an Érard belonging to Sir John Campbell and sent for by him from Edinburgh where it was stored. It was in a wooden case and proved a difficult job to get up the front steps of the hotel.

In the morning I found time to study the chapter on outposts in Brigadier General [Richard] Haking's *Company Training*. I had a somewhat heated altercation with McGrath at dinner. He has a tiresome habit of always taking up a paradoxical view and generally assuming the role of an advanced and enlightened thinker as against the humdrum conservative stupidity of the average Englishman. Harold Farrer and I did some Morse signalling before going to bed.

Sunday, 27 December 1914 – the house over Veitch's, Greenlaw

At Newton Don after tea we had a good heated argument as to whether (a) the Germans were a reprehensible race, and (b) whether the English were or were not prepared for this war. As the children were playing 'Up Jenkins' in the same room, there was somewhat of a noise.

'Up Jenkins' is a party game in which players conceal a small coin in their palm as they slap it on a table with their bare hands. The aim is for the players on the team without the coin to correctly identify which hand the coin is under.

Tuesday, 29 December 1914 – the house over Veitch's, Greenlaw

I was sent into Duns by motor at 9.45am to get pay for the two platoons going on leave and at the same time I drew two pairs of boots for two men in my platoon. Commander Campbell motored back with me and on the way sounded me [out] on the possibility of his requiring me to take over the post of deputy assistant quartermaster general [sic] to the battalion in place of Regan, a former PO who has been found to be incompetent at the job. I felt somewhat suspicious as to whether I was not being politely removed from the position of an executive officer, where I was reported to be no use. Ballantine and McHardy (who had just returned from leave) reassured me on this point, but in any case I suppose I shall have to accept it if they want me.

Wednesday, 30 December 1914 – 231A St James Court, Buckingham Gate, London

I left Greenlaw with my platoon at 11.50am by train and at Duns was joined by an officer in B Company. He is a ship owner from Newcastle and only joined some three weeks earlier. When we got to Berwick he stood me a drink and seemed to be complete master of the technique of rallying the barmaid. Lancelot Cherry, of D Company, motored to Berwick-on-Tweed to catch the 3.38pm train by which I was travelling and we had an interesting talk about artistic matters as far as York where we had to change. He has been [art historian Bernard] Berensen's private secretary.

231A Buckingham Gate was the home of Felix Walter Warre, another of Kelly's Balliol acquaintances and the 31-year-old son of Sir Edmond Warre, Kelly's Headmaster at Eton College. In 1909, four years after retiring from Eton, Sir Edmond had returned to take up the role of Provost (see Kelly's entry for 2 January 1915).

The 1911 Census lists Felix Warre as an auctioneer of 'literary property and works of art'. He served in the artillery during the First World War and survived to become an auctioneer at Sotheby's, His son Richard Warre, a regular soldier, was killed in the area of the present-day lighthouse during the defence of Calais in May 1940.

Thursday, 31 December 1914 – Bisham Grange, Marlow

I played [Felix Warre] my Xmas Prelude on 'Good King Wenceslas', my E Minor piece, and Op. 4 No.4 and he played me Scarlatti's D Major sonata. We then did some shopping and lunched at the Union Club after which I said goodbye. I caught the 5.50pm train to Marlow and was met by Maisie and [the dogs] Blackie and Wattle. Maisie took me straight to the Abbey and we saw the Vansittart-Neales, Mary Ethel Long-Innes [whose father had been born in Sydney] and 15 Belgian wounded. There is a nurse staying at the Grange.

Kelly and his sister Maisie rented Bisham Grange from the Vansittart-Neales of Bisham Abbey. In 1914 the ornate Warwick Room at Bisham Abbey was converted into a hospital ward for Belgian soldiers.

Friday, 1 January 1915 – Bisham Grange, Marlow

I went into Mrs Farrer's ward at [Bisham] Abbey at 10.50am to see her with her Belgian wounded. As I had expected she was inimitable and was chattering away in broken French and enjoying herself enormously. She was off duty at 11.00am and I went back with her to the Vicarage to see Mr Farrer and have a talk. Maisie and I sang and played to the Belgian wounded and we ended up by having 'Tipperary', 'The Brabancon', 'The Marseillaise' and 'God Save the King'. I played Scarlatti's 'C Major

Sonata', the Brahms – Gluck 'Gavotte', [a] Chopin 'Ballade', 'C Minor Waltz', my 'Xmas Prelude' (Good King Wenceslas) and Mendelssohn's 'Spring Song'. Maisie sang a French Bergerette, Paul Puget's 'Chanson de Route' and Bizet's 'Chanson d'Avril', 'Cold blew the Wind' and 'Aghadoe'.

The schoolroom had been brought into the hall and besides the twelve or so wounded Belgians there were three convalescent English privates, the nurses and the Vansittart-Neales and Aunt E Vansittart-Neale. I got back to the Grange at 6.45pm and hypnotised myself for an hour or so with 'Green Grow the Rushes O!'. There is something quite elemental in its symbolism and its haunting simplicity. After dinner Maisie sang it and a few other folk songs from Fuller Maitland's collection. I played Debussy's 'Berceuse Heroique' again and the jig from my E Minor flute serenade.

Saturday, 2 January 1915 – Bisham Grange, Marlow

I spent Friday at Eton, motoring over in Emma [the car] at 10.40am and spending half-an-hour with Dr Charles Harford Lloyd [his music teacher at Eton] at Hill Crest, Slough. I played him my Xmas Prelude on 'Good King Wenceslas' and later in the day at 6.15pm I took it up to Sir Walter Parratt and played it to him as well as my E Minor piece. He seemed genuinely to like both so I inscribed his name on the first and left the copy with him. He showed me a charcoal sketch which [John Singer] Sargent had done of him last summer and some points like the length of neck, are exaggerated, but it seemed to me rather striking.

Just as I was motoring into Eton at 12.30pm I was convulsed to see a party of boy scouts approaching me headed by [Eton Housemaster, Edward Littleton] 'Toddy' Vaughn [aged 63] dressed as a boy scout and limping along as best he could.

I lunched at the Provost's Lodge with Mrs Warre [and five other members of the Warre family including Felix] and I had two games of fives after lunch and at 3.15pm Edmond Waugh took Ernald Waugh's place and we had another game. It was a lovely bright day and the floods at Eton (the water was up to the drive of the Grange) looked lovely in the sunlight.

Sir Walter Parratt was Master of the Queen's Music from 1893 and of the King's Music through the reigns of King Edward VII and King George V. Sargent's head and shoulders study in charcoal, depicts the bearded Parratt wearing a jacket, waistcoat, white shirt and thin tie. It is now in the collection of the Museum of the Royal College of Music.

Sunday, 3 January 1915 – Bisham Grange, Marlow

For an hour-and-three-quarters before dinner I looked through most of my recent unpublished songs and revised some passages, and before going to bed I made some alterations in my B Minor, G Minor Studies (on which I had already made up my mind). In view of my going to the front, I am somewhat conscious of the spirit of Keats' sonnet:

> When I have fears that I may cease to be
> Before my pen has gleaned my teeming brain

and am anxious to leave my unpublished work as far as possible ready for the press.

I hope to be able to make a revised version of 'Away! The Moor is Dark Beneath the Moon' – having got all the details of revision ready to hand. Unfortunately there is no time for any of the Lyric Phantasy (for large orchestra), the F Minor Piano Sonata, the Aubade for Flute with accompaniment of strings, horn, bassoon and harp, a string quartet in E Minor, and about a dozen songs.

Monday, 4 January 1915 – 29 Queen Anne Street, London

I spent the morning writing letters and packing. I had an early lunch and drove in with Maisie and Mary Ethel Long-Innes, Blackie and Wattle, just managing to catch the 1.22pm from Maidenhead [to London]. At Taplow, Julian Grenfell got into my carriage and told me some interesting things about life at the front. He managed to get through the enemy's lines one day and after sniping three men got back again and was eventually awarded the DSO for it.

Julian Grenfell was another product of Eton College and Balliol, where he was a contemporary and friend of Patrick Shaw-Stewart. He was a popular member of the university, being a capable rower, boxer and an accomplished horseman, as well as an aspiring artist and poet. His father was William Grenfell – Lord Desborough – who presided over the 1908 London Olympic Games and gave a speech after Kelly won his gold medal with the Great Britain Eight in 1908. Lady Desborough – Ettie Grenfell – presented Leander Club with a bronze statue of Pallas Athene (which is today on display at the River and Rowing Museum in Henley) and each individual oarsman with their gold medals, Kelly recording that 'there was a good deal of pomp and circumstance in the atmosphere created by flourishes of trumpets followed by announcements from a sort of municipal herald with a splendid voice'.

Grenfell joined the 1st Royal Dragoons after leaving Oxford in 1910 and served in India and South Africa. In addition to receiving the DSO in November 1914, he was twice Mentioned in Despatches. Just over four months after meeting Kelly, Grenfell was struck on the head by a shell fragment. He died on 26 May 1915 with his parents and sister in attendance and is buried at Boulogne Eastern Cemetery. His best-known poem, 'Into Battle',was published in The Times *the following day.*

Thursday, 7 January 1915 – Duns Cottage, Duns

I came back from leave fully prepared to give my men lectures three times a week and generally speaking to smarten them up in every way but at lunch Sir John Campbell handed me a memorandum from Commander Campbell telling me to report to the brigade office, Duns and bring my kit. I spent the afternoon packing up and at 6.00pm I reached Duns by motor. I fully expected to spend a very uncomfortable night but to my great surprise and delight the commander had arranged that tonight I should sleep at Duns Cottage, (a sort of Dower House to Duns Castle), and that tomorrow I should move over to Duns Castle. Duns Cottage has been lent to the Drake Battalion and is at present occupied by Commander Campbell and [Senior Medical Officer, later Staff Surgeon Aloysius] Fleming with whom I had a very comfortable little dinner.

Friday, 8 January 1915 – Duns Castle, Duns

I walked down to the brigade office with Commander Campbell and Fleming, at 9.45am and I spent the morning and afternoon finding out my new duties as a battalion quartermaster. The book-keeping seems as though it would not be beyond my powers but there are so many regulations 'ungetatable' [regarding] the procedure to be adopted in indenting for clothes that I feel there are grave difficulties ahead in that line.

Tuesday, 12 January 1915 – Duns Castle, Duns

After tea (at Duns Castle) I read *The Times* and puzzled over my income tax forms for the current year. At dinner we were Mr and Mrs Hay, his nephew Brigadier General Mercer, the Brigade Major Wilson, the Adjutant Major Barker, Mlle. de la Riviere (the French Lady who teaches the Hay's nephew French) and myself. After dinner the brigadier general, Major Wilson, Mr Hay and myself had two rubbers of bridge [best of three games] in the smoking room. The brigadier had something to say about Henley and the Diamond Sculls. He plays golf at Huntercombe and seems to regard me with favour!

Wednesday, 13 January 1915 – Duns Castle, Duns

I spent most of the day in the quartermaster's office. My term as quartermaster promises to be short as another (new) officer was appointed in today's brigade orders.

Friday, 15 January 1915 – Duns Castle, Duns

I caught the 7.20am train to Edinburgh, having arranged an appointment with Dr Dickson the dentist. I spent an hour-and-a-half in visiting firstly a gallery of modern Scotch paintings, and, secondly, the National Gallery which I had seen once with Felix Warre in 1908. I had a good look at the Raeburns – some of which are excellent – and I also greatly admired the Rembrandt and the two Franz Halses (portraits of a Dutch gentleman and lady) on either side of it. I got my photograph taken before going to the Caledonian Railway Hotel for lunch. When I got back to the castle I wrote down nearly half of the organ prelude which I had been working at most of the day. I have had the framework in my head some weeks but the detail needed working out.

Wednesday, 20 January 1915 – Duns Castle, Duns
Wells read out battalion orders at dinner and in them I saw I was down to proceed to Blandford tomorrow with D Company from Chirnside.

The Drake Battalion was now under orders to join the rest of the RND at Blandford Camp, Dorset and the following day Kelly and an advance party of one company of the Drake embarked on their 400-mile journey south.

Thursday, 21 January 1915 – journey from Chirnside to Blandford
It was a lovely day and I took the opportunity after lunch of walking round the lake by Duns Castle which I had never had an opportunity of doing. I spent the morning in my office, clearing up papers and deciding what books relating to the store I would take with me. I left by motor from Duns Castle at 8.50pm for Chirnside, where I boarded the special train which had been ordered for D Company. I have enjoyed my stay at Duns Castle very much. The Hays have been very kind and life has been very comfortable.

Friday, 22 January 1915 – Drake Battalion, Naval Camp, Blandford
From comfort to the extreme of discomfort. We breakfasted at Gloucester where I bought the *The Times* and *Land & Water* and read them on the train on our way back to Blandford. At Blandford I marched up to the camp with D Company through an average of two inches deep of mud along the roads. We were met by Henry King, the second-in-command of Drake Battalion and after showing us our quarters he explained to me my duties of quartermaster. They were: (1) to draw the whole of the battalion stores and serve their portion of them out to D Company and (2) to feed the company by indenting for the food. The drawing of the battalion stores from the brigade store house nearby was a six-hour job or more and by the time it was dark not more than half the things were drawn and

people were clamouring for lamps, kitchen utensils and other necessaries. Of course, it was quite hopeless to try to draw the stores and serve them out at the same time and we all spent a very uncomfortable night.

To put a characteristic finish to a very uncomfortable day I missed the rest of the officers at 7.20pm when they all went off to dine with Brigadier General Mercer and though I ran off in the direction someone said they had taken, I failed to catch them and spent an hour-and-a-quarter wandering about the camp trying to find the 1st Brigade Headquarters. No-one seemed to have any idea where they were and after I had waded through mud, which sometimes came well over my ankle, in three different directions, I found my way back to the Drake lines with some difficulty. I reached them just ten minutes after Philip Kershaw, who had done exactly as I had done and he, Baker and I ate the remains of cold tongue, which we had had for lunch, on the floor with our pocket knives. It was one of the most depressing days I have every spent and yet it was amusing, especially the dreadful hunt for the general.

It was thoroughly characteristic of the authorities to plant us down here with no preparation (practically speaking) for our reception. King had ordered in a few stores which were sufficient to supply the men with a very scanty dinner and bed but the officers subsisted on a hamper which they demolished on the floor *a la Japonaise*. The huts of the camp seem to be practical and comfortable but the ground turns into deep mud whenever traffic or men's feet have passed over.

Saturday, 23 January 1915 – Drake Battalion, Naval Camp, Blandford

It was a nice fine day. I spent the whole of it drawing stores, issuing them to D Company. There was no time to attend to the men's food and at 6.00pm we discovered there was no breakfast for the men the next morning. I set out with a PO who helps me in the store, and after another unspeakable journey through the mud, firstly to the brigade headquarters (where I failed to get my information) I arrived at the store of the Anson Battalion, where I arranged to send a working party to draw some bloaters, haddock and butter. Sub Lieutenant [Edward Henry Swinburne] Bligh of D Company, undertook to fit out the officers' quarters from the things drawn for that purpose and we actually had a meal on the table and with chairs at lunch. As it was imperative that D Company should draw their stores, they rather insisted on their officers invading the store and taking their share of necessaries for their men and it was a nightmare to feel that I couldn't satisfy myself as to the number of things being taken!

Thursday, 28 January 1915 – Drake Battalion, Pimperne Camp, Blandford

We worked hard from 7.15am till 12.30pm (with an interval for breakfast), trying to get the camp ready for the remainder of the battalion and had succeeded in preparing each hut with the requisite for each platoon. We had worked on the assumption that each platoon would occupy one hut and Lieutenant Commander [Sydney] Searle said he had written to battalion headquarters at Duns to say what we were doing. When they did come, however, King – second-in-command – presented Searle with a revised plan in which each company fitted into three huts instead of four, and the scouts, band, and the machine-gun section occupied two more huts. Of course, all our plans were upset and the inventories of things I had prepared for platoon commanders to sign on taking possession of each hut were valueless. Confusion reigned throughout the afternoon and after dinner I had no palliasses [straw mattresses] to serve out, although 1,000 had been drawn from the brigade stores. I got to bed about 11.45pm after reading the paper in bed. I was rather struck by a phrase of a speech Kipling had made the day before about the necessity for providing bands for the new armies. After saying music was essential to the training of troops he made the statement, 'Melody for the mind and rhythm for the body'.

Friday, 29 January 1915 – Drake Battalion, Pimperne Camp, Blandford

The general and some other exalted personages rode around the camp about 11.30am and in consequence of a chance remark he passed to Commander Campbell and the adjutant about how half a battalion of Crystal Palace recruits down here were all at sea and what a good thing it would be if Drake Battalion lent them its quartermaster to assist them in drawing stores, I was sent out on a wild goose chase to help a battalion whose name I was given and whose position in the camp no–one seemed to know.

After spending an hour-and-a-half running them to earth, it appeared their commanding officer, Lieutenant Hill, didn't need any assistance. I heard a platoon had been sent up from our A Company to help, but I didn't know of their being sent nor where they were sent to when the bugler brought a message to say they were waiting for me. This incident seems to be typical of the lack of organisation in the Naval Brigade.

Sunday, 31 January 1915 – Drake Battalion, Pimperne Camp, Blandford

I spent the morning in the quartermaster's office writing indents for rations etc. I had an inspection of the officers' quarters after lunch to see whether they had the requisite number of lamps and water pails. Dr Hamilton took up his quarters with us last night and could not get hold of either of these articles, although he should have found them in his cabin. I found one lamp and one pail too many in the commander's quarters and boldly confiscated them from his servant. I was somewhat nervous when his servant told me at 4.30pm that the commander wished to see me as soon as he had finished his tea, but luckily he had left the camp for Bournemouth when I went to his cabin.

Tuesday, 2 February 1915 – Drake Battalion, Pimperne Camp, Blandford

Some half-a-dozen officers who belong to the first draft of a battalion, the whole of which had not arrived, joined our mess for dinner and there was singing and the usual kind of merry evening. I was obliged to play and after beginning with Grieg's C Minor Waltz I had recourse to

Carmen, as I usually do on such occasions. I had a talk with Cherry in his room as soon as I could escape.

Thursday, 4 February 1915 – Drake Battalion, Pimperne Camp, Blandford

There was a good deal of talk in camp as to the very good chance we had just missed by being sent out to Syria to make raids on the Turkish communications, in place of the two battalions of Marines whom they eventually decided to send and who start on Saturday. We are all very disappointed.

Saturday, 6 February, 1915 – Drake Battalion, Pimperne Camp, Blandford

The meat arrived at 5.45pm and I was present at the weighing, for which the butcher brought his own scales. It was short again as usual – this time [by] only five lbs. I was undressed at 11.30pm when the alarm sounded. On reporting myself in my dressing gown the adjutant told me he didn't require me but the remainder of the battalion turned out and were dismissed at 12 midnight.

12.30am – A very funny thing seems to have taken place. Apparently the officers' servants were summoned at 11.15pm with a threat that if they didn't turn out at once the battalion would be turned out. Two were missing so the alarm was sounded. Not only the Drakes turned out, however, for anxious officers rushed over from Collingwood lines and the general, Mercer, was early on the scene. The orderly officer was also in a great state of excitement and when the general told him to send an orderly to all the other battalions in the camp to say that though the alarm had sounded there was no need to turn out, he sent a man packing to tell the other battalions the alarm had sounded! I expect each battalion will turn out at intervals of 20 minutes throughout the night!

Monday, 8 February 1915 – Drake Battalion, Pimperne Camp, Blandford

The meat was reported bad to me as soon as I reached the quartermaster's office and I went straight up to Stewart [the 1st Naval Brigade Medical Officer] and brought him down to test it. He condemned 183lbs, in consequence of which the supply officer, a promoted NCO, came up after lunch. He began by saying he had often seen me at Henley and then went on to convince me quarter mastering was no job for me. He rather pooh-pooh-ed the fact of the meat being bad and tried to convince me it was owing to our butcher having cut it up the same night it was delivered, and to the window in the butcher's shop being shut. The butcher replaced the condemned beef with good mutton at 2.00pm and at 3.30pm he brought tomorrow's meat supply. This again turned out to be 9lbs. short until he had weighed it a second time on his own steelyard balls, when it made up the 9lbs. it was lacking!

Sunday, 14 Feburary 1915 – Drake Battalion, Pimperne Camp, Blandford

Harold Farrer produced a book of folk songs Mrs Watson had copied out for the Drake Battalion at lunch time and characteristically wanted something arranged at once about teaching them to the men. We decided to gather men into the recreation room at 6.00pm and spent part of the afternoon copying out the words of the ones we decided to do. At the appointed time Philip Kershaw, Farrer, Cherry, Campbell (the sub lieutenant in D Company), [Sub Lieutenant Sidney] Bonning, Cotton and myself went over to No. 1 hut and made rather an unpromising start with about half-a-dozen men. The number quickly grew, however, and before we had finished our programme at 5.50pm we had about 40, who showed some enthusiasm to the songs they had caught on to. We did 'The Girl I Left Behind' (three times), 'The Mermaid' (twice), 'Green Grow the Rushes O!' (three times), and 'Marching to Georgia' (twice). At the end I played Chopin's C Minor Waltz, the Brahms-Gluck 'Gavotte' and the overture to *Carmen*. It was the first time since I have played to members of the Drake Battalion that I have been listened to in silence! We were a good deal encouraged by our experiment and decided to get type written copies of a number of songs made in view of future meetings. The men evidently liked it, but there was a moment shortly after the beginning when it was uncertain whether the men would catch on.

Monday, 15 February 1915 – Drake Battalion, Pimperne Camp, Blandford

About 9.45pm Commander Campbell produced a book of photographs of his southern expedition 1910–1913 and talked about his experiences to [Lieutenant Commander Alexander] Gibson Smith, Philip Kershaw, Francis Henley and myself. This was very interesting, especially his account of the winter in the igloo.

Wednesday, 17 February 1915 – Drake Battalion, Pimperne Camp, Blandford

We woke up to find a blizzard blowing with driving rain. It was the day of the review of the two naval brigades by the First Lord of the Admiralty, Winston Churchill, and we all thought it would be put off. He turned up, however, and the review and march past took place in the rain at midday. I saw Geoffrey Howard, who only returned from the front yesterday and I witnessed the review with Eddie Marsh and one of the guests.

Thursday, 18 February 1915 – Drake Battalion, Pimperne Camp, Blandford

Two Admiralty clerks presented themselves at my store at 12.50pm and said they had come to take stock of the contractor's work. As they rather made themselves at home and showed me no signs of getting on with their work I began to ask them questions as to what they had to do. They immediately became supercilious and we finally fell foul over the question of my leaving them in my store while everyone was away at lunch. I resisted their gibes at my apparent distrust of them and finally bundled them out and locked up. The whole episode was somewhat ludicrous since in the first place they rather foisted themselves upon me like adepts in the art of the confidence trick and when I tried to get at why they should make my stores their headquarters they fell back on the very suspicious line of argument that this was the first time they had ever had any trouble with a battalion.

The second issue of khaki clothing arrived about 3.00pm. In the anteroom after dinner someone produced a rifle and several of us tried to press the trigger on aim without knocking off a penny that was balanced on the wings of the foresights. I only succeeded about four times in ten attempts and the majority of those who tried were no better.

Saturday, 20 February 1915 – 29 Queen Anne Street, London

I went first of all to Concert Direction E L Robinson to have 'High Germany' and a few other songs from [folk pioneer] Cecil Sharpe's collection of *Folk Songs for Schools* inserted into a book of words I am having printed for the Drake Battalion and from there I went to Schott and Co., 48 Marlborough Street, where I left my monographs and studies to be copied.

A telegram came from Burnett, my [quartermaster sergeant] at 7.00pm: 'Route march cancelled new quartermaster arrives today we leave Saturday next', and I am wondering with great curiosity where we go to.

Sunday, 21 February 1915 – 29 Queen Anne Street, London

At 10.30am I presented myself at 31 Tite Street, Chelsea, to sit for a charcoal drawing by [leading portrait artist] John [Singer] Sargent. Maisie wrote to him on Friday night asking him whether he would do me and he telegraphed to her early on Saturday morning and wrote her a delightful letter to say he had often wanted to draw me and would present her with the drawing if it turned out successful. I found a Major Armstrong with him – a retired officer from the Indian Army – and he spent a couple of hours talking with us as Sargent drew me. I found him very sympathetic.

Sargent was delightful and the conversation flowed so easily that I felt no sense of strain, nor any self-consciousness. He turned on some very interesting records of Spanish singers on his gramophone and one Egyptian song, accompanied by a queer mixture of instruments that sounded like a flute, violin (native) and xylophone. I played through Percy Grainger's version for the piano of his setting of 'My Robin is to the Greenwood Gone'. Maisie turned up about 12.15pm. The drawing was finished by 1.00pm and seemed to me quite excellent, though whether it is characteristic of me I couldn't tell. He promised he would do a drawing of Maisie later on, but of course I insisted in its being a professional commission. There were some delightful pictures of his in the studio and several bright chromatic water colours which I coveted a good deal. I told him his pictures often affected me like fresh modern harmonies in music and he seemed to be pleased with the comparison. It was altogether a most interesting morning.

Henry Warre and his wife and Edmond Lancelot Warre and Mary Long-Innes lunched with Maisie and me at Claridge's. Henry Warre was sent back from the front because of his rheumatism and has been working at the War Office some time. Mary Long-Innes took Maisie and me to see Percy Selwyn Long-Innes at a hospital in Vincent Square, SW at 3.45pm. He has been wounded in the right arm by a revolver bullet at close quarters and will not be well for three months or so.

I went from there to the Albert Hall where I was attracted by [Dvořák's] *New World Symphony*, but I found to my disgust that only the first two movements were performed and of these I missed most of the first movement by arriving late. I had tea at the Union Club and revised my songs 'There be None of Beauty's Daughters' and 'Earl March' before and after dinner. I dined with Maisie *tete-a-tete* at Claridge's.

I found H Golden on my return to 29 Queen Anne Street, and after revising my songs played about ten of Mendelssohn's songs without words, his characteristic piece in A Major, 'Scherzo a Capriccio' and 'Rondo Brillante' (for piano and orchestra). It is all very sympathetic to me at present. I also showed him my cadenzas to Beethoven's G Major Concerto.

The man Kelly had visited in hospital that day had been wounded in an action that would mark two 'firsts' of the First World War; namely the first Victoria Cross (VC) of 1915 and, more important, the first awarded to an Irish-born soldier.

After several days of fierce fighting around the railway embankment on the banks of the La Bassée Canal, near Cuinchy, the Germans captured an advanced post south of the railway on 1 February 1915. The Coldstream and Irish Guards charged along the railway embankment towards the German position under heavy fire but failed to take it. Two officers were killed and two more, including Captain Percival Selwyn Long-Innes, were wounded. Four hours later another attack went in: Lance Corporal Michael O'Leary racing ahead to shoot five Germans at the first barricade then three more at a second, before taking two prisoners. By this time O'Leary had already run out of bullets! O'Leary was feted as a national hero in Britain. Thousands turned out to see him in London after he received his VC and a poem, a song and even a play by George Bernard Shaw were written about him. His face – cap at a jaunty angle – appeared on government recruiting posters in an effort to attract Irishmen to join the British Army.

Monday, 22 February 1915 – Drake Battalion, Blandford

I caught the 8.50am train from Waterloo to Salisbury. I had heard by telegram on Saturday that a new quartermaster had been appointed. It thus remained for me to find out what I had been appointed to. A few words with Commander Campbell impressed me with the seriousness of the situation as I got a strong impression that when the battalion pushed off I should be left behind. I decided to strike quickly, so I went up at once to headquarters and in looking for the brigade major I stumbled across General Mercer to whom I presented my case. He told me to come again at tea time when the brigade major would be back, but though I turned up at 4.15pm and had tea with Stewart and a few other junior officers, the general did not put in an appearance until 5.30pm or the brigade major till 6.30pm. I put my case and they were both very sympathetic and the general said he would see General Paris to see whether I could squeeze in somewhere among the battalions who are going abroad on Saturday.

It appears that we are going to the Dardanelles and I am determined not to be left behind. There seems a chance of my getting into Hood Battalion, which would suit me very well as I should find myself with Denis Browne, Rupert Brooke and 'Ock' Asquith.

Major General Sir Archibald Paris of the Royal Marines was the much loved commander of the RND. He had commanded the Kimberley Column in the South African War and the RND from its formation in 1914 – including the Antwerp expedition and would do so throughout the entire Gallipoli campaign.

Tuesday, 23 February 1915 – Hood Battalion, Blandford

Feeling that it would be wise to turn a few more stones I went over to Hood Battalion after breakfast and explained my predicament to Denis Browne who took me over to the adjutant, [Lieutenant Commander Alexander Cecil] Graham, and the colonel, [Arnold] Quilter. They were short of officers and said they would be very glad to have me and during the course of the morning my transfer was arranged and I left Drake without belongings at 6.00pm.

Both Bonning and I, who have to leave Drake, feel somewhat ill-used, since if the battalion, through inadvertency, is over strength, it seems hardly fair that two of the senior subalterns should be got rid of. Commander Campbell professed himself very sorry to lose me and I think I was the victim only of his slackness. He has given me the impression, however, of having a convenient memory, he went back twice on what he had said. There was quite a feeling of distrust of him among several officers. One would have distrusted him less if he had not been over-pleasant when he meant to be nice. I was allotted to B Company in Hood and I share a cabin with Denis Browne in a chaos of clothes, books and equipment.

GALLIPOLI

FEBRUARY 1915–JANUARY 1916

'Regatta day'

*N*ow taken into the bosom of the Hood, Kelly's contacts and determination had finally turned his desperate wish of serving his country on active service overseas into reality. The destination was an open secret. Kelly and his fellow officers knew quite well that they were bound for Gallipoli but beyond that broad outline they had little further information. Would they be attached to the army and used in the initial assault? Would they provide reinforcements? Such questions were for the future however, and as Kelly settled into the routines of a new battalion as it put the finishing touches to its period of training, he was content in the knowledge that he would at last be part of a British campaign abroad. Serving with the Mediterranean Expeditionary Force (MEF), however, meant that while he had missed – rather fortuitously – being a part of one of Winston Churchill's misadventures (at Antwerp) he was about to be plunged into an even greater one: Gallipoli.

The campaign in the Dardanelles is seen as one of the great blunders of British military history. At the time of writing this has been the case for a hundred years and despite other campaigns and battles being reassessed and re-evaluated, when it comes to Gallipoli, the conclusion is almost always the same: an unmitigated failure.

THE LOST OLYMPIAN OF THE SOMME

It was Churchill's grand scheme to bring an end to the stalemate which had gripped the First World War, at least on the Western Front. The roots of the failure are arguably diplomatic. Both sides had made overtures towards the Ottoman Empire and its new regime, the Young Turks who seized power in 1908, but it was Germany who eventually secured an alliance with the so-called 'sick man of Europe'. Churchill's plan was to end Turkey's involvement in the war. To do this forces from the British Empire and Dominions and France would seize control of the Dardanelles – the route from the Aegean Sea to the Black Sea which linked the Mediterranean with Russia, the third partner in the Allied cause. In turn Constantinople would fall and Turkey would be knocked out of the war.

Such was the Allies' misplaced confidence – and so badly were the defending forces underestimated – that there was a widespread belief the Royal Navy would blast their way through – that a naval campaign and bombardment would see the Turks capitulate. The first shots were fired on 19 February 1915, the main attack coming on 18 March. From the start it was doomed to fail. The ships the Royal Navy sent were ageing and unsuitable for their task. The Turkish defences were much stronger than anticipated and the men much more determined. And the mines laid in the Straits proved to be lethal to British and French ships. It quickly became apparent that any hopes of an easy victory were futile and an amphibious assault would be required.

Kelly's diary shows us just how widely known it was that the RND would be going to the Dardanelles. His words also reveal how much he and his comrades were enthused by the task ahead. For men such as Kelly, Rupert Brooke, Patrick Shaw-Stewart and Arthur Asquith there could scarcely be a more exciting place to taste battle. For these academics, intellectuals and artists of the 'Latin Club' en-route to the Aegean, the Dardanelles – or Hellespont as it was known to the Greeks – lay at the heart of the Classical World. It was here that Troy once stood, on the western end of the Straits; Xerxes I of Persia and Alexander the Great both crossed the Dardanelles to do battle; and it was across this narrow stretch of water that in Greek mythology Leander – the man after whom Kelly's rowing club in Henley-on-Thames was named – swam every night to lie with his lover Hero. It is

*not difficult to see that for a group of men with an already heightened sense
of adventure, the prospect of heading to this corner of the Classical World,
where Europe fuses with Asia, was utterly enticing.*

*Few nerves are betrayed by Kelly in his diary. There appears neither little
concern about what lies ahead nor is there particular excitement about the
voyage – he was after all a relatively well-travelled man, having already
sailed several times between Britain and Australia in his lifetime. Of greater
significance for him were the friendships which developed amongst his fellow
adventurers. The Latin Club may well have appeared rather pompous and
elitist to outsiders, but they shared a genuine yearning for knowledge as well
as for each other's company. As they sailed on the* Grantully Castle, *they
talked and dined together, took Greek lessons, swapped poetry, sang, argued
and played together. And of these relationships, the most important for Kelly
was that with the great poet Rupert Brooke. It was to have a profound and
ultimately life-changing impact on him and in particular on his music. In
Brooke, Kelly found his muse and in Gallipoli he would find his elusive
musical voice.*

Thursday, 25 February 1915 – Hood Battalion, Blandford

We paraded at 7.40am and marched out to beyond Three-Mile Point
across the Salisbury Road where we were first inspected by Winston
Churchill at 9.30am and at 11.30am by the King, before whom we
also marched past. It was a lovely bright, frosty day and during the
long waits, we got very cold. There were some nine battalions parading;
those that go abroad tomorrow and the day after. I have had a bad
throat and could not shout at my men. Mrs Asquith, Violet Asquith,
Mrs Winston Churchill, Lady Gwendolen Churchill and a Mrs Guest
(née Lyttleton) lunched with the Hood Battalion after the review and I
met Mrs Asquith for the first time. I also saw Lady Quilter and Roger
Quilter, who lunched with Colonel Quilter in his cabin.

I joined Harold Farrer, Mrs Farrer and Maisie in the Drake Lines
at 4.00pm and Maisie came back to Hood with me to fetch my coat
prior to our motoring down to Blandford with Mrs Farrer. I fetched

the 200 booklets of folk songs I had had printed for the men to sing from the station and here there may be a chance of teaching them on the ship.

I wrote a good many letters after dinner and did not get to bed till midnight – with the discomforting prospect of having to be in Blandford at 8.30am, to see my company get its fair share of ammunition. I received a copy of *New Numbers* [magazine] in the afternoon and found some poems by Rupert Brooke (of this battalion) which struck a sympathetic note in me.

Saturday, 27 February 1915 – journey from Shillingstone to Avonmouth

The day was spent in packing up. The battalion left Pimperne Camp in three batches at 4.00pm, 6.00pm and 8.00pm to march nine miles or more to Shillingstone where they entrained for Avonmouth. I was in the last batch with my own platoon (the 5th), the company commander [Lieutenant Commander Sidney] Burnett and D Company. I have lost my voice for the last week and so was rather at a loss in trying to deal with men falling out.

We all found our web equipment extremely heavy and in addition the officers carried Webley and Scott automatic pistols and rifles. The marching was extremely heavy – the step being changed every five minutes. We reached Shillingstone about 11.30pm and had to wait there for three-quarters-of-an-hour before we got into a train. I never felt so partial to outdoor relief as I did when some ladies came round with hot coffee in hot water cans. I heard afterwards that it was Lady Baker who organised the little party and she obtained many blessings. I got fairly hot marching and so was correspondingly cold in sleeping. I had a carriage to myself and felt fairly comfortable with the air cushion Maisie gave me on Thursday.

In the afternoon I finished Bernhardi's book *Germany and the Next War*, of which I read the greater part in August and September. It didn't shock me as it appears to have shocked a great many people. It is really only a practical application of principles which at all events a good many people feel to be inevitable and it is mild after Machiavelli.

Sunday, 29 February 1915 – SS *Grantully Castle*, Bristol Channel
We reached Avonmouth at 6.30am and embarked on His Majesty's Transport the SS *Grantully Castle* which was lying a few yards away from the train. Most of the officers went up to Bristol for lunch, but one officer from each company had to remain behind and, as I was the one from B Company, I took on the job of officer of the watch for Rupert Brooke in exchange for my watch a day or two later.

I am at rather close quarters in a small cabin with [Sub Lieutenant Edward Beesley] Trimmer and a sub lieutenant who joined Hood after me. As we were the 'newest comers' we had no choice. I got in some sleep before breakfast and dinner and had a long night's rest from 9.30pm till 8.00am. We have all been very short of sleep recently. After dinner I finished J A Cramb's book *England and Germany* which I found very interesting. I have been brought up in such a different school of thought that it is hard for me to believe that anyone can seriously think the will to dominate others is the highest human aspiration. He appears to be in sympathy with this part of German modern thought.

Scottish historian and academic John Adam Cramb's book was actually titled Germany and England. *The author had been preparing a series of essays on Anglo-German relations for publication when he died unexpectedly in late 1913. The book Kelly had read was the posthumous result.*

Monday, 1 March 1915 – SS *Grantully Castle*
I slept from 2.00pm till 5.00pm, after which I had made up for the recent deficiency in sleep we have all undergone. I read the first three chapters of Haking's *Company Training* during the course of the day. The piano is not encouraging but both Browne and I played a little.

Tuesday, 2 March 1915 – SS *Grantully Castle*

There was a lovely sunset and Denis Browne and I amused ourselves in tracing a landscape in it. I read most of John Drinkwater's poem 'A Carver in Stone' in *New Numbers* and was not much impressed.

Wednesday, 3 March 1915 – SS *Grantully Castle*

Maxwell, the brigade major gave us an interesting lecture on the Dardanelles, dealing with the subject first historically and secondly strategically. [Oliver] Backhouse, the commodore of the 2nd Naval Brigade, ended the lecture by saying a few words. He confessed to complete ignorance of the operations we were being sent out to perform and he assured us the First Lord [of the Admiralty] hadn't any plans for us – beyond getting us on the spot for any possible use.

Thursday, 4 March 1915 – SS *Grantully Castle*

I was on watch from 4.00am till 8.00am and took the opportunity of writing down the bass part of my 'Waltz Pageant' to play with Denis Browne. I finished seven waltzes before breakfast and had completed 11 by teatime. We tried them through after tea – Denis Browne reading them fairly well at sight. He seemed to think them nice and fresh. We tried them through twice. During my watch I had to visit all the Hood sentries once an hour with the leading seamen of the picket and report them correct for the ship's officer on the bridge.

We paraded at 9.45am while the commodore went the rounds of the ship and at 2.30pm my company and part of A Company did three quarters of an hour's physical drill, consisting mostly of marching, doubling, stepping high and skipping. Colonel Quilter showed much interest in the last two exercises as he gave us a demonstration of how they should be done. It was quite warm and one could sit out after dark without a coat. We [officers] did some skipping at sundown. I played a rubber of cut-throat [bridge] with Patrick Shaw-Stewart and Bernard Freyberg before going to bed.

GALLIPOLI

Friday, 5 March 1915 – SS *Grantully Castle*, Straits of Gibraltar

We passed through the Straits of Gibraltar early in the morning in sight of the African shore, but at some distance from it. Colonel Quilter had the officers out at 7.15am and gave us half an hour's marching, doubling, stepping high and skipping. It was rather like Levey's class for officers at Crystal Palace over again, as we were chevvied about and rattled to an almost equal extent.

Lieutenant Joseph Henry Levey was second-in-command to the Chief Military Instructor at Crystal Palace and had been Kelly's military instructor during training. He was described in the official history of the RND thus: 'The best drill instructor is he who can deal with every lapse or negligence, however trivial, as though it were an unprecedented phenomenon, a demonstration deliberately planned to sap loyalty, to sow dissension in the ranks, to debauch the nation, to enhearten the enemy, and to bring the Empire crashing to the ground. Such a drill-instructor was Lieutenant Levey'. He was seen as 'a man without bowels, an expert in insult, a flail, a tempest, a tiger'.

A private soldier in 1899 Levey ended the First World War as a lieutenant colonel commanding a battalion having earned the DSO in 1917 during the capture of St Julien near Ypres. He became a legend in the RND but his legendary status was further enhanced by his actions on the eve of the outbreak of the Second World War when, as acting Chairman of British ORT – the Jewish educational and training organisation – he ventured into the very heart of darkness of Hitler's Third Reich to negotiate the evacuation of the students and staff at Berlin's ORT Technical School. As a result of his negotiations – this uncompromising man apparently strode into meetings with the Nazis in the full dress uniform of the Gordon Highlanders – 106 Jewish boys aged between 15 and 17, along with eight instructors and their families, left Germany for England on 29 August, 1939 – five days before Britain declared war. A second transport, with a further 100 boys and the school's Director, Dr Warner Simon, were not so lucky – they failed to get out due to the outbreak of war and died in the death camps of Europe. Levey died in 1970 but a plaque on the wall in the British ORT House in London commemorates his deeds.

Saturday, 6 March 1915 – SS *Grantully Castle*

The inevitable lecture, which has been on my conscience for some months, had at last to be given after 9.30am parade and I made use of some notes I had made about Christmas time on the subject of 'discipline'. I found a convenient place down on the men's mess deck, where I could seat my platoon and where I was free of disturbance, and I managed to spin out something for about 35 minutes. I did rather better than I expected, but I couldn't have held their attention for many more minutes.

We passed Algiers at a distance of some seven miles at 2.45pm and we got a good view of the snow-clad mountains further east. My company commander [Sidney Burnett] gave me some details of his life, before lunch. He ran away from school at Highgate when he was 15 to escape being turned into a priest; from then, when he enlisted, till now he seems to have signed on to any force which had any chance of taking part in any war!

Sunday, 7 March 1915 – SS *Grantully Castle*, South of Sicily

Smallwood, the colonel of Anson Battalion, gave the officers a lecture on bush fighting at 5.30pm and found some difficulty in spinning out what he had to say to fill in a half hour. He took part in the Ashanti campaign of 1900.

Patrick Shaw-Stewart, whom I sat next to at dinner, was in good conversational form. He, Rupert Brooke, Arthur Asquith, William Denis Browne, a subaltern called Trimmer and I sit together. Shaw-Stewart is still just a little the brilliant undergraduate and his talk savours a good deal of the classics.

Monday, 8 March 1915 – SS *Grantully Castle*, Malta

We [put] into Valetta after lunch. I just arrived at the Royal Opera House in time for the second act of Puccini's *Tosca*, which was extremely well given. I have seen it once before a year or so ago at Covent Garden – when the second act struck me as good, the first fair and the last poor. I got a similar impression of the last two acts again. I sat with Lancelot Cherry (of Drake) Rupert Brooke and Denis Browne and saw a good deal of Philip Kershaw and the two doctors, Hamilton and Williamson. We went to an eating house afterwards and had a gay time for half an hour.

Tuesday, 9 March 1915 – SS *Grantully Castle*

We left Malta about 11.00am. Denis Browne had bought some volumes of duets in Malta at my instigation and some waltzes for four hands by Moszkowski which were fresh and nice, Grieg's *Holberg Suite* arranged for four hands and a miscellaneous volume containing a Polonaise by Dvořák, which was not quite uninteresting. We tried through the Moszkowski waltzes.

Thursday, 11 March 1915 – SS *Grantully Castle*, Lemnos

We had a bright sunny day passing between Euboea and Andros and with distant views of Mytilene, Chios, the Sporades and Mount Athos – which showed up from some 60 miles or more very distinctly. We got into Lemnos at 6.00pm, taking anchor off Mudros. We spent the morning serving out ammunition and mustering kit bags.

Friday, 12 March 1915 – SS *Grantully Castle*, Lemnos

We paraded at 9.30am and after dismissing for half an hour we fell in again at 10.15am to do physical drill. I had noticed a speckled light cruiser at breakfast time and later on in the morning a signal message came to ask whether Sub Lieutenant [Frederick] Kelly was on board, this made me quite sure it was Joe Kelly's ship [HMS *Dublin*]. Sure enough his galley arrived with a note about 11.15am asking to come over. I got leave and lunched with him, returning at 3.30pm on receipt of a signal message from HMS *Blenheim* to say the *Grantully Castle* was getting up steam. It was a false alarm; instead of going off to the Gallipoli Peninsula, she changed anchorage a few hundred yards. Joe must have divined this, for he came over at 6.30pm and fetched me back for dinner, after having a couple of cocktails with Commodore Backhouse and myself in the smoking room.

The ship had swung while he was on board, with the result that he started steering in the wrong direction. I got completely bewildered when it was evident we had not been steering a right course, but luckily we struck the *Dublin* after roving for nearly an hour. For my return journey a bearing had been taken, so I did not have much difficulty in finding the *Grantully Castle*.

Joe has been out in the Levant since he was at Bisham in July and has been watching the Dardanelles. He was within range of the big guns of the Dardanelles forts at 10,000 yards and got 'straddled' – shots falling just short and just beyond him – and quite recently he was at anchor in the Gulf of Xeros observing military movements on shore, when 4-inch guns opened fire at him at 3,000 yards and scored several hits before he got underway and could reply. I saw some of the holes they had made on the deck and in the funnels. Joe had not slept off his ship for seven months and then had only slept in his bed three times. He was rather depressing about the task which awaits us in clearing the Gallipoli Peninsula of Turks and Germans. He thinks there are a great many of the latter there and that they have made excellent preparations. He also has a high opinion of the shooting of the fort-guns.

He introduced me to his commander, Mosse, who had a glass of wine with us in the captain's cabin after dinner. We had fresh fish, which was a delicious luxury after the so-called fresh herrings we have been having on the *Grantully Castle*. It was delightful seeing Joe and I was very much interested at being on a warship under active service conditions. The captain's quarters were pretty spacious – consisting of a fairly large sitting room (over the crew), a dining room, a bedroom, a bathroom and WC. The sides of the ship look like a cubist picture.

We discussed the war a good deal. He put down the escape of the *Goeben* from Messina to Sir Berkeley Milne and exonerated Admiral Troubridge. He lay in wait [for the *Goeben*] with the *Dublin* and two torpedo boats further east, but missed it. When he came on to the

Grantully Castle I felt conscious of having a very big fish in my net as there is no four-striper [captain] on board with the exception of Backhouse, who is acting commodore!

John Donald Kelly – always known as 'Joe' – was no relation to Kelly but they had known each other for some years and had become friends. He had entered the navy in 1884, was promoted to lieutenant in 1893, commander in 1904 and captain in 1911, serving on various foreign stations in the east and the Antipodes. As captain of the light cruiser Dublin *in 1914 in the Mediterranean he was part of the operation which attempted to locate and attack the German raider* Goeben. *Always seen as a 'sailor's sailor' he was promoted to rear-admiral in 1921 and on the verge of retirement in 1932 was called upon to take command of the Atlantic – later the Home – Fleet after the Invergordon Mutiny. His final post was as Commander-in-Chief, Portsmouth, from 1934 to 1936 and he was made Admiral of the Fleet just before his 65th birthday.*

He died in November 1936 and was accorded a naval funeral of due pomp and circumstance in London – watched by thousands and filmed by Pathé News – before burial at sea off the Isle of Wight. The famous destroyer commanded by Lord Louis Mountbatten during the early years of the Second World War was named after him. Joe Kelly would assume an even greater role in Kelly's life in the weeks following their serendipitous surprise reunion in March 1915.

Saturday, 13 March 1915 – SS *Grantully Castle*, Lemnos

The *Dublin* galley called for me at 7.00pm and I went over. Joe sent me back early (at 9.00pm) because he was under orders to sail at daybreak. I caused some commotion on my return from the *Dublin* because I was [mistaken for] Commodore Backhouse and had the Officer of the Day and sundry other men on duty all turning out to receive me.

Sunday, 14 March 1915 – SS *Grantully Castle*, Lemnos

They have arranged that one company each from Hood and Anson shall go on shore for training each day and today it was B Company's turn.

Mine was the first platoon to leave and we had to await the remainder of the company by the water's edge. We landed on the north-eastern shore of Port Mudros Bay and did a route march going first of all east and then north-west till we got on to some high ground on the neck of land between Port Mudros and the sea north of it, and here ate our ration.

We reached the landing place at 2.30pm but had to wait some time for a boat. The island is very rocky and treeless. The villages and people were much cleaner than I expected to find them. Most of the inhabitants were rather good-looking and wore nice bright clothes. Colonel Quilter gave the Hood officers a talk after dinner in which he said we might have to wait weeks before we should be needed and calling upon us to make special efforts not to get slack.

Wednesday, 17 March 1915 – SS *Grantully Castle*, Port Mudros, Lemnos

Sub Lieutenant [Leslie] Shadbolt of D Company took a boat load of his men off to bathe at 11.00am and I went with him. We found a little promontory on the west side of the bay, on one side of which Shadbolt and I bathed and on the other side the men. We had shallow water with a nice, white beach under foot. The water was about the same temperature as on an ordinary summer's day in England.

Thursday, 18 March 1915 – SS *Grantully Castle* – voyage from Lemnos to Gallipoli Peninsula

I relieved Denis Browne on watch at 3.00am and was on duty till 8.00am. I got on shore with a boatload of recruits and had about two miles more to walk before I picked up the company which I could see marching along opposite me on the other side of a bay. We marched west as far as Kondia where we turned around and marched east, off our tracks for a mile or two and then halted for lunch. Shortly after lunch we did an impromptu attack up a hill, during which I found myself doing extended order with my new platoon for the first time. They seemed to know it fairly well. We marched back to the boats along the harbour shore. Burnett wouldn't let us bathe – for which I was hoping with some eagerness.

The Greek villages we passed through, especially Kondia, were picturesque and I longed to go into some of the *kafenia* [cafes] we passed to see whether they had anything that might give one an idea of the taste of coffee: after three weeks on board, I have not been able to touch the coffee supplied. When we got on board again at 4.00pm we heard we were off to the Dardanelles at 6.00pm, and we immediately served out an additional 80 rounds of ammunition apiece, making 200 rounds per man. Six transports left, some of them containing French troops and I felt a good deal thrilled at the sight of the flotilla steaming in formation in the light of the young moon. We didn't expect to do more than make reconnaissance in force, but as it occurred to me that probably none of the skippers of the transports had ever steamed in line before, I felt the expedition might not be without its dangers. We spent the evening packing up.

Friday, 19 March 1915 – SS *Grantully Castle*, Port Mudros, Lemnos
We breakfasted at 5.00am and fell in silently on deck ready for landing at 5.30am. We were steaming in a southerly direction so that Hood Battalion, on the starboard deck could not see the Gallipoli Peninsula. The *Dublin* was manoeuvring like a sheepdog around a flock of sheep and there was another warship in attendance. When the light came we were dismissed from parade with orders to wait in readiness for landing, but the word soon went round that we were going back to Port Mudros. We located ourselves as being some five miles north of Suvla Bay and an hour and a half later we passed the mouth of the Dardanelles at about four miles distance or less. The sea was perhaps a little rough for landing, but from the fact that we were told to fall in without packs it looked as though we were not intended to land but to serve some strategic purpose by making a demonstration of force. We saw several warships off the mouth of the Dardanelles. At dinner time we had rumours of several battleships having been lost today in the Dardanelles.

Saturday, 20 March 1915 – SS _Grantully Castle_, Mudros Bay, Lemnos

At 11.30am we held a mock court martial (for instructional purposes) on the paymaster [Herbert] Gillard. It provided some amusement, but as I acted as prisoner's escort and had to stand for an hour and a half I didn't altogether appreciate it.

We heard from two of the men of HMS _Irresistible_, who were on HMT _Royal George_, that their ship, after suffering 160 men killed from shell fire, had struck a mine and been beached in the Dardanelles yesterday, that [another] had been mined and beached on Rabbit Island and that the _Inflexible_ had been mined in one compartment but had made Tenedos. Also that the French battleship _Bouvet_ had been sunk and that the _Gaulois_ had been beached after being mined. It seems as though the attempt to force the Dardanelles has not been very successful. Reports say that both shores are lined with torpedoes which are let off at ships attempting to pass. There was a rumour we were sailing shortly for Alexandria.

Based on what he had been told and with the full details still to emerge, Kelly's remarks regarding the Anglo-French naval operations were understandably muted. In fact the operation had been a dispiriting failure. British ships had first shelled the forts guarding the mouth of the Dardanelles as early as 3 November 1914 in response to a Turkish bombardment of Black Sea ports. More than three months were to pass before Britain again attempted to force the Dardanelles using 'ships alone'. The intention was to smash the Turkish forts and neutralise their guns before sending the fleet up through the narrows into the Sea of Marmara as far as Constantinople to re-establish a warm water route to Russia via the Black Sea.

By early March it was clear that little progress was being made and plans began to be put in train for the large-scale landing of troops with Secretary of State for War Lord Kitchener entrusting Sir Ian Hamilton with the command of the MEF on 12 March. Another all-out, all-naval assault was planned to commence on 18 March with an Anglo-French fleet consisting of most of the 14 British and four French capital ships arrayed in three groups in line abreast, reducing the forts with gunfire and proceeding up the Straits after a path had been cleared by minesweepers. But the minesweeping proved hazardous and when the assault began unknown threats lurked in the waters and the Turkish gunners in the forts proved themselves remarkably resilient and more than a match for the gunners on the Allied ships. What followed was a severe mauling for the Allies as the Turks responded to the assault with venom.

The first two vessels to become casualties were French: the Gaulois was hit and had to retire then the Bouvet struck a mine and went down in two minutes with almost all her crew. HMS Irresistible was mined next followed by HMS Ocean two hours later. HMS Inflexible and the Suffren were also put out of action. These losses could not be sustained and the attack was called off.

The final attempt to smash a way through to Constantinople by using ships alone was over in a single day. The disaster served to reinforce the view in London that in order to silence the guns and secure the Dardanelles to ensure the safe passage of the navy, the landing of large numbers of troops was inevitable. By the time Kelly heard news of the dreadful losses at sea it was a certainty.

Tuesday, 23 March 1915 – SS *Grantully Castle*, Mudros Bay, Lemnos

A strong north-easterly wind was still blowing and it was rather cold. A Greek interpreter has come to live on the ship and I was one of those who took a lesson at 2.15pm. He taught three of us – [Sub Lieutenant Eric] Gamage, [Lieutenant Ernest] Nobbs and myself – the alphabet and after we had done he took Shaw-Stewart, Denis Browne, Asquith and [Sub Lieutenant Arthur] Tisdall, who were more advanced.

Kelly's assessment that Arthur Walderne 'Wally' St. Clair Tisdall, a young officer in the Anson Battalion, was 'more advanced' in Greek was an understatement. His academic and sporting careers were studded with glittering prizes which he continued to accumulate when he went up to Trinity

College, Cambridge. There he gained a double first in Classical Honours and the Chancellor's Gold Medal for Classics.

Tisdall was only a month away from going down in history as the first man of the RND to be awarded the VC for his actions on 25 April 1915 during the Gallipoli landings. On hearing wounded men on the beach calling for assistance, Tisdall, 'jumped into the water, and, pushing a boat in front of him, made four or five trips between the ship and the shore and was responsible for rescuing several wounded men under heavy and accurate fire'. He was killed on 6 May 1915.

Wednesday, 24 March 1915 – SS *Grantully Castle*, Aegean Sea

The strong north-east breeze was still blowing. After a number of rumours during the last few days as to our sailing, we finally weighed anchor about 5.00pm on receipt of orders that were brought by a despatch steamboat. It was interesting looking at the warships – including the *Queen Elizabeth* with her eight, huge 15-inch guns – as we passed close by them, and as we left the bay the view of the ships with the snow-clad heights of Samothrace in the background made a lovely picture.

Thursday, 25 March 1915 – SS *Grantully Castle*

We passed between Delos and Nikaria and Patmos in the morning and at tea time we passed fairly close to Rhodes. The morning was spent in inspecting men's blankets. I had a Greek lesson with Arthur Asquith, Rupert Brooke and Denis Browne at 2.30pm.

One of the Anson officers – Sub Lieutenant [Alan] Campbell is ill and word had got to Denis Browne that he would like to be played to. The two colonels were playing bridge in the salon so I played Schumann's F Major Romance on the piano in the companion [room]. Campbell, however, found it too awful, at which I didn't wonder.

Before dinner I finished writing out a polka I have been under promise to write for Patricia ever since she left England in 1912. This is about my third attempt to carry out the contract – the two former ones being just tinged with a suspicion of vulgarity in the rhythm.

I did semaphore with my section leaders at 3.30pm and at 4.45pm. I attended a lecture by Lieutenant Nelson (of Scott's South Pole expedition) on the prismatic compass. I have lost the key to my tin box – which does not promise well for a possible disembarkation tomorrow.

Alan Urquhart 'Beo' Campbell was the son of the famous late nineteenth-century actress Mrs Patrick Campbell, for whom George Bernard Shaw specifically wrote the part of Eliza Doolittle in Pygmalion. *Campbell was killed in France on 30 December 1917 serving with the Howe Battalion and is buried in Metz-en-Couture Communal Cemetery, British Extension.*

Lieutenant Edward Nelson was the marine biologist on Scott's Antarctic Expedition. He assumed temporary command of the Hood for a short period in the summer of 1915 and later commanded the Nelson Battalion.

Saturday, 27 March 1915 – SS *Grantully Castle*, Port Said

We were off Port Said at 6.10am and I hurried down again to get a bath before we entered the Suez Canal. We spent part of the morning examining the men's packs and seeing they had the right articles put away in them. At 11.30am I did semaphore with my section leaders and petty officers. In the afternoon Denis Browne and I took our platoons ashore and marched them through the town to bathe on the sea beach. The water was rather full of black sand, but it was very pleasant.

We got leave to dine on shore and Ock Asquith, Denis Browne, Rupert Brooke and I left the ship at 5.45pm. After dinner we got our hair clipped short as an example to the men. There was talk of our going out to the trenches on Monday to repel a probable attack from the Turks.

Sunday, 28 March 1915 – Hood Battalion Camp, Port Said

B Company had orders to leave the ship after breakfast, with all their gear, and move their line of tents the other side of the railway line about half-a-mile from the outskirts of Port Said. It rained fairly heavily while we were disembarking and moving into camp. There were only two tents per platoon supplied, so that about 24 of the men had one tent among them. We arranged for them to put their gear in their tent and sleep out.

Monday, 29 March 1915 – Hood Battalion camp, Port Said

It was rather windy and the sand got into everything. I am in a tent with Denis Browne, Patrick Shaw-Stewart and Charles Lister who has just joined up with the battalion as a platoon commander from the divisional staff to which he was attached as interpreter. Browne and I sleep out in the open. We were duty company and I had to take my platoon on to the *Grantully Castle* in the morning and again in the afternoon, to assist in unloading and cleaning the mess decks. It is said things were packed into the ship at Avonmouth with so little forethought that the only way of getting them into the right place is to unload and reload all the transports.

I spent over an hour of the morning playing the piano in the saloon. There was no-one else there and I played two organ preludes, my recent setting of the 'Song of David' (Smart), my Allegro de Concert and the first two movements of my F Minor piano sonata.

Tuesday, 30 March 1915 – Hood Battalion camp, Port Said

There is a piece of enclosed water – part of the lagoon – at the back of the camp which is deep and clean and makes an excellent bathing place in the early morning. The battalion did a route march from 8.00am till 12.15pm. We marched through Port Said and out for about three-and-a-half miles west along the sea beach. At the furthest point we reached, we halted and had a delightful surf bathe. The breakers were coming in quite like they do on the Australian beaches, the only difference being that the sand was not quite so clean.

Wednesday, 31 March 1915 – Shepheard's Hotel, Cairo

I raced Freyberg, OC, A Company, Hood Battalion, in our morning swim and was very easily outdistanced. He was champion of New Zealand for three years. The four companies spent the morning carrying out tactical exercises at the back of the camp. B Company spent most of the morning practising the attack and as I was for some considerable time in the firing line with my own platoon alone I had a good opportunity of practising fire orders.

Denis Browne, Johnny Dodge and I got leave to go to Cairo for 48 hours and we caught the 6.10pm train. On reaching Shepheard's Hotel we engaged rooms and then motored straight to the pyramids, where we spent an hour walking about them and gazing at the Sphinx in the light of the full moon. There were some Australian troops about, one or two of whom were a little too friendly according to English military standards. We all enjoyed some quiet contemplation of the Sphinx after the guide had finished his explanations. We got back to the hotels about 2.00am.

Shepheard's Hotel was originally founded by Englishman Samuel Shepheard in 1841. In the late nineteenth century, when Cairo became a hub of international commerce, Shepheard's became a focal point where its famous terrace became the place to be seen for European tourists and travellers including members of the international monarchy and aristocracy. Its guest book boasted such names as Winston Churchill, Lord Kitchener of Khartoum, Theodore Roosevelt and T E Lawrence. Shepheard's has also become a favoured location for several feature films including the multi-Oscar winning The English Patient.

Thursday, 1 April 1915 – Shepheard's Hotel, Cairo
Denis Browne, Johnny Dodge and I spent an hour at the Museum of Egyptian Antiquities after breakfast and I was glad of the opportunity to revisit the Sheikh el Beled, one of the 4th Dynasty scribes, and other things. At 11.30am we made for the Mosque Al Azhar – the University Mosque – and visited the bazaars on the way home. I had an amusing bargain for a Persian rug which I brought down from Egyptian £5-10-0 to £4-0-0 inclusive of charges for postage to England. In the afternoon we want to the Sultan Hassan Mosque and the Kait Bey and Sultan Barbuk mosques in the tombs of the Khalifs and ended up at sunset

on the citadel terrace. We climbed the minaret of the Sultan Hassan Mosque (280-ft high).

I saw [George] Lloyd in Shepheard's after lunch and when I told him some of the RND had gone to El Kantara to repel an attack of the Turks on the canal he looked at me with rather an amused smile and invited me to go to his office in the War Office to see the disposition of the Turkish forces according to the latest information. I went at about 7.00pm and found his room covered with large maps with Turkish Army Corps – represented by patches of paper – pinned on to them in the localities where his spies had last reported them to be. It was most interesting and he struck me as doing some very good work. There were apparently very few Turks anywhere near the canal – most of them being in the Caucasus and round about Constantinople and the Gallipoli Peninsula. He said we should get a very hot reception.

I was very sorry to hear from him of the death of S P Cockerell who had been flying on the Suez Canal. He had apparently not been vaccinated since he was a child and died of smallpox after two days illness. I have known him ever since he went to Eton and liked him. He has always struck me as being a very capable man and his death is a considerable loss to his generation. Lloyd said he had been doing very useful and plucky work on the canal.

Sir George Ambrose Lloyd (First Baron Lloyd), a near contemporary of Kelly at Eton, had coxed the Cambridge crew to victory in the boat races of 1899 and 1900. He was an honorary attaché at the British embassy in Constantinople (Istanbul) travelling widely in the old Ottoman Empire. By late 1914 he was seconded to the intelligence department of the general staff in Egypt and when Kelly bumped into him at Shepheard's he was serving on the staff of General Sir Ian Hamilton, the Commander-in-Chief of the MEF, as he made his final preparations for the British landings on Gallipoli.

Thirty-four-year-old Lieutenant Samuel Pepys Cockerell, Eton and Trinity College, Cambridge (1900) and also a member of the Cambridge crew in the university boat race of 1900, was serving with a Royal Flying Corps (RFC) detachment operating out of Camp Moascar, Ismailia. He was employed flying reconnaissance missions against the Ottoman Turk Army in the region of the Suez Canal. He died on 20 March 1915 and lies today in Ismailia War Memorial Cemetery.

Friday, 2 April 1915 – Hood Battalion, Port Said
In the afternoon Johnny Dodge and I spent an hour at the zoo and I was delighted to see the same jungle cat I had seen four-and-a-half years ago, with its eyes all squeezed in with sleepy contentment. We saw two of the pontoons on which the Turks tried to cross the Suez Canal. We reached Port Said about 11.00pm.

Saturday, 3 April 1915 – Hood Battalion, Port Said
Sir Ian Hamilton reviewed the Naval Division at 9.00am and if our colonel could be believed, declared himself very well satisfied with the Hood Battalion. I went into Port Said at 11.00am to do some shopping and get some money and I finished up by lunching with Patrick Shaw-Stewart at the Eastern Exchange Hotel. I dined with Charles Lister at the Casino Hotel.

Rupert Brooke was taken ill during the morning and after lying out under an awning most of the day was moved to the Casino Hotel at tea time. Both Shaw-Stewart and he seem to have a touch of the sun. It was one of the most uncomfortable days I have ever spent, as a strong wind made the air thick with eddying sand and everything in and out of the tent got covered with it. There was nothing to do but get through the day by sleeping or doing nothing, as any company training was out of the question.

**Friday, 9 April 1915 – Hood Battalion, SS *Grantully Castle*,
Port Said**
We had had orders overnight to breakfast at 5.30am prior to the battalion going out on landing operations. At 4.30am, however, a counter order came cancelling it and telling us we were to embark on the *Grantully Castle*.

Saturday, 10 April 1915 – Hood Battalion, SS *Grantully Castle*, Levant

I was officer of the watch from 6.00am till 9.00am and put in my time between visiting sentries and reading the French [*Yellow Book* of diplomatic documents] on the war. I found it as exciting as a detective story. We left Port Said about breakfast time with a lighter in tow. This is for landing purposes on the Gallipoli Peninsula. We are steaming at six-and-a-half knots on account of the lighter.

Asquith noted later that the lighters being towed were full of drinking water and that fortunately at this time hostile submarines were still rare in the Aegean.

Monday, 12 April 1915 – Hood Battalion, SS *Grantully Castle*

B Company spent the morning getting the sand and dust out of their web equipment and off their ammunition and chargers. At 2.15pm they did physical drill. I read through Rupert Brooke's sonnets, 'The Treasure', 'Peace', 'Safety', 'The Dead' (Nos. 1 and 2) and 'The Soldier' from *New Numbers* for the second time, also *The Staircase* a one act play by Lascelles Abercrombie. The latter struck me as being good – the sonnets I like a good deal.

I finished the French [*Yellow Book*] of diplomatic documents relating to the war before going to bed. I found it a little redundant considered merely as literature but on the whole extremely interesting. Jules Cambon comes out of it as a pretty acute observer of Germany's intentions.

Tuesday, 13 April 1915 – Hood Battalion, SS *Grantully Castle*, Aegean Sea

Our lighter, which we have towed from Port Said, broke loose at 4.00am and we spent the day standing by to keep it in sight. There was a fairly strong wind blowing and the captain, rightly or wrongly, decided it was impossible to launch a boat to secure it. Our signalling officer, however, announced at 9.00pm that [another ship] had picked up five lighters in spite of the weather. It is an odd and somewhat humiliating occurrence that several ships of a large expedition should all be hanging about in the sea looking on helplessly at their drifting lighters.

I read a book called *Why We Are at War* by members of the Oxford Faculty of Modern History and had a short discussion of literary matters with Rupert Brooke before dinner. He thinks Dr Johnson's prose style quite perfect and apart from Shakespeare who is supreme, he seems to like Keats best of the poets. He is very fond of Belloc and G K Chesterton and does not care much for R L Stevenson.

Wednesday, 14 April 1915 – Hood Battalion, SS *Grantully Castle*
I rested from 2.00pm till 4.30pm when I was woken up by a severe squall. For about half an hour the wind blew the waves away in sheets of water. Patrick Shaw-Stewart, Ock Asquith and I had a Greek lesson after tea and with the conversation getting round to the Greek for musical instruments, playing, etc, the interpreter said he sang and volunteered [to sing] after the lesson was over. It is the song, according to him, which the Greeks sing on setting out in ships to fight the Turks. I played three games of chess with Lieutenant Nelson after dinner and won two of them.

Thursday, 15 April 1915 – Hood Battalion, SS *Grantully Castle*, off Lemnos
There was a fancy dress dance in the evening and about 25 men paraded in their get ups at 6.15pm and caused a great deal of amusement. As they have left their kit bags behind at Port Said it was remarkable what they achieved. The whole thing was redolent of a very nice sentiment uniting all ranks. Two men got up as CPO [Frederick] Flynn, the Battalion CPO and imitated him, which caused considerable amusement.

I read some of Anatole France's *Pierre Nozière* after dinner. We were in sight of the lighthouse on Lemnos late at night.

Friday, 16 April 1915 – Hood Battalion, SS *Grantully Castle*, Skyros
We entered Mudros Bay, Lemnos, at 8.00am and anchored in the mouth of it, as further inland it was crowded up with transports and

warships. About 10.30am we got orders to proceed to Skyros, but we had not gone a couple of miles before a destroyer came after us at about 27 knots and ordered us back. It appeared that a transport (No. B12) had been torpedoed by Turkish destroyers off Skyros at 10.00am. Just as we were entering Mudros Bay, however, we got the order to proceed to Skyros. We reached it about 5.30pm and after hanging about for some time finally entered the harbour about 6.45pm to find several transports and warships already there. The entrance is only about a quarter-of-a-mile broad and the shores are coloured with a great variety of rock. There is a big mountain – about 1,500 feet high, I should imagine – which gives quite an impressive touch to the little harbour.

We have no definite news of the torpedoed transport, but the captain said he had heard that three Turkish destroyers had fired at her in vain, without hitting her, and without doing much damage. According to his story the Turks had given the crew ten minutes in which to leave the ship and it was in the ensuing panic alone that any casualties occurred. Forty men were said to have been lost.

I had a delightful talk about literature and poetry with Rupert Brooke after tea and again after dinner. He strikes me as being made of really fine stuff – both physically and mentally. He talked of his own work, too.

Saturday, 17 April 1915 – Hood Battalion, SS *Grantully Castle*, Skyros

About half of A and C Companies, consisting almost entirely of stokers, left the ship at 8.00am with Sub Lieutenants John Dodge, Shadbolt and Trimmer for HMT *Royal George* and at 10.30am she left Skyros. It was said they were to act as boat's crews for the landing force at Gallipoli and possibly as crews for the minesweepers. There was considerable depression at the battalion being depleted in this way as it was thought that if further working parties were required the authorities would be likely to take them from a battalion that had already been tapped for the purpose.

GALLIPOLI

I received a letter addressed in Maisie's handwriting without a stamp, [in it was enclosed another from Joe Kelly in pencil – both below] which gave me one of the greatest surprises I have ever experienced:

HMS *Dublin*, Malta, 9 April 1915
My dear Koochface,

I daresay you will be speechless as the dogs were when you got our telegram of Tuesday. Joe sent me a wire to Bisham asking me to come out here and have a look at him – he had been Paying me Court as they say since last July. So as I was going to Antibes I decided to risk it and got here on Sunday – we had decided we couldn't get engaged or anything until we had met, and this was the only chance of seeing him. I am very glad I did come for I couldn't be happier. I wish I could have told you about it before, but I never thought Joe would get leave till the war was over, and you would be at home yourself. He goes back to the Dardanelles on Sunday, and I go to Antibes to stay with Diana for a bit on Wednesday before going home to the dogs and May. Won't Mrs Bill be sick at being done out of a wedding at Bisham!

The only thing I regret about the hurried wedding is that you knew nothing about it and couldn't be there. I sent you a telegram signed Bootface and had it returned by the censor.

Good bye and good luck, yours affectly...

HMS *Dublin*, Malta, 9 April
Dear old Sep,

Maisie has the only pen. I hope we have your blessing – we sent you a telegram after our wedding, there was no time for doing so before, she is happy, I hope and think – I certainly am. We – the ship – have to return to the Dardanelles – Maisie for Antibes.

I am sending this by a transport on the point of sailing.

So long old boy – all the good luck and hope to see you in a few days.

yrs ever, Joe.

Of all incredible events! But after-all it saves a good deal of trouble and as the marriage, if unexpected, is extremely welcome, the circumstances add rather a fillip. But fancy old Joe and Maisie, of all people in the world! I wonder how she got to Malta and what excuse she made for going, etc etc!

I was preparing to go to bed at 8.45pm when Rupert Brooke came into my cabin and we had a talk about literary matters. I asked him to read me his five sonnets, 'Peace', 'Safety', 'The Dead' (Nos. 1 & 2) and 'The Soldier'. I enjoyed the sound of his voice and the way he read them a good deal but I don't know that I was conscious of any new light being shed upon the lines. I don't understand 'Safety' – the others I like very much.

Even by the time of Kelly's first meeting with Brooke in September 1914, the 27-year-old was already seen as a huge star in the poetry firmament, although his fame was yet to spread into the mainstream.

Born in Rugby in 1887, he had studied at Rugby School, where his father was a housemaster, before going on to King's College, Cambridge. Brooke was well acquainted with the Bloomsbury group of writers and also came to be viewed as central to the Dymock poets, along with the likes of Robert Frost, Lascelles Abercrombie and John Drinkwater.

From 1909 he lived in the Cambridgeshire village of Grantchester and his first volume of poems was published in 1911. King's elected him a fellow in 1913 – the year in which he also travelled widely, visiting North America, the Pacific Islands and New Zealand.

Known for his good looks as well as his poetry - W B Yeats is said to have called him 'the handsomest young man in England' - the poem which was to elevate him to unprecedented levels of attention, 'The Soldier', would be written towards the end of 1914. Beginning 'If I should die, think only this of me/That there's some corner of a foreign field/That is forever England', its entry into national consciousness began with its publication in The Times Literary Supplement *on 11 March 1915. It was read by the Dean of St Paul's Cathedral as part of his Easter Sunday sermon on 4 April that year. It would become one of the twentieth century's most famous poems, viewed as the epitome of the idealistic, optimistic and naïve mood of the country in the early months of the First World War.*

Monday, 19 April 1915 – Hood Battalion, SS *Grantully Castle*, Skyros

The battalion started landing about 8.00am and B Company, or most of it, was in the first party. Eventually we came to a stop at the top of the hill, about three-quarters-of-a-mile away and about 300 feet high. We just lay down for an hour or more in the sun, overlooking a large harbour, about a mile-and-a-half in front of us.

The island is a divine paradise of wild thyme and other scented herbs, lizards and, people said, large tortoises. The part we traversed was very difficult going, consisting mostly of rocks, pieces of marble and a short prickly shrub, but the atmosphere was almost aggressively sweet with the smell of herbs. One can well imagine the patriotism this scent must have awakened in the breasts of Greeks.

Tuesday, 20 April 1915 – Hood Battalion, SS *Grantully Castle*, Skyros

The whole RND landed between 7.30am and 9.00am and took part in a kind of field day. Hood Battalion put in a pleasant two hours or so in a delicious rocky dry water course before it got orders to advance in support of Howe Battalion up a steep hill against imaginary Turks. Before we got to the top the staff had discovered a flank attack or the necessity, more likely, of diverting some of the forces away from an already crowded spot, and we descended again and proceeded to try and find our way up the same little valley in which we had spent most of the morning. Through reading a signal intended for Howe [Battalion] apparently, we soon got the order to halt, and after half-an-hour or so we returned to the olive grove which had been chosen as the rendezvous of the 2nd [Naval] Brigade, with the other battalions.

Philip Kershaw and Lancelot Cherry came to dinner from the *Franconia* and we had a jolly evening. I sit at [the chief engineer's] table with Patrick Shaw-Stewart, Denis Brown, Arthur Asquith, Rupert Brooke and Charles Lister and we're a happy party.

Wednesday, 21 April 1915 – Hood Battalion, SS *Grantully Castle*, Skyros

At 5.45pm Colonel Quilter explained to us the plan of operations on the Gallipoli Peninsula and the part we are to play in them.

Thursday, 22 April 1915 – Hood Battalion, SS *Grantully Castle*, Skyros

We were to have left early in the morning but owing to the weather all operations were cancelled for 24 hours. I had a very odd dream about a concert in which I found myself playing Bach's A Minor organ fugue without having had time to look it up. In the middle it became apparent that if I was to finish it I should have to improvise, which I proceeded to do for a few bars. Things began to go from bad to worse, however, and finally in seizing on to a loud entry in the bass I found to my horror my right hand playing Mendelssohn's 'Wedding March'!

B Company was duty company so there was practically nothing to do, I spent an hour or two colouring the two large maps of the Gallipoli Peninsula they have given us. Rupert Brooke, who was taken ill the night before last, was found to be seriously ill this morning and when several doctors came for a consultation in the afternoon they held out very small hope of his living. The pneumococcus germ has poisoned his blood through a bad lip and his face is all swollen up. I looked into his cabin before breakfast, when I found him very dazed, but I had no

Son of Empire: Despite being the son of an Irishman, Kelly was accurately described by the *Sydney Morning Herald* in 1906 as an 'Anglo-Australian'. The young Kelly was shaped both by the land of his birth and that which became 'home' for the rest of his life. In his outlook and attitudes, he was a man of the British Empire and of its ancient institutions.

(Courtesy George Newlands, McLaren Books, Helensburgh)

Right: 'Typical young Australian': News of Kelly's success as a rower spanned the world, with reports in the Australian media proclaiming his many successes at Henley Royal Regatta. This sketch of the 21-year-old Kelly appeared in *The Referee* in August 1902. Coverage of Henley eclipsed even the Olympic regatta, indicating that the Royal Regatta was considered the most prestigious rowing event.

F. S. KELLY
(Winner of the Diamond Sculls at Henley, 1902.)

Left: Undergraduate: Frederick Septimus Kelly photographed in 1903 at the age of 22.

(Courtesy Balliol College, Oxford)

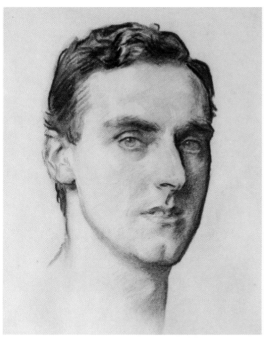

Left: Historic sketch: The famous artist John Singer Sargent captured the essence of the sitter's personality when Kelly sat for this charcoal study in Sargent's studio on Tite Street in Chelsea on 21 February 1915.

(Courtesy Kevin Gordon via Carol Jones)

Right: Beloved sister: John Singer Sargent also immortalised Maisie Kelly in charcoal not long after he had sketched her brother. Stricken with grief Maisie ensured his name was not forgotten by funding the Bisham War Memorial. Today the original Singer Sargent portraits of Frederick and Maisie Kelly hang side-by-side in the home of portrait artist Kevin Gordon in the USA.

(Courtesy Kevin Gordon via Carol Jones)

Above: Oxford Blue: Kelly (*back row, second left*) with the rest of the 1903 Oxford Boat Race crew which lost to Cambridge by six lengths. Despite his prowess as a sculler and rower, Kelly was not awarded his Blue until 1903. Oxford's chances were scuppered by Cambridge's false start, which was allowed to go unpunished by the umpire, former Cambridge Blue Frederick Pitman.

Below: 'Dashing sculler': Kelly demonstrates stroke technique on the Thames at Henley, outside the Leander Club boathouse – many of the buildings on the street called Thameside beyond still stand today. It was said that when he was at the height of his powers, his sculling stroke was 'like the downward beat of a swallow's wing'.

(Courtesy George Newlands, McLaren Books, Helensburgh)

LEANDER CLUB.
OLYMPIC CREW 1908
St. lbs.
Bow A.C.Gladstone. 11.6
2. F.S Kelly. 12.1
3. B.C.Johnstone 12.11
4. Guy Nickalls. 12.6
5. C.D.Burnell. 14.2
6. R.H.Sanderson. 13.6
7. R.B.Etherington Smith 12.7
Stroke. H.C.Bucknall.11.6
Cox. C.S.Maclagan. 8.8

Left: Olympic gold: The medal awarded to Charles Burnell for Great Britain/Leander's victory in the Olympic eights rowing final at Henley in 1908, with the winning crew's names engraved on a separate plaque.

Below: Olympic champion: Kelly poses for posterity with fellow Leander Club Olympic rowing medallists on the steps of the clubhouse at Henley-on-Thames. It is a ritual often performed today with Leander medallists after an Olympic Games. *(Courtesy Leander Club)*

Above: In the Hood: Officers of the Hood Battalion at Blandford Camp, Dorset in February 1915. Kelly is pictured middle row, fifth from the right. His close friends Rupert Brooke, Arthur Asquith and Bernard Freyberg are pictured respectively on the middle row second from left, back row, extreme left and seated, third from left. *(Courtesy Imperial War Museum)*

Below: Early morning exercise: Kelly (*centre*) stretches his muscles with fellow officers Lieutenant Eric Nobbs (*extreme right*) and Lieutenant Commander Alexander Graham (second right) aboard the *Grantully Castle* bound for Gallipoli via Egypt – March 1915. *(Courtesy Len Sellers)*

Above left: Champion swimmer: New Zealander Bernard Freyberg, whose marathon solo swim on the night of 25/26 April 1915, was one of the most daring escapades of the Gallipoli campaign.

Above right: Original editor: Arthur Asquith, the son of British Prime Minister Herbert Asquith edited Kelly's unpublished war diary.

(Courtesy John Rous)

'Forever England': Rupert Brooke's original grave on Skyros. The funeral and location inspired Kelly to write his 'Elegy in Memoriam Rupert Brooke'.

(Courtesy Mike Read)

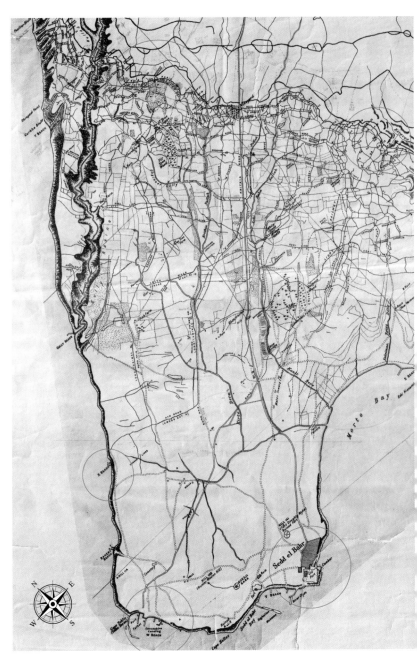

Helles front: A trench map of Cape Helles and the Krithia front showing the sectors and locations (*circled*) which would have been well known to Frederick Kelly during his time on the peninsula.

idea he was dangerously ill. The doctors made me realise, however, that it was far more than likely that he will not live and I felt very much depressed. I have had a foreboding that he is one of those, like Keats, Shelly and Schubert, who are not suffered to deliver their full message; but there seems to be just the slenderest chance he may live. I saw him carried on to the deck and lowered down into one of the ship's boats to be taken in a steam pinnace – from HMS *Canopus* – to a French hospital ship [the *Duguay-Trouin*] which is in the harbour. Ock Asquith went over with him and by the time of writing this (10.15pm) has not returned. I am conscious that a really fine talent and rare character hangs in the balance and it is very galling to hear from the doctors that they can do little but watch the progress of his illness.

Friday, 23 April 1915 – Hood Battalion, SS *Grantully Castle*, Skyros

The events of today made a deep impression on me. Rupert Brooke died on board the French hospital ship at 4.45pm and, in view of the ship's orders to sail at 5.00am the following morning, arrangements were at once made to bury him on the island he loved so well.

I left the ship at 8.15pm with the colonel, second-in-command (Myburgh) and about a dozen officers from this battalion and a steam pinnace from HMS *Dartmouth*, containing General Paris, a few officers of the staff and Harold Farrer and Lancelot Cherry, took us in tow to the French hospital ship. Here we took on the coffin and Arthur Asquith, who with Denis Browne had been tending Rupert, and a further boat, in which were about a dozen French officers who came to attend the burial, was added to the tow.

Charles Lister had gone with Denis Browne and a working party to dig a grave in the olive grove, which had served as a rendezvous for the 2nd Naval Brigade in the divisional field day last Tuesday – when Rupert began to sicken. It was about a mile from the shore to the grove, over very difficult stony ground and the petty officers who bore the coffin were obliged to go very slowly. We reached the grove at

10.45pm where, in the light of a clouded half-moon, the burial service was read by the Chaplain of the 1st Naval Brigade and a firing party under command of Sub Lieutenant Patrick Shaw-Stewart accorded the body military honours. It was a most moving experience. The small olive grove in the narrow valley and the scent of the wild sage gave a strong classic tone which was so in harmony with the poet we were burying that to some of us the Christian ceremony seemed out of keeping.

When all the others had gone back to the boats, Lieutenant Commander Freyberg – Rupert's company commander – Ock Asquith, Charles Lister, Denis Browne and I covered the grave with stones and as many pieces of marble as we could find. At the head and feet there were two wooden crosses with the name and the date of death and on the larger of them our Greek interpreter wrote the following inscription:

Ενθαδε Κειται 'ο
ξουδος Του θεου
Ανθυπολοχαγος Του
Αγγλικου Ναυτικου
ἀποθανων Επαρ Της
Α'απα λαυθερωσαως Της
Κων / πουλεως Απο
Των Τουεκων.

[Here lies the servant of God, sub lieutenant in the English Navy, who died for the deliverance of Constantinople from the Turks.]

The body lies looking down the valley towards the harbour and from behind an olive tree bends itself over the grave as though sheltering it from the sun and rain. No more fitting resting place for a poet could be found than this small grove, and it seems as though the gods had jealously snatched him away to enrich this scented island.

For the whole day I was oppressed with the sense of loss but when the officers and men had gone and when at last the five of us, his friends, had covered his grave with stones and took a last look in silence – then the sense of tragedy gave place to a sense of passionless beauty, engendered both by the poet and the place. On getting back to the ship I copied out the contents of his notebook before going to bed – as a precaution lest the original should be lost in being sent to England.

Saturday, 24 April 1915 – Hood Battalion, SS *Grantully Castle*, Gulf of Xeros

We left Skyros at 5.30am in company with most of the Naval Division and were escorted by HMS *Canopus*, *Dartmouth* and some destroyers in the direction of the Gulf of Xeros. Colonel Quilter gave the officers an excellent talk on the active service which awaits the Naval Division in the course of the next few days.

Sunday, 25 April 1915 – Hood Battalion, SS *Grantully Castle*, Gulf of Xeros

It was a perfectly still, hot and sunny day – an ideal one for the landing of the Australians and New Zealanders, the 29th Division and the French at Kapa [Gaba] Tepe, Cape Helles and on the Asiatic side of the mouth of the Dardanelles, respectively. The function of the RND was to demonstrate off Bulair and towards evening to make a feint of landing on the north shore of the Gulf.

We were told overnight that a bombardment of some of the forts by our ships would begin and I woke up at 5.30am in expectation and waited to see what was happening. The *Dartmouth* and another smaller ship were firing – the former with 6-inch guns, but at the distance we were away, some five miles I should think, one could scarcely hear the reports although one could see the flashes and see the smoke of the shells on the hills. The day was deliciously warm and still and had far more the feel of the regatta day about it than the prelude to our landing for really hard fighting.

Colonel Quilter gave B Company a first rate talk about the hardships of war on morning parade. After it was dismissed I showed my platoon, about ten men at a time, several maps and explained to them our plan of operations – which seems to be that we demonstrate off Bulair and then go back to reinforce either the 29th Division or the Australians and New Zealanders.

After dinner we had news that both had effected satisfactory landings and were making good progress. I slept from 3.00pm till 4.30pm and spent several hours of the day colouring two of the large scale maps of the Gallipoli Peninsula we have been given, with blue and red pencil – so as to bring out the heights. Lieutenant Commander Freyberg left the ship for his swim ashore after dinner.

Anyone reading Kelly's final sentence might be forgiven for thinking that his friend, Bernard Freyberg, was embarking on a post-prandial dip. In fact Freyberg's actions that night turned out to be one of the most astonishing individual feats of courage and endurance of the entire Gallipoli campaign.

As Kelly had noted, the RND were to be deployed in a deception plan to menace the neck of land forming the narrowest point of the peninsula, at a position known as the Bulair Lines. The hope was that the sight of a fleet of warships and packed transports lying offshore in the Gulf of Xeros would unnerve the Turks into thinking that a night landing was about to take place with the aim of cutting off their forces to the south. The overriding intention, however, was to peg down Turkish troops in the north which might otherwise be despatched to assist in repelling the planned British landings on the toe of the peninsula, 50 miles to the south-west, and that of the Australians and New Zealanders at Gaba Tepe on the west coast.

Although the original deception plan called for boats, packed with selected men of Kelly's Hood battalion, to land and create the diversion, it was felt that such a course would lead to unnecessary casualties, so when one such boat got to within two miles of the shore at 12.40am, Lieutenant Commander Bernard Freyberg, New Zealand 100 – and 400-yards freestyle swimming champion in 1906 – volunteered to 'go it alone' by swimming the remaining distance in 'bitterly cold water', towing a raft of flares to emerge on the shore at several points to mimic an amphibious landing and gain information about the Turkish positions. Setting a compass bearing as the ships could not show any lights, he then swam back out to sea in the inky darkness and was mercifully picked up at 3.00am, half-a-mile out, at the very limit of his endurance, suffering from severe cramp and half dead with hypothermia.

The deception worked: two Turkish divisions were held ready around Bulair to repel an invasion and Bernard Freyberg thoroughly deserved the DSO he was awarded. Arthur Asquith, who, along with Chares Lister, had requested to be included in Freyberg's endeavour later noted that Kelly, also a strong swimmer, 'had asked and been refused leave to accompany Freyberg on this enterprise'. Asquith was of the opinion that in acting alone and swimming ashore Freyberg had achieved the same results that a landing with a far larger force could have hoped for and 'thus probably averted the sacrifice of a number of men. The Greek press of about this date had news of Turkish troops despatched to deal with a landing in the Gulf of Xeros, so presumably the feint was successful'.

Monday, 26 April 1915 – Hood Battalion, SS *Grantully Castle*, Gulf of Xeros

Another delightful, hot day. We were still opposite Bulair Lines and had orders to 'demonstrate'. No shelling, however, took place as far as I was aware. Charles Lister called me at 2.00am to see Lieutenant Commander Freyberg's flares on the northern shore of the Gulf. He had gone within a mile or so of the shore in one of the ship's boats under escort of a torpedo boat – HMS *Kennet* (I think) – and from there he swam ashore towing a little canvas boat – the *Queen Elizabeth* – containing flares and a pistol, etc. His object was to light flares on the shores to make the Turks think it was the prelude to a landing in force. After the flares were lit the *Kennet* was to open fire. I saw the flashes of the guns from the bridge. As a matter of fact, he found no Turks there at all though he crawled uphill some way. His only excitement was the discovery during his swim, of the proximity of a porpoise which gave him a start. It was a clever idea finely carried out and might have achieved much in deceiving the enemy if they were there.

During the afternoon we got orders to steam to Cape Helles at 8.00pm so we spent the afternoon thinking of our gear in view of an early landing in support of the 29th Division the following morning. I got in an hour's sleep before lunch and another hour before tea. Before dinner I played Scarlatti's C Minor Sonata. Chopin's F Minor Ballade and my studies in E Minor and B Minor. We all expect to be in action tomorrow.

Tuesday, 27 April 1915 – Hood Battalion, SS *Grantully Castle* off Cape Helles, Gallipoli Peninsula

We had breakfast at 1.00am and spent the rest of the day ready to disembark at short notice. No orders, however, came and we spent the day watching the bombardment of Achi Baba and Pasha Dagh by the warships. I saw 6-inch guns being fired mostly and missed the *Queen Elizabeth*'s 15-inch guns, which I was told did some firing. I finished packing after breakfast and slept in my clothes for a couple of hours. I spent the afternoon from 2.00pm till 6.00pm sleeping in my cabin.

There was a great fleet of transports lying off Cape Helles and Sedd el Bahr and far in the distance some nine miles off we could see the Australian troops' transports off Kapa Tepe. It was interesting seeing the flashes of the guns and the bursts on the land. Stores, it looked like, were being landed near Cape Helles. We were only about two or three miles from the shore and could see things quite plainly through glasses. I saw no Turks nor did anyone else. It was another nice warm day.

Wednesday, 28 April 1915 – Hood Battalion, SS *Grantully Castle*, off Kapa Tepe, Gallipoli Peninsula

We breakfasted at 5.30am – nominally speaking the majority of officers being convinced that after our fruitless early breakfast the day before, there was no real necessity for such an early rise. I appeared at 6.15am. We spent the morning off Cape Helles and witnessed an attack of the 29th Division on Achi Baba. A heavy bombardment was kept up by several of our warships, much of the fire being directed on Krithia. We could see our troops advancing in extended order along the cliff by the sea-shore (some two miles off) but I never caught sight of any Turks.

The *Dublin*, now painted a pale grey, steamed quite close to us about 7.15am and Joe Kelly and I waved to one another. He sent me a semaphore message asking whether I had received his letter from Malta. He very obligingly opened fire quite close to us and continued planting shells on Krithia and Achi Baba all the morning. The *Queen Elizabeth* also steamed fairly close to us and it was with great excitement that we watched her training her 15-inch guns shorewards. She did open fire, but unfortunately only with her 6-inch guns.

About 11.30am we steamed up to Kapa Tepe where we spent the afternoon. Here we saw the Australians on the beach and halfway up the hill (north of Kapa Tepe) under hostile shrapnel fire. It was difficult in both cases to see where the firing line was. We again saw no Turks, but it seemed as though they had here been driven over the brow of the hill which was covered with shrub. The enemy had a concealed howitzer in action behind Achi Baba. On her way to Kapa Tepe in front of us, the *Franconia*, with the Drake Battalion and the divisional staff on board, was fired at from the shore and three shells dropped abaft of her. Off Cape Helles one or two shells dropped among the ships.

In the late afternoon news came that the admiral had commandeered two of the RND's battalions of Marines whose landing had raised our expectations, and as a message was also received to the effect that it was unlikely that we should land here there was considerable disappointment. Some of the keener spirits construe 'here' as meaning Gallipoli Peninsula and view our chances of taking part in the operations very pessimistically. The RND is certainly very much shrunk in numbers, the

Anson and much of the Hood and Howe Battalions having been taken for beach parties. It now does not consist of much more than a brigade. I slept from 2.00 till 4.30pm. I really did think I had packed for the last time prior to landing.

I played cut-throat bridge with Patrick Shaw-Stewart and Gamage after dinner. I don't suppose anyone ever viewed a battle in progress in greater comfort than we did the attack on Achi Baba. It was warm and still this morning, and we all had our glasses trained on the scene of operations and the bursting shells. Several of us were nonplussed at the absence of aeroplanes on our side (the enemy had none). I only saw one aeroplane or seaplane – I am not quite sure which – and it didn't do any reconnaissance work as far as we could see.

Thursday, 29 April 1915 – SS *Grantully Castle*, Cape Helles, Gallipoli Peninsula

We were a decidedly depressed set of officers for the greater part of the day, as it seemed as though there was little likelihood of our landing. The Marine battalions have been taken from the RND and it seemed as though it was being broken up into working and beach parties and for anything, save fighting. At 5.00pm however, orders came that we were to proceed to Cape Helles in readiness for immediate disembarkation and when we took a number of stretcher bearers and medical stores on board from a trawler, it really looked as though we were at last going to do something. We were without further orders at 10.00pm when we went to bed, but at 11.35pm the Officer of the Watch came round with the order to embark at once.

Major Sketchley of the divisional staff came on board at 6.00pm and stayed to dinner. He gave us some very interesting news of the landings at Cape Helles and at Kapa Tepe. Both the 29th Division and the Australians seemed to have behaved heroically and won a footing though suffering heavy casualties. He warned us against the Turkish use of the white flag.

*The officers' briefing given by Major Ernest Frederick Powys Sketchley, of the
Royal Marine Light Infantry, was as near an honest account of the current
state of affairs ashore as any junior battalion officer was likely to hear. It was
relatively peaceful when Kelly finally got his wish and set foot on Turkish
soil on W Beach on that cold, moonlit April night. Just five days earlier the
enclosed, semi-circular amphitheatre of W Beach, overlooked on three sides by
low, sandstone cliffs, had been the bloody stage for scenes of carnage.*

*Accompanied by the crackling frenzy of well-aimed fire from some 180
Turkish rifles, the assaulting British troops had gone ashore in slow-moving
open boats in broad daylight in the biggest amphibious operation of the war.
Those who were not shot on the boats or were hit and fell in the surf, or were
drowned due to the weight of their equipment, charged on to W Beach in the
teeth of tenacious Turkish resistance. Half a dozen men of the 1st Battalion of
the Lancashire Fusiliers were famously awarded 'Six VCs Before Breakfast' in
the process.*

*With the dead floating in the water or fringing the waterline behind
them the survivors fought on; negotiating the bodies strewn across the beach
and battling through barbed-wire entanglements to grasp the merest of
toeholds on the cliffs above and then to cling on desperately to their gains
by nightfall. But, as Kelly had noted, the Turks had exacted a high price
from the 'invaders'; out of an attacking force of 999 officers and men of
the Lancashire Fusiliers, for example, only 426 answered their names at
roll call the next day. Almost 200 were killed or died of wounds during the
assault and the hard fighting during the afternoon. The beach is still known
as Lancashire Landing in their honour and many of the dead lie today in a
cemetery of that name on a knoll 500 yards beyond the sand. A handful of
Anson Battalion men from a platoon attached to the assaulting battalions
had also been killed.*

*By the time Kelly's turn came to get ashore at Lancashire Landing, the
British at Cape Helles on the toe of the peninsula, the Anzacs on the west
coast at Ari Burnu and the French on the Asiatic coast of the Dardanelles
Straits had succeeded in wresting control of their landing beaches from the
Turks and – at Cape Helles at least – had followed up the Turkish retirement*

to a second and arguably stronger line of defences some two miles inland and almost stretching across the width of the peninsula.

Behind this line stood the village of Krithia – modern-day Alçıtepe – and behind that towered the looming presence of Achi Baba, rising to a height of 706 feet and offering superb views of the ground captured by the Allies to the south. Both Krithia and Achi Baba had been initial Allied objectives on 25 April 1915 but had thus far resisted all attempts at capture during the costly attack which became known as the First Battle of Krithia, fought on 28 April, and witnessed by Kelly from the Grantully Castle.

From W Beach Kelly and the Hood would head north towards the Allied line which was now, after that first battle, hunkered down still some way short of Krithia itself and under the ever-watchful glare of Turkish observers on the heights of Achi Baba beyond.

Major Sketchley, who had briefed Kelly, would later be mentioned in despatches on three occasions and go on to earn the DSO on 13 July 1915 during fighting south of Achi Baba. With the assistance of a corporal he managed to stem a retirement which had turned into a headlong retreat then gathered together about 40 men and lead them forward to reoccupy some trenches. His citation notes that he 'exhibited great courage, presence of mind and powers of personal leadership in a moment of crisis.'

Friday, 30 April 1915 – Cape Helles

I landed with my platoon (No. 5, B Company) in the second tow to leave the *Grantully Castle* at 1.30am. It was full moon and a lovely, clear but very cold night. I met Lieutenant Commander Burnett on the beach (W Beach, where the Lancashire Fusiliers landed last Sunday) and we marched up to the right of the beach where A Company and most of B Company had already piled arms and turned in. PO [Joseph] Kirkbride lent me a blanket which I shared with Burnett and [Lieutenant Alan] Hughes (second-in-command of B Company) but in spite of huddling together we were all miserably cold.

It was a nice sunny day, which the battalion spent in marching out to a shallow trench some mile-and-a-half on the way to Krithia, and in digging it into fairly deep holes and traverses. Shells were passing over us both ways most of the day, but none fell near us. On the way back, however, we had not left the part of the line on which the platoon had been working ten minutes before a shell pitched quite close by.

The Naval Brigade is bivouacking on the top of the cliff between Capes Tekke [Tekke Burnu] and Helles. We are within range but not within view of the Turkish batteries. It was my first experience of shell fire, and as none of the shells pitched closer than a quarter-of-a-mile, it was not very alarming. Much more alarming was the sound of one of our ships' guns replying to the enemy's fire. Though a mile-and-a-half or more away the report and the scream of the shells were very nerve-racking.

On getting back to our bivouac I went with Charles Lister and Denis Browne to Cape Helles, where we inspected the ruins of the lighthouse, the twisted mountings of the guns in a Turkish battery, a formidable Turkish barbed-wire entanglement, and we finally had a good view down on to the beach where the French are landing. They seem to have got things into a more orderly state than obtains on our beaches.

Saturday, 1 May 1915 – Hood Battalion bivouac between Capes Helles and Tekke, Gallipoli Peninsula

Another warm sunny day, which we spent like yesterday in preparing supporting trenches. Nothing happened in the firing line, but the intermittent shell fire continued like a colossal game of tennis over our heads. The country up as far as Achi Baba is quite delightful – open, with a certain number of small trees, some orchards and a profusion of wild flowers – among which I saw lavender, burridge [borage] and an iris which smelt sweet. I was warmer last night owing to our packs having been brought up to camp; but it was still very dewy and cold.

Sunday, 2 May 1915 – Hood Battalion, farm building on north side of peninsula

After finishing my diary and turning in last night, what promised to be a very comfortable night was interrupted by two alarms at 11.15pm or so, and half-an-hour later, after which we lay down in our kit, and finally marched off for the firing line about 1.00am. I had borrowed one of the doctor's stretchers, with which to keep out the dew, and it was annoying to be robbed of the prospect of a really warm and dry bed.

We marched out first to a supporting trench some 100 yards in the rear of the firing line, and had not been there many minutes when a staff officer sent me off in charge of a party of ten men to take up ammunition to the firing line. This proved to be an exciting job, as our orders were to run along the line for half-a-mile or more, shouting 'ammunition' to the left, where it was said they were badly in need of it.

We were shot at a good deal in some places both from in front and from snipers behind and I found it difficult to get the men along quickly. When I got to my limit I found only three of the men with me, but I managed to pick up most of them on my way back. About three-quarters-of-an-hour after I had joined B Company trench again, the battalion advanced to take part in an attack. The Turks had carried out a night attack but had been repulsed, and it was deemed advisable, I suppose, to follow this up with a counter attack. I was on the left of my battalion in a gully running up to Achi Baba and after finding myself in front of the entrenched line I finally decided to retire for it. We [all] retired some two hours later driven back by the enemy's shrapnel, which was well directed.

We got back in the afternoon about 4.00pm and took up our new camping quarters. My platoon during its advance killed three snipers – or rather the six scouts I sent ahead for the purpose. The place seems to be infested with them and it is very difficult to see them. I was thoroughly tired and short of sleep by the end of the day. It was my first real day of active service and shrapnel burst near me several times.

After writing the above and in anticipation of a good night's rest, I heard the order that the battalion was falling in, and about 8.00pm, when it was quite dark, we marched out single file through several Indian [soldiers'] camping grounds, stumbling into trenches, and were led over to the sea side of the peninsula where we spent an uncomfortable night, huddled up in and around a farm in readiness to support some regulars in the trenches in front of us. There was no room to lie down and the B Company officers huddled together under a wall. We started back for the camp about 3.30am and halted as a sort of picket some half-mile in rear of the farm until it was light. On the way out in the dark one of my men fell down from a little stone bridge and seriously injured himself. Burnett, my company commander, was wounded in the arm in the morning attack.

During the nights of 1 and 2 May 1915, the Turks had launched a series of failed assaults to try and drive the Allies back towards Cape Helles. An Allied counter attack was organised and, as they rushed forward without artillery support to take up a position astride a creek known as the Achi Baba Nullah in support of the French on their right, the men of the 2nd Naval Brigade came under intense fire for the first time. Kelly's battalion had been 'blooded'.

Arthur Asquith later noted that 'the Hood Battalion suffered about 90 casualties in about 20 minutes, mainly from enemy shrapnel. The remains of the 2nd Battalion of the Hampshire Regiment, who had been fighting continuously since the landing, were sent up in support, and came up over the heather as stiff as a wall, led by an officer with his arm in a sling. He conferred with Colonel Quilter; they decided that the exposed ridge upon which we were trying to dig in with entrenching tools was untenable; and a retirement was ordered'.

Lieutenant Commander Sidney Burnett was evacuated from the peninsula, first to the Blue Sisters Hospital, Malta then 'invalided home' back to England. He transferred to the army in August 1916 and joined the South Staffordshire Regiment.

Monday, 3 May 1915 – Hood Battalion Camp, some three-quarters-of-a-mile inland from Cape Helles, Gallipoli Peninsula
The battalion, after its return from the farm building at daylight, settled

down in a camping ground, just vacated by some Indian regiment, with the prospect of a day's rest. There were a good many fatigues, however, to be got through and in the afternoon I had to take a battalion working party of about 120 men to the first camp we occupied on the shore to fetch the men's packs and all picks and shovels. I managed to get in a much needed bathe on W Beach, where I saw Francis Henley and Quartermaster Sergeant Marlow gave me some tea afterwards. On the way back to the camp in the dusk I saw John Houghton Gibbon, who is out here with Battery No. 460 (I think he said).

What was intended to be a night's rest turned out to be a very nerve-shattering experience; by way of protecting the camp from shell fire, our ships' guns and the recently landed field batteries kept up a terrific bombardment of the Turkish positions, almost incessantly. The enemy, however, were not prevented from dropping shrapnel all around and in our camp and when one adds that several snipers were trying to pick off any men walking about our lines, it is difficult to imagine more unpleasant circumstances for sleeping. Oddly enough, I did manage to get some sleep and was quite unaffected by the noise.

On arrival back at the camp I found I had practically no cover in which to sleep and before I could get to rest I was obliged to dig myself a trench in the dark. My servant, while I was thus engaged, came to me quite unhinged and cowering at the roar of the French .75s [75mm quick-firing field guns] and was completely out of his senses. Denis Browne was extremely good and comforted him like a child while I finished digging my trench so that we had him in between us. The doctor, McCracken, had given him an opiate and he was soon asleep. Later on in the night the doctor himself came running to where we B Company officers were sleeping, considerably frightened at finding six bullets lodging in his bed trench. One of the snipers had marked him down.

Kelly was acquainted with Major John Houghton Gibbon, 406 Battery RFA, through their mutual connections with Eton and rowing. After Eton, Gibbon had attended Trinity College, Cambridge where he had earned his rowing

'Blue' in 1899 and 1900. Commissioned as a second lieutenant in the Royal Artillery in 1900, he had served in Africa from 1901–1906 where he had fought in Nigeria in the Anglo-Aro War of 1901–02. He was awarded the DSO and mentioned in despatches for his services at Gallipoli doing 'good work at the landing, and on 1st/2nd May when the Turks broke through the French line'. Later in the war he rose to command divisional artillery, became garrison commander of the RA depot at Woolwich in the 1930s and was a steward at Henley Regatta.

Surgeon, later Staff Surgeon, William McCracken, served with the Hood Battalion throughout the war and was much-loved and respected by all who served with him. A highly-skilled doctor, he was fearless and tenacious in trying to attend to the wounded on the battlefield, being twice wounded himself. He was recommended for the VC for his actions north of Passchendaele in October 1917 by, among others, his then commanding officer Arthur Asquith. Although he was overlooked for the VC he did receive the DSO and Bar and the Military Cross by war's end.

Tuesday, 4 May 1915 – Hood Battalion, firing line, trench between French on right and [British infantry] regulars on left

A fairly restful day of fatigue in which, luckily, I had to take no part. At 3.00pm Patrick Shaw-Stewart and I bathed. The battalion fell in at 4.30pm and marched out to the firing line, running from the main Kilid Bahr – Krithia road, about 300 yards of which we took over from some French troops who had been holding it. On our left were some regulars, on our right Howe Battalion and beyond them the French extending to the Dardanelles. I was on the left on the road and compared notes with the regulars on the other side of it before dark.

There was no Turkish line in front of us and I believe the scrubby country on our front was free of them for half-a-mile at least. It was the battalion's first night in the trenches and it behaved admirably. There was perfect fire discipline, the men only firing on order. B Company officers sat up all night without relief – and very sleepy work it was in the early hours. The French kept up a perfect fusillade all night.

Wednesday, 5 May 1915 – Hood Battalion, firing line, trench between French on right and [British infantry] regulars on left

There was nothing much to do in the morning and I was glad to find John Gibbon had established an observation station for his battery in our line. I spent part of the morning listening to him taking range and giving instructions. I moved down after tea into some trenches supporting the firing line occupied by A Company and had a fairly quiet night.

With the Turks still in possession of the village of Krithia and Achi Baba, along with the stretches of four major gullies (or nullahs) – Achi Baba Nullah being one such – which threaded their way down from the heights behind their lines towards the sea, the Allied advance up the peninsula was effectively hamstrung. The Turkish trenches, machine guns and strong points had been organised with considerable attention to detail while the defence of the sector could be orchestrated by observers on Achi Baba. In order for the Allies to make progress the Turks had to be flushed from the trenches and nullahs, evicted from Krithia and toppled from the summit of Achi Baba so that the high ground could be used by the Allies in turn as a spring board for further advances.

And so the British and the French sat down to plan their second large-scale attack at Helles, little more than a week after their first costly assault. The date was set for 6 May 1915; zero hour would be 11.00am – in broad, bright daylight – after a short preliminary bombardment consisting mainly of shrapnel shells. Frederick Kelly was about to take part in the Second Battle of Krithia.

Thursday, 6 May 1915 – firing line about two-and-a-half miles from Achi Baba

We had gone to rest overnight in pleasant expectation of a great advance to be made the following day. After breakfast orders came as to our dispositions and what seemed a very promising plan of attack was expounded to us through our company commanders. It was that the French, with the Naval Brigade on their left, should make good a line

2,000 yards to their front by 12 noon. This they were to hold at all costs while the regulars on the left of the whole line made a great sweeping movement which was to envelop Krithia and Achi Baba. The Naval Brigade's front was to be 400 yards and our task seemed a feasible one. The following was our [Hood Battalion] plan of advance, one company forming the firing line, while there were to be several supporting lines [each] moving up at 200 yards distance in rear.

First wave – whole of A Company
Second wave – two platoons of C Company
Third wave – two platoons of C Company
Fourth wave – two platoons of B Company (5th Platoon – [Kelly] – on right)
Fifth wave – two platoons of B Company
D Company – ammunition parties
Anson Battalion – supports

We were to start at 11.00am and reach our objective by midday. Just before we started word came that the French (under whose direction the Naval Brigade was acting) had changed their plan and had decided to form the whole of the firing line themselves, while we were to act as supports. As it was already 11.00am however, and there seemed to be doubt about their intentions, it was decided to advance as arranged above.

A Company moved off, so I was afterwards told, at a great rate and left the supporting lines in rear. However that may be, it was a considerable time before C Company moved off in front of me, and in the meanwhile the brigade major, Maxwell, came and tried to urge me to go through C Company, under the impression they and I were holding back. The left hand of our line moved at a greater rate than the right half and I missed getting off with Denis Browne's platoon, with which I was to form one of the supporting lines, but I carried out what I could of the orders by following on in rear of the right half of C Company's lines.

We were very soon under heavy rifle fire and I was delighted with the way my men stood it. After about our third rush, however, the pieces of cover for which men naturally made tended to split up our line, moreover, the lines in front began to bear away very markedly to the left instead of keeping straight on as intended. I decided to keep my original direction and was soon isolated with my PO and about 12 men. There was no sign of the French on our right, but very soon Anson Battalion had come up from behind and very rightly tried to continue the line to the right.

On my right some 200 yards or more on, there was a line of men which, after scrutiny with my [field] glasses, seemed to contain some of our own men, so I decided to make for that in two rushes through very heavy rifle fire. We all arrived safely and found ourselves amongst about 200 Anson men, who – no more than I did – had any idea where they had got to. On their left no-one was to be seen at all and on their right was a gap to the French. Our position was critical if the Turks – of whom I knew nothing except for their rifle fire coming from uneven scrub in front – counter attacked. They, however, seemed to be as confused as we were, and we immediately set to work digging on the left and extending our line on to where we hoped to find the rest of Hood, of whom there were no signs.

The French supports soon joined up on our right, but it was not till early next morning that we got into touch with anyone on our left. I found Lieutenant Nelson of A Company, who had been in the first advancing line, with about four Hood men, but with this exception

I had no idea where my battalion had got to. I collected Hood men together somewhere on the left of the Anson [Battalion] and we all got to work deepening what was not much more than a ditch and making a parapet to keep out the fire of about six very active snipers. I had lost two men killed, 12 wounded, three missing, in the short advance of at most 1,200 yards – but I didn't find out these figures till we were relieved in the firing line two days later and could get news of the rest of my platoon. One of my men, Patrick McKeown, showed great *sang-froid* in volunteering to pick up an important message from the hand of a previous messenger, just shot dead 200 yards in rear of the trench, and take it to headquarters in rear.

As I learned afterwards, the French, the regulars and our own staff thought very highly of the advance of the Naval Brigade. The rest of Hood on our left had pushed forward in advance of the line I got to and quite unsupported on either side had held on till dark and thus formed an important hand hold on to which supports could climb up on either side. After dark they moved back several hundred yards to bring themselves into line with the regulars and the Anson, thus forming somewhat of a continuous line across the peninsula. We didn't have an easy task for instead of a front of 400 yards we found ourselves lost in a gap of something over 1,000 and with no knowledge of what it really was. I don't suppose there were more than 1,000 all told in Hood and Anson before the advance began and as our losses during its progress were very heavy, our numbers were wholly inadequate.

During the night the snipers were very active in trying to make us believe they were really a strong force in front of us. There was not much fire from a strong Turkish trench 400 yards in front of us. Lieutenant Nelson and I took alternate watches of two hours and we made every alternate man relieve their neighbours in hourly watches. We had a very short field of fire if the Turks had decided to attack.

Able Seaman Patrick McKeown, whose actions Kelly thought so gallant that he named him in his diary, was a 20-year-old Glaswegian. A carpenter before joining the navy in April 1913, he received the Distinguished Service Medal (DSM) for 'services in the Gallipoli Peninsula'. Invalided home with recurrent eye infections he survived the war.

Friday, 7 May 1915 – Firing line about two-and-a-half miles from Achi Baba

There was not much activity on the part of the enemy throughout the day, but several snipers kept a very close watch on our trenches and made it unsafe for one to expose oneself.

The 20 Hood men had little to do, but Anson spent the day in continuing our trench to the left. The remainder of Hood away on our left were relieved at nightfall but our isolated party had to spend another night in the trench.

Saturday, 8 May 1915 – Same supporting trenches as I occupied on Wednesday night, 5 May

Lieutenant Nelson's and my little party of Hood men were relieved soon after daybreak and found our way back to the part of the old firing line 1,000 yards back, that Hood had occupied on the nights of 4 and 5 May. There we found the remainder of the battalion and counted up losses. We are not to mention anything in diaries that might give information to the enemy, so I am not mentioning casualties. We had lost Colonel Quilter who had already been buried where we were assembling. I don't know what his military qualities in the field were, but for peace training, smartness in drill and for a thoroughly impartial solicitude for all his men and officers alike he struck me as being an ideal battalion commander.

Denis Browne and I were the only officers left in B Company and during the course of the morning he was wounded in the back of the neck by a sniper and sent back to the base. His wound does not appear to be serious and as it will put him out of harm's way for a month or so

I regarded it merely as a piece of good luck than bad. Ock Asquith had been wounded in the knee in the attack so that Patrick Shaw-Stewart and I were the only sound ones of our little coterie on board ship, which had included the two above, Rupert Brooke and Charles Lister. We re-organised the battalion into two companies. I wrote up my diary from 3 May to 6 May.

The fighting on 6 May 1915 had raged all day. Once more coming under French General d'Amade's command to reinforce his troops on their right, Kelly's battalion had advanced more than 1,000 yards under heavy enfilade fire from Turks on a ridge 300 yards to their right. Driving further, initially without the promised support of the French on their right, by 12.30pm the Hood had captured the forward Turkish trenches near a ruined and roofless shack known as 'The White House'. While some of the Hood men began to dig for all they were worth to hold on to their gains, others set off again and forced their way forward another quarter of a mile, before they hit a wall of Turkish bullets and were forced to go to ground. It was all over at 3.30pm; the Turkish main positions remained unmolested, Krithia was still in Turkish hands and the ultimate prize of Achi Baba appeared as distant as ever.

An hour later all units along the entire Allied line received orders to hold fast and dig in where they stood. Further attacks on 7 and 8 May resulted in piecemeal gains but not the great breakthrough everyone had hoped for. Far from being the key to unlocking the inertia which had gripped the war on the Western Front in France and Flanders, in little more than two weeks, and despite the advances and yards gained, the fighting had quickly degenerated into almost the same bloody trench stalemate that the Gallipoli landings had sought to overcome.

Charles Lister – wounded four days before Kelly and the Hood had gone into action in the Second Battle of Krithia – escaped the fighting but as Kelly revealed casualties had been heavy: 20 men of the Hood and 24 more of the Anson were killed on 6 May alone and many more were wounded. The highest ranking casualty was Kelly's commanding officer. Lieutenant Colonel

Arnold Quilter, an ex-officer of the Grenadier Guards who had earned the DSO during the South African War at the turn of the nineteenth century, was seen by his men as a perfect gentleman. Somewhat shy but undoubtedly brave and resolutely soldierly, his subordinates thought him an inspiring commander who was responsible for establishing the enduring foundation of esprit de corps which proved to be so strong in the Hood. He is buried today at Skew Bridge Cemetery, Cape Helles.

Sunday, 9 May 1915 – Supporting trench, 300 yards in rear of firing line, left of White House

We spent a slack day during which I found my way to Tinirid Farm with Sub Lieutenant Martin of the Hood machine-gun section and had a good wash. At 6.30pm we moved forward, one and a half companies into the firing line trench, and the other half, in which my reconstituted platoon was, into a supporting trench 300 yards in rear of it. About three times during the night the enemy poured in a fairly heavy fire, of which the bullets came whizzing just over our trench. We stood to arms in readiness to move up as supports if required. My men were split up in the supporting trench, but of the 20 under my charge we had four sentries on watch and PO Kirkbride and myself kept two-hour watches throughout the night.

Just before the battalion left for the firing line we heard two snipers had been captured in our rear. They are very daring and active and it is said they paint their faces green for protective purposes.

Monday, 10 May 1915 – Supporting trench, 300 yards in rear of firing line, left of White House

A slack day in the trench. I got a mail.

Tuesday, 11 May 1915 – Part of the old firing line, 300 yards or so in rear

Another day in the support trench 300 yards in rear of the firing line. I got hold of a *Weekly Times* and two copies of *Land & Water*. 16 and

23 April. I was glad to see Belloc thinks that the tide, as far as superiority of numbers, has turned in favour of the Allies.

We were relieved by some Territorials at 10.00pm and moved back to the old firing line 1,000 yards in rear. It rained during the night and we woke up next morning very wet and miserable.

Thursday, 12 May 1915 – Camp on high ground about three-quarters-of-a-mile from Cape Helles

I saw some Drake officers who had spent the night quite close to us, early in the morning, and learnt from Farrer, Pinks and McHardy of Lancelot Cherry's and Harold Edgar's deaths. They have not had nearly so many casualties as Hood have. We moved back to a camp on high ground about three quarters of a mile inland from Cape Helles and took up our quarters in two delightful small fields with flowers and a sprinkling of olives, a quince and fig tree. I bathed to the left of W Beach with Patrick Shaw-Stewart and Leslie Shadbolt in the afternoon.

Friday, 14 May 1915 – same camp

Shadbolt and I missed a visit from General d'Amade [then in command of the French *Corps Expeditionnaire d'Orient* – their Eastern Expeditionary Force] who thanked the Naval Brigade for the recent assistance they afforded the French in the attack last Thursday.

I went to Morto Bay in the Dardanelles with Patrick Shaw-Stewart and Shadbolt to bathe at 2.00pm and we spent a deliciously lazy afternoon. The water is very shallow with a bottom of white sand. We saw several Turkish shells pitch within a quarter of a mile or so of a battleship in front of us.

More letters to censor after tea.

Saturday, 15 May 1915 – same camp

I left camp at 5.30am with a working party of 50 men to work on W Beach and didn't leave work till 12.30pm. The beach was a scene of great activity and the reason we were kept so hard at work was, I was told, that they are anxious to land as much as possible before the arrival of two German submarines which are said to be on their way out. Several shells fell in the neighbourhood about 10.00am and work was stopped for me to take cover until things were quiet again.

I went for a walk with Patrick Shaw-Stewart and Leslie Shadbolt at 3.00pm through Sedd el Bahr to see the effects of the naval bombardment. It was a mass of ruins. They wouldn't let us in the fort. We had a bathe afterwards in Morto Bay.

Tuesday, 18 May 1915 – communicating trench in rear of firing line

The battalion left camp in two parties at 3.00am and 3.30am for the firing line. I was in the second party with Lieutenant Commander Parsons. It was decided to advance silently at 9.00pm and try to dig in 400 yards in advance. This was carried out with complete success without a single casualty. The Turkish trenches facing us were about some 800 yards away and the advance was made without their being aware of it. The result of the achievement was that the present line runs straight from the sea on the left to the French right where the conformation of the ground on the right bank of Kereves Dere necessitates a bend backwards to the sea.

Generally speaking instructions are far too vague; a company being sent out in the dark to make their own way to an objective, the exact whereabouts of which don't seem to be known to those who issue the orders and each officer just shifts the responsibility on to his subordinates. It would be difficult enough to find one's way if the country were clear but in this part, where 150 men lost their way last night, it was a network of disused trenches facing in all directions.

Kelly is recording his thoughts having been given the task of guiding the party of 150 men who had lost their way in the dark.

Thursday, 20 May 1915 – at work on communicating trench to firing line

After knocking off work at 4.00am I took my men back to one of the supporting trenches where I had left their waterproof sheets and blankets on our way up to work the night before. Since then a platoon returning from the firing line had been put into the same trench, and being themselves without blankets and waterproof sheets and finding ours there, they had lost no time in making themselves snug. The direct intimation I had of the state of affairs was the sudden violation of the order as to silence, which had up to then been pretty well observed.

Now, however, shouting to my men to follow me, blankets or no blankets, was like calling one's dog to come out of a dog fight, and though I made more noise and was more violent than anyone else, I didn't succeed in getting them to do what I wanted until the great majority of blankets had changed hands and the losing party was left rubbing their eyes and cold.

We slept in a neighbouring trench till 8.00am when I went back to the White House to headquarters for orders. These were to bring my men back there to spend the day resting. As the CO had promised us two slack days after last night's digging, I didn't take the opportunity to sleep, but spent the entire day having a clean-up and a bath. It was still, hot and sunny, so I spread out all my clothes in the sun and sat with only my Burberry on reading the *Weekly Times* and talking to Lieutenant Commander Parsons and Patrick Shaw-Stewart.

At 6.00pm I got orders to the effect that my platoon must spend another night digging, though this time we had only to work for four hours, when another platoon was to take over. It must be half-a-mile up to the old firing line, by the circuitous line of trench we had to follow to avoid snipers, and we had to carry our provisions and ten dixies [cooking pots] full of tea to the firing line 300 yards further on. In the narrow trench with several bodies of men to pass this was no easy job and it took an hour to reach the firing line.

We spent from 9.45pm till 1.45am deepening and broadening the trench on which we were at work the night before and again we were unmolested by the enemy. I spent part of the time in conveying back the ten empty dixies from the firing line to the support trench, where my men could more conveniently get them on finishing work.

Friday, 21 May 1915 – near headquarters at the White House

[There are] two arch-grousers; [one of them] perhaps not so much addicted to grousing as to an unrelieved pessimistic outlook to which he gives very forcible expressions; the more forcible according to the greater proximity of snipers or shells. It is interesting to observe the effect of bullets on the highly-strung. Only one or two of us – Patrick Shaw-Stewart and Leslie Shadbolt for example – are quite unmoved.

Our doctor, McCracken was unfortunately sniped (through the right hip) in the afternoon while he was sitting within ten yards of my dugout. There is a very active body of snipers somewhere up by the firing line who have a line on the White House and the whole of the afternoon bullets have been whistling continuously over my dugout.

Ever since the day of Rupert Brooke's death I have been composing an elegy for string orchestra, the ideas of which are coloured by the surrounding of his grave and circumstances of his death. Today I felt my way right through to the end of it, though of course, much of it has still to take on definite shape. The modal character of the music seems to be suggested by the Greek surroundings as well as Rupert's character, some passage-work by the rustling of the olive tree which bends over his grave. It should work out to some nine minutes in performance.

In the *Weekly Times* I noted the death of another victim to blood-poisoning, [composer Alexander] Scriabin, at the age of 43, if I remember right.

Saturday, 22 May 1915 – Hood Battalion, base camp we occupied from 12 to 17 May

I moved to the camp in the middle of the tail of the peninsula about three-quarters-of-a-mile from Cape Helles at 5.15am with my platoon. There was nothing to do all day except that I took some men, who wanted to bathe, to X Beach at 2.30pm. We had intended to go to Morto Bay but were warned by some Howe men that French sentries were stopping all bathing parties on account of the beach being shelled.

I sent PO Kirkbride, Leading Seaman [LS] Anderson and two men to W Beach to spend £3 buying cigarettes and chocolates for the platoon while I took the rest of the party back after our bathe. This is part of [older brother] Thomas Herbert Kelly's gift of £20 which he sent me for my platoon just before I left England as it occurred to me, now that they have established a canteen I had better start spending it.

I had to put a hot compress on a boil on my cheek which McCracken, our doctor, cut just before he was wounded two days ago. It is a great bore having another one after all my inoculations last summer.

We were told officially that Italy had declared war on Austria and even Patrick Shaw-Stewart believed the news. I confess to some doubt pending fuller information.

Tuesday, 25 May 1915 – Hood Battalion, same camp

News came shortly after we arrived at the beach that an enemy submarine had just sunk HMS *Triumph* at Kapa Teke. Several of the transports put to sea during the afternoon.

Wednesday, 26 May 1915 – Hood Battalion, same camp

The camp was shelled a good deal in the afternoon and at dusk one of our cooks was killed. I was very sorry to hear, too, that the Anson [Battalion] officer, Lieutenant Commander Grant was severely wounded in the neighbouring lines at the same time. He was the officer in Benbow [Battalion] who did so well in getting some men back from Antwerp.

Lieutenant Commander Gerald Grant was certainly one of the RND heroes of the ill-starred Antwerp expedition of October 1914. Asquith noted that 'During the retreat from Antwerp, Grant, refusing to obey his company commander's

*order to enter Holland and be interned, was put under arrest. He managed to
hang back until his company commander had crossed the frontier and then
inviting the petty officers of his escort and some stragglers to avoid internment,
led a party of 35 by byways along the Dutch frontier, evaded the Germans,
and escaped to the coast'. Grant received the Distinguished Service Cross
(DSC) for his service and audacity at Antwerp. During the shelling Kelly
mentions Grant was severely wounded by shrapnel which lodged in the area
of the left shoulder blade and spine. The Hood cook who was killed was Stoker
1st Class Edwin Hillard Hawthorn of Grimsby, who was hit in the head by
shrapnel and died of his wounds. He was buried the next day at the expanding
cemetery at Cape Helles in a ceremony conducted by Chaplain C Beardmore
and today lies in Lancashire Landing Cemetery above W Beach.*

Thursday, 27 May 1915 – Hood Battalion, same camp

I took a working party of 36 men down to X Beach reporting there
at 6.00am. There was no lighter for us to unload as expected so they
turned us on to improving the road. After we had been there half-an-
hour or so [Sub Lieutenant Alfred] Brandt put in an appearance and
told us HMS *Majestic* had just been torpedoed by a submarine off
W Beach. I took a walk round the cliffs and saw her ram and about 100
feet of her bottom showing above water. She was only 400 yards or so
from the shore and surrounded by transports and destroyers so that
it must have been smart torpedo work. Following on the loss of HMS
Triumph two days before this is a distinct score for the enemy.

*Kelly's reference to the sinking of two British warships in as many days
proved how quickly news could spread around the peninsula and served as a
reminder that the war was raging just as fiercely in the waters off Gallipoli
as it was on land.*

*He had mentioned the sinking of the pre-dreadnought battleship
HMS Triumph on 25 May and was now lamenting the loss of the Majestic,
the stricken hull of which he had seen with his own eyes.*

The Triumph had been torpedoed and capsized after ten minutes – before which time many of the crew were rescued by HMS Chelmer – *but went down 30 minutes later with, according to records held by the Commonwealth War Graves Commission (CWGC), the loss of 55 officers and men. The* Triumph's *sinking was noteworthy in that she became the first victim of German U-Boats operating off the coast of Gallipoli, a campaign which had begun that very day. The man responsible for sinking both ships was* Kapitänleutnant *Otto Hersing, the captain of the U-21, who on 5 September 1914, sank the first ship to be torpedoed in the First World War when he attacked and struck HMS* Pathfinder *off St Abbs Head, Scotland with the loss of 254 men.*

Now, two days after sinking the Triumph, *Hersing had put two torpedoes into the* Majestic *as she lay at anchor in 54 feet of water, surrounded by other vessels off W Beach: 'smart torpedo work', to use Kelly's own words. Forty-two men were lost as the* Majestic *capsized in seven minutes.*

The emergence of the U-Boat threat in the seas off the Aegean coast of the peninsula was indeed a 'distinct score' for the Ottoman Turks, effectively ending relatively continuous naval gunfire support for the Anzac and Helles fronts.

Friday, 28 May 1915 – Hood Battalion, same camp

I had another hot, slack day, except for an hour and a half after lunch when I had to take a party of eight men to the Naval Divisional Engineers, not far from the pylons where an officer taught us how to manufacture hand grenades with jam-pots. Finally, when we all watched the officer who instructed us, light the fuse and throw it, a great anti-climax ensued, as the grenade he had made himself didn't explode and we had to watch another ten minutes while he re-fused it.

I went to Morto Bay with Harold Farrer to bathe at 6.00pm.

Saturday, 29 May 1915 – Hood Battalion, supports to firing line

Another hot day which I spent in devouring *Land & Water* of 8 May and two *Spectators*. I went to Morto Bay with Leslie Shadbolt and Patrick Shaw-Stewart to bathe at 5.00pm. We moved up toward the firing line about 9.45pm, my company remaining in the supporting trenches.

The firing line has moved forward some 300 yards since we were last there a week ago. We marched as far as brigade headquarters where we halted an hour and a half and after resuming our march we entered an elaborate series of communicating trenches which now extend from the White House to the firing line. My party had to carry ammunition and got left behind in the trenches.

Sunday, 30 May 1915 – Hood Battalion, supports to firing line

A slack, hot day in the supporting trench. Life is very squalid here, meals being very unappetising in the surroundings. There are four dead Turks lying in front and behind our trench and the stench is far from pleasant. We are going to bury them as soon as it's dark.

We heard the *Goeben* and two torpedo boats had been sunk by our submarine in the Dardanelles. This should make a Russian landing near Constantinople much more possible.

Monday, 31 May 1915 – Hood Battalion, supports to firing line

Our Turk burying last night was a tiresome business. We emerged at 10.30pm and had to finish before the moon rose. There was a good deal of firing going on, with stray bullets whistling by us and I found the men very anxious for me to pronounce the trench deep enough before it would have scarcely contained even one of the bodies. We had to dispose of three highly-scented bodies and it took us till [midnight].

Wednesday, 2 June 1915 – base camp

I had a slack day which I spent in an elaborate dugout I constructed for myself with the help of one of my men before breakfast. A rumour came down the trench that Austria had 'thrown her hand in'! If this is so it only remains for Germany to take sides with us too and so we shall all happily find there is no further need for fighting!

We were relieved by Hawke Battalion in the firing line at 11.45pm, three hours late, and had an incredibly uncomfortable journey brushing by incoming battalions in the line of communicating trenches. We reached our base camp about 2.45am and to my great joy I found my Wolseley valise and for the first time since landing, slept in pyjamas – and not in my clothes.

Thursday, 3 June 1915 – base camp
I had a bath and put on a spare suit of khaki I found in my Wolseley valise, revelling in the possibility of changing my clothes. About midday Commodore Backhouse explained to the officers of the 2nd Naval Brigade the plan for a general attack on the Turkish positions all across the line. It was to be preceded by a furious artillery bombardment after which he confidently expected we should only find dazed Turks in their trenches. We, the 2nd Brigade, were only required to take two trenches, while all the reserve was to be used on the left, which by evening was to have passed Krithia and possibly swept Achi Baba by nightfall. He expected the attack would take place on 5 June or later, but as a matter of fact we heard in the afternoon that we were to move up overnight into the firing line and that the attack would take place the next day.

Friday, 4 June 1915 – aboard the SS *Reindeer*
We left our base camp at 12.30am and reached our part of the firing line just before dawn. I found my old dugout and slept in it till 8.00am. There were several things that required attending to between then and the attack which was timed to take place at midday.

This was preceded (a) by a fierce artillery bombardment of the Turkish trenches from about 10.50am till 11.20am; (b) by an interval of ten minutes, 11.20am to 11.30am during which the whole line fixed bayonets, ostentatiously waved them, cheering at the same time and then kept up a steady fire till 11.30am and (c) by a further fierce bombardment from 11.30am till midday.

Two-hundred-and-fifty Hood men all told under Colonel Charles Kennedy Craufurd-Stuart, Lieutenant Commander Raymond Parsons, Lieutenant Maurice Hood, Lieutenant John Ferguson, Sub Lieutenant W Denis Browne, Sub Lieutenant Leonard Cockey, Sub Lieutenant

Francis Baker and Sub Lieutenant Leslie Shadbolt, leapt over the trenches on a front of about 200 yards between Anson [Battalion] on the right and Howe [Battalion] on the left and doubled towards the Turkish trenches. Twenty minutes later some Collingwood [Battalion] supports, who entered our trench after [the Hood men] had left, followed them. For the next half hour I was spacing my platoon out so as to occupy 75 yards of the Anson trench on my right, and except that I heard heavy rifle fire in front I had no conception what was happening. Then, however, there was rather an alarming rush back to our trench of panic-stricken Collingwood and Anson men. I spent the next three-quarters-of-an-hour going up and down the trench pushing them out again and telling them to go and report themselves to any officer they found in front of the line. My temper was not of the best.

I got some 30 men or more over the parapet until our trench was pretty clear except for our own men but then on looking out in front, I found most of them merely lying down a few yards from the trench. I jumped out myself to give them a lead on and told them to make for a bank a hundred yards on when I had got them moving. We were under a heavy fire and on turning to get back to my trench I was hit on the inside of the right heel by a grazing bullet, which made a wound about two inches long and about half-an-inch deep in the centre. It cut the side of my boot open. As far as I can remember, I was out of the trench twice – this being the second time and firstly in trying to stem the first rush of men back to the trench. I turned a few of them about, but there were too many for me to cope with. I had no idea how things were going in front, as there was a skyline 300 yards in front. I afterwards heard that so many officers were put out of action by the terrific fire that met them that the men were leaderless and didn't know what to do.

The bombardment, from which so much was hoped, had apparently done little damage, some of our side saying the Turks had cleverly concealed their trench some way in rear of a very obvious parapet on the skyline on which our guns had wasted all their shells. I heard later in the day that all the officers of the Hood attacking party had been put out of action, Ferguson, Baker and [Sub Lieutenant Charles] Martin [of the machine-gun section] being killed and Parsons wounded and captured in an advance Turkish trench. The casualties seem to have been very heavy – practically all the attacking party, though at the time of writing (5 June, 8.30pm) I have no definite news. Collingwood are said to have lost 600 out of 850 men.

Everyone is blaming the French for failing to advance and take [Haricot] Redoubt from which the RND attacking parties were enfiladed. We seem to have got into the second Turkish trench but could not stay there on account of the fire. The left of our line was said to have made good progress. It was here that the chief attack was intended. On being wounded I reported to Lieutenant Nelson, the other Hood officer, in command of the trench, who told me to make my way back to the rear. I could get along the trench with little difficulty and in fact walked back to the divisional field dressing station to the south east of Hood base camp. Here I had tea with Fleming, the principal medical officer of the 1st Naval Brigade and then went down to the medical station on W Beach where I found our CO, Craufurd-Stuart, with a bullet through his jaw, Lieutenant Hew Hedderwick and Leslie Shadbolt. We all got on to a small Channel Island steamer, the *Reindeer* about 6.30pm and early the next morning sailed for Lemnos. On the jetty I saw the [General Officer Commanding] Sir Ian Hamilton, who seemed to be pleased with the day's operations.

There was nothing to eat on the *Reindeer* but a few tins of bully beef and I was glad to make use of the contents of my haversack – a tin of sardines and some jam – which just went round among the seven or eight officers capable of sitting up. We slept in our clothes in the saloon.

Monday, 7 June 1915 – SS *Ascania*, Levant

It was fairly warm, owing to a following wind. I procured a Shakespeare from the ship's library and read *Titus Andronicus* for the first time. It struck me as being one of the great plays. Oddly enough I do not ever seem to have heard or read an opinion expressed concerning it.

THE LOST OLYMPIAN OF THE SOMME

Tuesday, 8 June 1915 – SS *Ascania*, Alexandria

We reached Alexandria about 3.00pm and until now – 11.00pm – have no orders for disembarkation. At 9.15pm Alexander Graham, our adjutant, came on the ship with his wife and Montagu of the RND. From the latter I heard that Denis Browne was missing after the attack and we are all anxious. Nelson Hood is also reported missing.

Under the circumstances Kelly's selection of the most violent and blood-soaked of the Shakespearean canon from the library of the hospital ship Ascania *– to which he had been transferred for onward passage to Egypt – could not have been more apt. The Third Battle of Krithia had been a disaster for the Allies in general and the RND in particular. The failure of the French to advance their line a single yard on the right had left the assaulting battalions of the Hood, Howe and Anson – with the Collingwood Battalion in support – exposed to the withering fire of every weapon the Turks could bring to bear on them.*

Forty-four men of the Hood lay dead out of a total of some 12 officers and 300 other ranks killed, wounded or taken prisoner. Of those whom Kelly had mentioned in his diary as leading the attack, the commanding officer Charles Kennedy Craufurd-Stuart had been seriously wounded (he survived the war only to die in a German air raid on Folkestone in August 1942) while C Company commander Lieutenant Commander Raymond Parsons, Lieutenant, The Honourable Maurice Henry Nelson Hood, Lieutenant John Ferguson, Sub Lieutenant Denis Browne and Sub Lieutenant Francis Baker had been killed.

Denis Browne's loss was felt keenly, not only by Kelly but throughout the battalion. Arthur Asquith noted, 'W Denis Brown was a contemporary and devoted friend of Rupert Brooke at Rugby and at Cambridge, and they joined the RND on the same day. Previously he was assistant musical critic to The Times *and lovers of music will remember him as the author of a beautiful setting of the songs 'Salathiel' and 'Gratiana'. Rare ebullitions of an underlying high and fiery spirit took by surprise acquaintances who were accustomed to his infinite gentleness, selflessness and sympathy. His zeal for the welfare and training of his men was unlimited and most of his brother officers would, I think, have voted him the Ideal Platoon Commander. At Blandford he arranged for the teeth of his men to be seen to by a dentist. They were mostly miners and at Malta, seeing that many of them were suffering from the glare of the sun, he bought blue spectacles for them all. He hurried back to the peninsula from Alexandria in less than a month, after receiving his first wound, just in time to take part in the costly attack of 4 June. Survivors of the attack described him as having shot and bayoneted several Turks in their second line of trench before he fell.'*

Other units of the RND had fared much worse. The Collingwood Battalion had been literally smashed to pieces, losing more than 600 men of which 153 – including Bernard Freyberg's brother Oscar – had been killed. It was so badly broken that it was disbanded soon afterwards. Of the 70 officers and 1,900 men of the three assaulting battalions of the RND who had risen from their trenches to attack the Turkish lines on 4 June 1915, 61 officers and 1,319 men had become casualties – 167 of them killed. Yet the heights of Achi Baba seemed as distant and impregnable as ever. There it stood, hunched and defiant, still barring the way to Constantinople and still glowering down menacingly on the Allied lines and on the fields of the corpses of those Allied soldiers who had tried and failed to take it on three occasions and the Turks who had given their lives to stop them.

Wednesday, 9 June 1915 – Deaconess' Hospital, Alexandria
We left the ship about 11.00am and with six other officers of the RND and one from the 'Motor Bandits' [the Armoured Car Section of the Royal Naval Air Service] I was taken to the Deaconess' Hospital in a motor ambulance. Our CO, Colonel Stuart, Hew Hedderwick and Leslie Shadbolt were all placed in the same ward, which is high and airy. Alan Hughes and [Sub Lieutenant William Mark] Egerton, who were wounded on 6 May, came in to see us shortly after our arrival, and later on, our doctor, McCracken, who was sniped on 21 May. He had just returned from Cairo. My heel was dressed about 2.00pm and I went to bed for the rest of the day. There was some dead flesh to be cut away.

Things struck me as being somewhat chaotic here and the ward we are in is not nearly as clean as it should be. I heard that the hospital had been in German hands till a week ago when they substituted English for German staff. I hear the English staff do not know where anything is.

Thursday, 10 June 1915 – Deaconess' Hospital, Alexandria

I got into the square at 5.15pm and did some shopping during the course of which I managed to procure some music paper. The woman in the shop was a German and very forlorn with no news from her relations. After a momentary look of suspicion, when I asked her whether she was German, she seemed to me very glad to be using her own language again and we had quite a little conversation.

I went to the Savoy Hotel at 6.45pm and met Philip Kershaw at 7.30pm. He was waiting for Mervyn Herbert, with whom he was dining, so I waited till 9.00pm when Mervyn turned up and dined with them. Mervyn is at the [British] Agency here. Kershaw has just recovered from a bullet wound through his lung received on 8 May and is returning to Gallipoli next week. He has made a record recovery for such a wound. I broke the hospital rules, I found out afterwards, by returning at 11.00pm and had to undress in the dark.

Educated at Eton and Oxford, The Honourable Mervyn Robert Howard Molyneux was a career diplomat in Egypt at the time he met Kelly. He was the third son of Henry Herbert, 4th Earl of Carnarvon at Highclere Castle, Hampshire and half-brother of George Herbert, the 5th Earl of Carnarvon, who financed the search for and, in 1922, the excavation of Tutankhamun's tomb.

Saturday, 12 June 1915 – Deaconess' Hospital, Alexandria

I drove out to the Summer Palace Hotel, Ramleh – some four miles – to dine with [a lady who is] somewhat Scotch in her disapproval of frivolity and was sure the war would give the average English girl a lesson in self-sacrifice. It wasn't that [English girls] had really been bad, but unthinking. At the next table were Ock, Violet Asquith and Charles Lister – just turned up from Malta on his my back to Gallipoli – and I was terrified lest I should be overheard agreeing with her!

Charles Lister had a car and gave me a lift back, but not before we had visited the Agency, where we had a talk with Mervyn Herbert and two attachés. I reached the hospital at midnight and my heart misgave me on finding the front door locked and all in darkness. It was with feelings long since unfamiliar that I slunk round one corner, then another and then into a long corridor – to find one of the nurses waiting for me! She gave me a bad scolding and said she had reported me to the major – who, I earnestly hope, is not the severe old lady with the spectacles. Military discipline rather than her!

Wednesday, 16 June 1915 – Majestic Hotel, Alexandria
In the afternoon I played for an hour on a fairly good Bechstein Grand in a music shop called Hugo Hackh, where I had the conversation with the German lady on 10 June. She refused to make any charge. I played Mendelssohn's 'Variations Serieuses', Brahms' 'Variations on an Original Theme', Mendelssohn's 'Scherzo a Capriccio', my D Minor study and my new 'Elegy for Strings in Memoriam of Rupert Brooke'. It is practically complete except for the writing down. I had never played it before and was pleased with it. Charles Lister and I hired a boat after tea and sailed out in a strong wind to the breakwater where we bathed.

The 'forlorn' German lady whom Kelly had met earlier and who had shown him a kindness by refusing his money had good reason to be fearful. Hugo Hackh, the German owner of the music shop on the Rue Cherif Pasha was shortly to become persona non-grata *in British-controlled Egypt. On 11 February 1916 he appeared in a list, drawn up by the Secretary of State for Foreign Affairs and published in the* London *Gazette, of 'persons and firms in Egypt with enemy interests, which have been licensed by the Egyptian Government, to carry on business for the purpose of liquidation only'.*

Thursday, 24 June 1915 – Shepheard's Hotel, Cairo

I spent a very happy day contriving at last to see the Arabic Museum – which I missed on my previous visits to Cairo – and visiting the bazaars again, where I bought two old Persian vases and finally poking about rare bookshops picking up suitable volumes for active service conditions. These consisted of Southey's *The Life of Nelson*, Pope's *Essay on Man*, *The Sorrows of [Young] Werther* and *Antony & Cleopatra*.

The Arabic Museum was no disappointment and it was satisfactory to find a not over-large collection, of which I could get somewhat of a grasp during the course of the morning. Some of the early stone work, the metal work, and above all the glass lamps, were the most beautiful contents of the museum. The glass lamps were like a dream of romance – like a poet's words catching form. I read some more of [George Henry] Lewes' *Life of Goethe* after dinner.

Friday, 25 June 1915 – Majestic Hotel, Alexandria

I went to Hugo Hackh's music shop about 6.00pm and played till 7.30pm. A young sergeant of the Ordnance Corps listened to me for some time before I finished, when he came and told me he was professional violinist and suggested our making music. He gave me a name which sounded like 'Furnal'. I dined with [Lieutenant] J T Colledge [Gloucestershire Yeomanry Hussars] at the Khedevial Club and met a Mr and Mrs Blagden – who live in Alexandria – and a Miss Shed. We went out for a sail in the harbour and ended up at a circus.

It was almost a full moon and the warm breeze and the lights of the harbour, combined with the lovely sail of our boat, set my mind in a romance.

Kelly subsequently played several times with the young Army Ordnance Corps sergeant, John William Furler from Kingsteignton in Devon, who had been in Egypt since 10 March 1915. He was commissioned as a second lieutenant on 10 September 1918.

Sunday, 27 June 1915 – Majestic Hotel, Alexandria

I worked at my 'Elegy for String Orchestra in Memoriam Rupert Brooke', all the morning and finished it by lunch time. I have still to put in the phrasing and expression marks. I went to the Deaconess' Hospital with Mr and Mrs Norman Holden at 4.45pm to report myself and while Holden was having his wound dressed I went up to see Eric Nobbs, of Hood Battalion who was only one day back on the peninsula when he was wounded a second time with a shrapnel bullet in his ankle-bone.

Forty-year-old Lieutenant Ernest Nobbs had enlisted in the ranks of the Royal Marines in October 1892 and had been discharged in October 1913 after twenty-one years' service. Re-enlisting with an honorary commission in 1914, he had exchanged quartermastering for a platoon. He went missing, believed killed, commanding a company of the Hood Battalion on 24 March 1918 during the German spring offensive on the Western Front.

Monday, 28 June 1915 – Majestic Hotel, Alexandria

I met John Furler at Hackh's music shop at 5.45pm and we played. I was much impressed with the nobility of the Rondo of Mozart's E Flat sonata. I have never come across Mendelssohn's Opus 4 before and found many interesting things in it. Grieg's C Minor sonata contains fine things. Whatever else may be the matter with his work, his instinct for harmony is unerring.

Tuesday, 29 June 1915 – Majestic Hotel, Alexandria

I worked at my 'Elegy for String Orchestra' in the morning and from 2.45pm till 4.45pm, by which time I had finished filling in the phrases and marks of expression. It seems to me to be an advance on my previous work as far as individuality of formed matter is concerned. It is so entirely bound up with Rupert Brooke and the circumstances of his burial that in a sense I feel myself the chronicler of its ideas rather than the composer. As we slowly made our way behind the coffin to the olive grove [a certain] phrase constantly recurred to my mind. The work is a true portrayal of my feelings that night – the passionless simplicity of the surroundings with occasionally a note of personal anguish.

I went to Mustapha Barracks to report at 12.15pm and to the Deaconess' Hospital at 5.30pm. I met John Furler at Hackh's at 6.30pm and we played Mozart's sonatas – violin and piano – in E Flat Major K v 481 and A Major K v 526 and Bach's E Major Sonata No. 3. The first movement of the latter is really divine.

Friday, 2 July 1915 – Majestic Hotel, Alexandria

I spent about an hour-and-a-half in Hugo Hackh's playing at different times during the day. The broad sweep of the melody of [Schubert's] *Ave Maria* surged through me for the rest of the day: what a marvellous tune!

I dined with [essayist and literary critic] Percy Lubbock [Eton, King's College, Cambridge] in my hotel and had a pleasant talk. It is nice in these surroundings to occasionally come across a man with intellectual interests. We went round to the Union Club afterwards where we were shortly disturbed by a considerable hubbub from the street. On looking out I saw half a dozen American bluejackets in full flight before a pack of Australian soldiers! Rumour has it that on a previous similar occasion the retreating Americans were followed with derisive shouts of, ''e's too proud to fight!' in reference to President Wilson's speech after the sinking of the *Lusitania*.

Wednesday, 7 July 1915 – HMT *Nile*, Mediterranean

I drove down to Quay No. 45 at 10.30am and succeeded in stowing away nine cases of Greek wine, whiskey and liqueurs in my cabin without protest from my embarkation officer. I secured a cabin with Egerton, but later on a third officer, from Nelson Battalion, was put in as well.

I lunched at the Union Club with Egerton and was lucky enough to get hold of the new *Land & Water* just arrived. I also read an incredibly prejudiced article by C V Stanford in the *Quarterly Review* (I think) about music in war time.

I found myself posted up as first officer of the guard and spent some time after dinner seeing sentries posted. The *Nile* is a ship of about 5,000 tons, fast and comfortable, though my first dinner didn't raise hopes as to the fare. It has a staff of Chinese stewards. I've enjoyed my convalescence in Alexandria a good deal and we're lucky to have such a place for our wounded.

Sunday, 11 July 1915 – Hood Battalion, RND base camp, Gallipoli Peninsula

I landed with Lieutenant Egerton and the 2nd Naval Brigade draft – about 54 men – on W Beach at 6.15am but did not get up to the base camp – the same camp as we occupied from 12 May till I got wounded – till about 10.30am, the men being provided with breakfast down on the beach. The battalion had been up in the trenches and were in process of arriving back by driblets. Of the old lot of Hood officers I found Major Myburgh in command, Lieutenant Commander Nelson as adjutant, Bernard Freyberg, second-in-command, Ock Asquith in charge of a company as a lieutenant commander – he was a sub lieutenant when I last saw him in Alexandria – Patrick Shaw-Stewart a lieutenant and Charles Lister and five new officers who had been drafted in from Collingwood and Benbow Battalions. Later in the day I was put into A Company under Freyberg.

The flies are thick over all foodstuffs.

Freyberg, Ock, Lister, Stewart, Egerton and I went bathing on X Beach at 5.30pm. I have been practising a different stroke since racing Freyberg at Port Said – when I took a leg stroke with each separate hand stroke. I now take two hand strokes – one hand after the other – to one stroke with the legs and I was interested to find I could keep up better with Freyberg. He took about a length off me in about 25 yards. Things were very peaceful on the peninsula, except for a mild bombardment of the Turkish lines in the morning. I felt quite glad to be back!

**Monday, 12 July 1915 – Hood Battalion, RND base camp,
Gallipoli Peninsula**

It was a hot day and for us there was nothing to do, though at 4.00pm
we got orders to stand by for an immediate move. There was a big
attack on the Turkish lines – in two places – one in the morning
and another about 5.30pm and from what we heard the net result
of operations was satisfactory, the famous redoubt on the left of the
French line being taken.

I was awake at 3.00am and heard about six shots from one of the
ships' big guns which seemed to me to have been a signal for a general
bombardment. I counted 60 shots in one minute which didn't seem
to be exceptional for the intensity of shots. When the bombardment
stopped there was a decidedly weak reply of rifle fire and I felt fairly
confident. At 4.30pm there was another fierce artillery bombardment
for an hour and the second part of the attack was carried out.

Both the morning and afternoon bombardments were a fine sight to
watch – the whole of Achi Baba from side to side of the peninsula being
at times completely hidden from view by a great curtain of dust and
smoke. In the afternoon there were several sensational hits on the very
summit itself, where an enemy observation station was reported to be.
It gave it the appearance of a volcano in eruption.

Our OC, Major Myburgh, went on the sick list in the afternoon so,
with Freyberg filling his place, I was left in charge of A Company.

**Tuesday, 13 July 1915 – Hood Battalion, RND base camp,
Gallipoli Peninsula**

We had nothing to do in spite of our orders to stand by all day. The
attack on the Turkish lines continued and seemed to be successful from
the very meagre news that got to us. A rumour came to us that some of
our dead officers were seen in the positions in which they had fallen on
4 June.

Wednesday, 14 July – Hood Battalion, RND base camp, Gallipoli Peninsula

There was a strong gale blowing all day, entailing great discomfort from the clouds of dust. We had nothing to do except stand by in case we were needed. I went bathing with Ock Asquith and Egerton at 5.45pm on X Beach. There seemed little doing in the firing line but no authentic news reached us of what the position of affairs up there really is.

Just as we were finishing dinner, orders came that Patrick Shaw-Stewart was to take up a party of about 180 men from A and B Companies with Charles Lister, [Sub Lieutenant William] Carnall and myself to report at Backhouse Post about 9.45pm.

We had to split up into several parties of about 40 men and take up ammunition, sand bags, chloride of lime and periscopes to the various RND battalions in the front trenches. My objective was the Chatham Battalion and I was supplied with a guide. He was not very certain of the exact situation, so when we had got somewhere near, I left my men where they were and went to look for them myself. [Kelly had, by this time, grown a thick, black beard – a naval privilege jealously guarded by the men of the RND throughout the war]. This led to my ludicrous arrest as a supposed German officer. It was a zealous sentry of the King's Own Scottish Borderers (KOSB) who was not to be restrained, even by one of his officers, and I was kept at the point of the bayonet for about 25 minutes before being allowed to proceed to the Chatham Battalion between two sentries as an escort!

The suspicious sentry had a whole string of questions which I couldn't answer, such as; if I had brought an ammunition party [up] to the Chatham Battalion, why was it they had not sent down for any? Who were their officers? Where was my party? 200 yards in rear being a very suspicious answer to the latter. This was all amongst the trenches taken since Sunday; a very confusing network I found them. I finally found my party after half-an-hour's search and delivered the various things we had been carrying at 3.00am. We were back at the base camp at 5.00am just about sunrise. It was very hot work and in places there was a considerable smell of dead Turk.

Thursday, 15 July – Hood Battalion, RND base camp, Gallipoli Peninsula

We stood by from 4.00pm expecting to go up to the trenches at 7.30pm. During dinner, however, word came that we were not to start till the following morning, so we had another night in peace.

I took a walk with Charles Lister at 2.00pm to the [SS] *River Clyde* – the stranded 'Wooden Horse of Troy' [run ashore on 25 April 1915 as a landing ship] – at V Beach, to try to secure some planks to cover in our officers' mess. We were very obligingly treated by a naval officer there. The ship has already been rifled and chiefly, he told me, by the RND.

We walked over to X Beach afterwards to bathe. The wine and liqueurs I brought back from Alexandria add greatly to the pleasures of the mess.

Friday, 16 July 1915 – Hood Battalion, support trench, middle of the line

We moved off at 7.15am and after some delay at Backhouse Post, owing to our guides being late in putting in an appearance, we marched up 'Oxford Street' to the front trenches – past many a savoury smell of dead Turk. We finally got squashed up in a communicating trench, leading to a trench occupied by Drake Battalion and in their trench itself.

Whoever had arranged for the 2nd Naval Brigade to relieve the 1st had not made a very good mathematical calculation, as we were two-and-a-half companies too many for our lines alone. We had to stand all huddled up in the burning sun for two hours – at the end of which time two companies were sent back to Backhouse Post. I was on watch from 12.30am till 3.30am but I got very little rest before then owing to parties coming through and enquiring their way. We have C and D Companies in front of us, but their trench further to the right is occupied by Turks.

The flies are very bad, but I got some sleep in the day by putting muslin over my head. I felt very depressed and a little faint with the heat and discomfort.

Arthur Asquith was of the opinion that the overpowering stench of Turkish corpses rotting under the blistering Aegean sun, each one covered in a thick, black blanket of flies, was amongst the most trying of ordeals to which the troops were subjected at any time: 'The Turks who had been killed on 12 July lay everywhere, unburied and half-buried, in these newly-captured trenches', he wrote. 'The weather was sweltering, the stench overwhelming, and many of our officers and men vomited again and again. Reluctance to face this nauseating experience was so strong that during the afternoon there were three cases of self-inflicted wounds among the two companies sent back temporarily to Backhouse Post – the only cases of self-inflicted wounds which I can remember in the battalion.'

Sunday, 18 July 1915 – Hood Battalion, support trench, middle of the line

At 8.45pm 100 men of A Company under Patrick Shaw-Stewart and myself stood ready to move out at [a position known as] Point 6 with 100 Howe men and a party of engineers to dig a sap [a trench extending forward from an existing position] connecting Point 6 with the firing line about 150 yards in front. This took us till 3.00am to finish – we didn't move out till about 11.30pm. Our presence was not detected by the Turks, but there were a good many stray shots flying about and we lost PO Jack, an able seaman called Graham, both killed and one Howe man killed – no wounded, except a few pick-wounds. Some of the men were rather rattled.

Patrick Shaw-Stewart and I walked up and down the line for the first hour or so. Later on we made the journey every half hour, however. There was one man who seemed to be a complete craven complaining of a pain in his chest. It was very interesting to find the next morning after the doctor had returned him, as having nothing the matter, that he was the man whom Patrick Shaw-Stewart a few days ago had had to tell off for some very impertinent criticisms of the Hood officers and its doctor in a couple of letters of his we had had to censor – impertinent because he knew they would be censored by us.

I got no sleep till 3.30am. I found I've missed out a day. This day of the night-digging party was a fairly hard working day – the commodore coming up and generally keeping us all busy with plans for better communications with the firing line.

Thirty-four-year-old PO Thomas Jack of Broughty Ferry had been one of the survivors of A Company of the Collingwood Battalion which had been practically annihilated during the Third Battle of Krithia on 4 June 1915. Transferred to the Hood on Collingwood's disbandment, he was killed on 19 July 1915 and was buried 'in [a] communication trench between 5 in E10 and 6 in E11. Cross marking grave'. Posthumously mentioned in Sir Ian Hamilton's despatch of 22 September 1915 his grave was subsequently lost and he is now commemorated on the Helles Memorial to the Missing as is Able Seaman Edward Graham (22) of Annitsford in Northumberland.

Monday, 19 July 1915 – Hood Battalion, same trench
I had orders to try to locate a machine gun in a Turkish trench some 400 yards or more away and this took up the greater part of my morning. About 12.30pm I took a journey up to the firing line some 175 yards in front and had a talk with Freyberg for an hour.

I got half a dozen letters from Maisie that had failed to reach me when I was wounded and I spent a very happy hour reading all the news they contained. She has a very happy gift of letter-writing, which one appreciates all the more under these conditions. I got a sleep in the afternoon.

Patrick Shaw-Stewart and I get our meals together in a dugout, and over a bottle of red Greek wine we had an interesting retrospective talk of our Eton and Oxford experiences – or more exactly, of his academic and my rowing careers respectively. There was nothing doing all night as far as A Company was concerned and after 12.30am when my watch came to an end I got some sleep.

Tuesday, 20 July 1915 – Hood Battalion, same trench

Thanks to Bernard Freyberg's keen activity an assault had been planned on a neighbouring trench leading back into the Turkish lines. Its object was to remove a barricade in it some 100 yards up it towards the Turks. After half-an-hour's artillery bombardment Charles Lister set out with a party of men preceded by some bomb throwers and quickly performed the task. He appears to have done extremely well under difficulties as two of the four bomb throwers faltered and the party of men required some persuasion before they would follow him.

Unfortunately Turkish shrapnel wounded both him – slightly – and Freyberg – a disquieting stomach wound – and one of the new draft of five officers for the Hood, whose first visit it was to the firing line, was killed by a rifle bullet in one of the saps leading to the firing line.

We have been very unlucky in officer casualties during these five days in the trenches as another of our officers, Paine, was killed a few days ago. I read Lewes' *Life of Goetha* for a couple of hours or so. I was told by our adjutant he had heard the Turks were reported to be preparing for a final attempt to drive us off the peninsula with 100,000 men, and that in the event of their failing they will give up.

The officer shot on his first visit to the firing line was Lieutenant Frank Blashfield Ramsey. Commissioned as a sub lieutenant in January 1915, he had been transferred from Benbow Battalion and had only joined the Hood in the trenches two days before he was killed. He has no known grave and is commemorated on the Helles Memorial.

Captain Charles Paine (38) of the Royal Marine Light Infantry, attached to the Hood, was killed on 17 July 1915. A special memorial stone records that he is buried somewhere in Redoubt Cemetery, three miles northeast of Cape Helles.

The doughty Bernard Freyberg hated the thought of leaving the battalion, even though his injuries were serious, and was back on the peninsula – his wound unhealed – in less than a month.

Thursday, 22 July 1915 – Hood Battalion, base camp, Gallipoli Peninsula

As a new draft of officers and 200 men had come for the battalion, a rearrangement of companies was necessary. Owing to the casualties in officers of the last few days, I found myself in charge of B Company. I had a fairly busy [time attending to] divisional orders as to respirators and sprayers etc.

Friday, 23 July 1915 – Hood Battalion, base camp, Gallipoli Peninsula

I found myself gazetted a lieutenant in one of the recent *Times*.

Saturday, 24 July 1915 – Hood Battalion, base camp, Gallipoli Peninsula

It was another hot, windy day with a great deal of dust in the air. My inside was out of order – like everyone else's – and I ate nothing all day. With [Sub Lieutenant] Ivan Heald, and Morrison ill, I was reduced to one sub lieutenant and had a great deal of company work to do – including 136 letters to censor.

Lieutenant James Morrison, of Edinburgh, who was, according to Arthur Asquith 'a most conscientious and reliable officer', was killed whilst commanding a company of the Hood at Gavrelle near Arras on the Western Front on 23 April 1917.

Monday, 26 July 1915 – Hood Battalion, base camp, Gallipoli Peninsula

I spent my spare time writing a letter to Eddie Marsh about Rupert Brooke and Denis Browne. After tea I bathed with Ock Asquith just above Sedd el Bahr. Francis Henley came to dinner. We have a company officer's mess consisting of the CO, Edward Nelson, the doctor, [Surgeon Eric Mackinnon] Molesworth and Ock, Egerton, Patrick Shaw-Stewart and myself. The battalion lost practically all its

stokers – about 140 – all of them taken to go to sea, and is much weakened in consequence.

**Wednesday, 28 July 1915 – Hood Battalion, base camp,
Gallipoli Peninsula**

Charles Lister arrived back after a very speedy recovery at Imbros and I
am delighted that he has been appointed to B Company as [my] second-
in-command.

*Amplifying Kelly's entries above, Arthur Asquith commented that, 'In
the Hood, the Naval Reservist Stokers – tough middle-aged types – were
concentrated in two companies. Prone to almost incessant 'grousing', they had
long felt that service afloat was their 'metier' and that in using them as soldiers
the Admiralty was simply trying to make sows' ears out of silk purses. They
allowed little to escape their dry and rather cynical sense of humour, and
nothing to surprise or ruffle their stoic calm. Dysentery and casualties were
causing kaleidoscopic changes in the personnel of the Hood, and the removal
of 140 of our sturdiest and most seasoned troops at such a crucial time in the
campaign increased the immediate difficulties of our battalion officers.'*

*Charles Lister, bored with being a patient in hospital at Imbros, had 'broken
out' of it in his eagerness to return to action with the Hood on the Gallipoli
Peninsula. Arthur Asquith recalled that 'some shallow wounds in his back
were still unhealed, and every morning he called loudly for his batman to dress
them. The batman, whom we will call "Brown", had perhaps been efficient [in
civilian life] as a bank clerk but was not seen as a servant. One morning after
calling for Brown repeatedly without result, Charles Lister turned to a brother
officer and said "Brown is impossible. He is hopelessly inefficient. What can
we do with him?" And then, after a pause, he added, "I think we shall have to
make him an officer!"'*

**Friday, 30 July 1915 – Hood Battalion, base camp,
Gallipoli Peninsula**

The days are peculiarly uniform as regards bright sunshine and a north-easterly wind, which, if it keeps us cooler than we otherwise should be, yet causes much dust to fly about. The nights are still and not too hot. Since I returned from Alexandria life has been far from uncomfortable when in the base camp with one's camp and base kit and the possibility of getting a bath each day, to say nothing of mosquito curtains and the improvements in the mess; one is living a different existence to what one did in May.

I bathed with Ock Asquith off Sedd el Bahr harbour (the little Turkish one north-east of the fort) at 6.00pm and we watched a Frenchman catching small fish with a hook and line. We came back to dinner with many regrets over our short-sightedness in not bringing any fishing tackle back from Alexandria, but we cheered up later in the evening when one of the new officers arrived with quite a decent catch which he had bombed. The staff captain, Greenwood, dined with us. A healthy argumentative spirit is manifesting itself and dinner seldom passes by without sides being taken and a subject thrashed out. Nelson and I always find each other on opposite sides.

Asquith noted that during these discussions Kelly by 'challenging and dissecting every generalisation was a prime promoter of many agreeable arguments'. He went on to say that 'Roughly speaking Nelson, the marine biologist, represented what at Oxford we should have regarded as a mathematical and Cambridge point of view. I remember Kelly tilting against the theory of 'De Mortuis' [of the dead, speak no ill]. Mendel's theories [of genetics/inheritance] were also under discussion and many aspects of the war, including the reasons for the non-return to the peninsula of certain unwounded and lightly-wounded officers'.

Saturday, 31 July 1915 – Hood Battalion, base camp, Gallipoli Peninsula

Nearly all our officers spent the morning down at divisional headquarters where instructions were given in bombs and bomb throwing. There was a catapult with which one threw them – an instrument like a large easel of an artist with a number of thick pieces of Indian rubber. In structure it seemed to be fairly simple and successful, but the workmanship was so gimcrack as to make it rather dangerous. Having lit the fuse of one bomb and done what I was required to do in order to release the pocket which held it, I was beside myself to find the releasing catch had not worked. The second smack I gave it made my hand quite sore.

I censored letters till 5.30pm and at 6.00pm I went to Sedd el Bahr port (the little one on the north side) with Ock Asquith and Egerton to bathe. It was a beautiful still evening and the Asiatic coast was bathed in a soft opalescence. On our walk back we saw a gorgeous sunset with Samothrace outlined in gold.

Monday, 2 August 1915 – Hood Battalion, base camp, Gallipoli Peninsula

Ock Asquith and I were detailed to meet a guide at the junction of the Eski Line [the 'old' original line reached after the landings] with the Krithia Nullah at 6.00am. But owing to a mistake in the instructions we missed him and had to find our own way up to the firing line. We were to get a hang of the trenches in the sector at present held by the 42nd Division in case the RND is called upon to occupy any of them.

The line began on the left of the trenches occupied by us a fortnight ago (on Achi Baba Nullah) and ran about three-quarters-of-a-mile to the left to a point about 300 yards beyond Krithia Nullah where it joined the sector held by the 29th Division. We had a very obliging set of officers to deal with and altogether spent an interesting three and a half hours. We rode out from the camp, but returned on foot.

General Mercer, to whose 1st Naval Brigade we have just been turned over to on the break-up of the 2nd Brigade, inspected our lines at 6.30pm and the battalion made a pretty good show as regards cleanliness. There was rather an unpleasant note struck, however, by a petition which all the RNVR men – including about eight POs – put in to be sent to sea. Last week the stokers were taken and they seem to regard it as a right that they should be taken too. They have been unfairly used, no doubt, as a force, but there was an absence of good motive about the present agitation – so several of us thought.

Wednesday, 4 August 1915 – Hood Battalion, base camp, Gallipoli Peninsula

More company matters in the morning and in addition I made a few notes on trench warfare with which to regale my POs and section leaders. This much dreaded ordeal [was] faced after 6.30pm muster. The GOC, [Major General Sir Archibald] Paris, was very anxious we should wake up our men's spirits for a final spurt, with the professed hopes that we should be off the peninsula in a few weeks.

The [men] were somewhat disappointed that nothing came of the promise in divisional orders some three weeks ago that the RND would leave the peninsula towards the end of July for a 'much-needed rest' or some such words and so they need bracing up to face the prospect of another month or so here. I talked [for] about 20 minutes.

By late July 1915, after three major battles and further fruitless fighting, it was clear that the southern sector at Cape Helles was a doomed front. The Turks had proved to be resilient and resourceful soldiers resulting in heavy battle casualties for the Allies. Disease had whisked thousands of others from the firing line and those who remained were physically and emotionally spent. The Allies needed more men – and more men meant a new plan.

It was decided that another 'front' be opened with amphibious landings at Suvla Bay on the Aegean coast, 18 miles north of Helles, combined with a 'breakout' battle involving the Australians and New Zealanders from the left flank of the Anzac beachhead six miles to the south. In spite of the extreme exhaustion and fragility of the forces at Helles, further diversionary attacks would be launched in support of the Suvla landings.

Friday, 6 August 1915 – Hood Battalion, base camp, Gallipoli Peninsula

The long hoped-for offensive opened with a heavy bombardment of

Turkish trenches west of Krithia Nullah at 2.30pm and at 3.50pm the 29th Division assaulted them – whether successfully or not we don't yet know (6.00pm). The battalion has been 'standing by' ready to move off since 4.00pm.

There was a huge batch of letters to censor. After dividing them with Webb, my share amounted to 108. After dinner we had news that the 29th Division had taken some trenches and that the 42nd Division had failed to take the trench allotted to them but were making another attempt after dark.

Saturday, 7 August 1915 – Hood Battalion, base camp, Gallipoli Peninsula

There was a bombardment of the Turkish trenches going on most of the day and we stood by for an immediate move – without, however, getting further orders to go.

I wrote a few letters and read some more of Lewes' *Life of Goethe* besides watching the effects of the bombardment. Some high explosive shells pitched on the summit of Achi Baba, again making a magnificent spectacle like a volcano in eruption. In the morning we got several shells quite close to our lines – shells that were after one of our batteries close by.

I was delighted to get Rupert Brooke's *1914, and Other Poems* by the afternoon post, Felix had very considerately sent them out. We got news of a further successful landing of three divisions [at] Suvla Bay.

Sunday, 8 August 1915 – Hood Battalion, base camp, Gallipoli Peninsula

My only other officer, Webb, went ill, so I had to attend to all the company affairs myself. I read some of Rupert Brooke's poems and was delighted with them. So far, the only work of his I know is the great sonnet sequence *1914* and it seems almost too good to be true that more of his work can be up to the same level, if in a different vein. I bathed by myself off Cape Helles at 6.45pm after attending the B Company rum issue.

Monday, 9 August 1915 – same camp

There is somewhat of a lull in the news of the new landing operations at Suvla Bay and though a great deal of country is reported as under our occupation one is still waiting for news of the occupation of Sari Bair, the 973-feet high hill. It looks as though this might hold up the new advance and cause it to develop into trench warfare like Achi Baba did to our original landing at Cape Helles.

Wednesday, 11 August 1915 – Hood Battalion, base camp, Gallipoli Peninsula

Matters at Anzac and north of Anzac seems to be getting down into the usual trench warfare, but one still hopes that reinforcements may enable them to push on towards Maidos. The Indian Brigade are rumoured to have been in possession of Sari Bair hill but to have been driven off again.

Kelly's assessment of the situation was correct. The optimism generated by the initial momentum following the landings at Suvla Bay gradually gave way to dismay as Turkish tenacity, poor intelligence and dire leadership at the highest levels of the British command ensured that this offensive too ground to a halt in two weeks. The British dug in on their meagre gains.

Saturday, 14 August 1915 – Hood Battalion, base camp, Gallipoli Peninsula

There was a concert in the evening, lasting a couple of hours. I rather shrank from the thought of sitting through it, but it turned out to be much more entertaining than I had expected – there being more humour than sentiment. I took an instructional class in the parts of the short [magazine Lee Enfield] rifle from 10.00am till 11.00am.

Patrick Shaw-Stewart [now attached to general headquarters as liaison officer with the French forces] dined with us. We have acquired an excellent French cook, who was directed to us by our quarter-master, Gillard, to whom he showed a chit directing him to 'report to the General'. We hope that by keeping quiet about the matter and rigging him out in a Hood uniform, he may drift into being a permanent acquisition. The difference in the treatment of our service rations was very noticeable.

Sunday, 15 August 1915 – Hood Battalion, base camp, Gallipoli Peninsula

I read a good deal of Lewes' *Life of Goethe* before breakfast. I spent a fairly busy morning occupied with company matters – among which were applications on the part of the men to subscribe to the War Loan. Yesterday they were like shy animals and behaved as though I were trying to lure them into a trap; but to-day I got over £150 from them.

Monday, 16 August 1915 – Hood Battalion, Eski Lines west of Krithia Nullah, Gallipoli Peninsula

We spent the morning preparing to move up to the trenches and at 12.30pm the first company left the camp. We are in reserve in the Eski Lines to the 2nd Naval Brigade – now [consisting of] the Marine Brigade plus the Howe Battalion – and are in very comfortable quarters about half a mile behind the firing line. With Morrison's return I now have two sub lieutenants under me.

Wednesday, 18 August 1915 – Hood Battalion, Eski Lines, Gallipoli Peninsula

I finished Lewes' *Life of Goethe*, which consists of nothing but interesting information and sound judgment. The style, however, is heavy-footed and annoyed me in the same way that a slightly dull man would who talked slowly and surely about a subject he knew well. I knew practically nothing of Goethe's life before this. For a great writer his work seems to be curiously unequal.

I explored the trenches occupied by A and C Companies in the afternoon and extended my walk by going down the dry nullah to Clapham Junction with Egerton. I began reading Moliere's *Les Precieuses Ridicules*.

Thursday, 19 August 1915 – Hood Battalion base camp near Sedd el Bahr

As the flies in my dugout were particularly tiresome I decided to try a policy of *Schrecklichkeit* and accordingly slaughtered large numbers. For the rest of the morning the ants were busy carrying off the dead and wounded, each dragging a burden about twice the size of itself over impassable obstacles, to their holes in the loose earth on top. In many cases their Herculean task was performed in the face of determined resistance on the part of their victims who would cling to every stone or twig which lay in their path.

We left the trench (B Company) at 3.30pm and came back to the base camp down Gully Ravine. I had not been down it before and was surprised to find it much deeper than the other nullahs, with precipitous sandstone cliffs about 60 feet or more high, which gave it quite a majesty. I managed to get in a bathe at Sedd el Bahr with Ock Asquith and Patrick Shaw-Stewart before dinner. After three days without washing in the trenches it was an indescribable joy diving in, 'like swimmers into cleanness leaping'.

Freyberg had arranged a fine spread for dinner with what he had brought back from Alexandria, and with Buckland and Shaw-Stewart added to the company commanders' mess, we had nine of the old Hood officers. The evening, as usual, ended in an argument between Nelson and myself.

Schrecklichkeit *is the German term for what, in English, can be translated as 'frightfulness'. As the German Army had driven through Belgium and northern France in the summer and autumn of 1914 some of its units had perpetrated atrocities against civilians – rounding them up and executing them – in cities like Dinant and Louvain (Leuven). Many in England thought that such acts of terror were an extension of Germany's military strategy to the civilian populations of the countries which it had invaded. Kelly's use of the term in German reflects both his understanding of the language from his time studying in Germany before the war and what it had come to mean.*

It is interesting to note that Kelly used a direct quotation from the first stanza of Rupert Brooke's poem 'Peace', to describe the sheer pleasure and exhilaration of being able to wash away the foetid corruption of the trenches in the clear waters of the Aegean. 'Peace' was the first of Brooke's five war sonnets written in 1914 and it is clear that Kelly was processing his thoughts and emotions about his friend and fellow officer through reading Brooke's poetry in the collection 1914, and Other Poems *he had received less than two weeks earlier.*

Monday, 23 August 1915 – Hood Battalion, support trench to firing line, just before Krithia

I spent all the morning in preparation to move up to the trenches. B Company moved at 5.50pm and reached the support trench which we took over from D Company.

Tuesday, 24 August 1915 – Hood Battalion, support trench to firing line, just before Krithia

I had a good many things to keep me occupied, putting my new officers on to their various jobs. In the middle of the day I spent an hour going round the firing line (at present occupied by A Company) with Charles Lister and Wallace, one of my new officers. There are two saps which lead out towards the Turkish trenches and the men in them were set for sniping and listening posts. I tried a couple of shots with the two periscope rifles but found them very gimcrack and unsatisfactory. There were two of the cyclists told off to work a trench mortar and [a] catapult for hurling bombs.

Late in the afternoon the firing line and support trench were subjected to some shell fire and Charles Lister was hit again (for the third time this campaign.) He came down to my trench looking a dreadful pale green colour and wouldn't wait for a stretcher. Two men helped him to the doctor 80 yards further down and I saw him dressed. He has two wounds and in both cases as there is no exit wound, it looks as though the projectiles were still in. One piece of high explosive shell entered just behind and below his right hip bone and the other the back of his calf. We're all anxious to know the first piece has not got in deep. Four or five other men were knocked out by the same shell.

[Lister] has a great name in the battalion for complete disregard of his own safety, but on the three occasions in which he has been hit he was taking no risks – which makes his ill-luck all the more accentuated. Several times he has walked out to Turkish trenches and saps to see whether they were occupied!

I had orders about 9.00pm to prepare to move at 4.00am to 'Lancashire Street', some 500 yards in rear of our present trench and I was up till 10.00pm exploring in rear to find out where we could fit in.

Wednesday, 25 August 1915 – Hood Battalion, firing line, 'Worcester Flat' [trenches] and barricade

I moved up to the firing line at 2.00pm and took over 'Essex Knoll' and Sap 5. In the latter there is a complicated system of sentry routine for constant sniping observation and, at night, listening, and the first platoon which took it over was some time in taking over from the outgoing men. It contained a large catapult for jam-tin bombs, a Garland Gun for Garland bombs, two periscope rifles and an iron tube through which a sentry kept a constant look out on the Turkish continuation of the sap. The Turkish line is about 40 yards away from the end.

It was not unlike a fair and I immediately set to work trying all the 'side shows' by ordering the catapult and Garland Gun to be used and sniping myself from all the sniping posts. I only had my company really set up by about 8.30pm when I spent an hour or more going round the lines held by D Company on our left with Ock Asquith. I turned in at 11.00pm and took a round an hour-and-a-half later. Things were quiet.

Thursday, 26 August 1915 – Hood Battalion, firing line, Worcester Flat and barricade

I was settling down for a sleep after the morning stand-to-arms, when it was reported to me that R Winship, of my old platoon, had been shot through the head in Barricade 5. He had been sniping over the side of the trench and was hit by an enfilade shot that came from the Turkish trench beyond and to the left of the barricade-head some 50 yards away. The configuration of the ground is very deceptive and no-one had realised that an apparently safe parapet on the left side of the sap – running to the Turkish trenches – afforded no cover to the head of a man sniping out the other way.

All sniping had to be stopped during daylight. From having things all our own way the day before we were somewhat dominated by enemy snipers today. Whereas we only had a barricade head to fire from, a Turkish sniper had a length of some 20 or 30 yards, so that he could train [his rifle] on where he knew was the only position we could fire from, while we never knew which position he would choose. They smashed several of our periscopes and our periscope rifle and stand.

A section of our battalion bombers was told off for Barricade 5 in the afternoon, to take the place of the two cyclists. They've had five days' training at divisional headquarters (DHQ). Their first attempt at putting their art into practice was not reassuring as they wounded one of themselves by a premature burst after the bomb – a jam pot – had left the catapult. It seemed to me the operator waited too long after lighting the fuse, but I don't believe the interval till the burst came was seven seconds as it should have been. The jam-pot bombs are made at DHQ and are said by the majority of people to be very unreliable – especially so if they are kept some days before use.

About 10.00pm, when I was sent for to Barricade 5, I ordered two of [the bombs] to be thrown by hand on to a patch of scrub some 15 yards away, where both my officers and men said they had soon someone moving. This was hardly more of a success than the first attempt. First the fuse matches would not light and then, when some minutes had elapsed while a box of matches was being borrowed, two bomb fuses wouldn't light. However, two were finally hurled and burst.

This last experience of them was the occasion of a ludicrous little panic occasioned by both my junior officers who were in the barricade, a number of men mistaking their own sentries – who were keeping watch in a listening post ten yards to the left of the barricade – for Turks. Luckily I thought of withdrawing them before sending off the bombs to search the ground! It was the two officers' first experience of fire trenches but I took the opportunity to read everyone a lesson and told them 'off'. It was a miracle the sentries weren't shot. In replacing them myself, one of the men further down the sap blazed off at us. It was a hard dénouement but when I arrived in the trench it was unpleasant to find all the men huddled about with no-one keeping a lookout and two rather helpless officers. But I suppose one must expect this sort of thing when about three quarters of them are from the new drafts, of whom one knows very little except that they have done very little musketry.

Winship's death is a distinct loss of a good man. I remember him once on board the *Grantully Castle*, displaying considerable character and reliability as a sentry in running in a man who refused to obey his orders.

The various weapons that Kelly thought were akin to fairground 'side shows' and which he appeared to have so little faith in, reflected the paucity of effective equipment and ammunition which the men in the trenches needed to fight the static siege warfare which had gripped the peninsula. He had already tried his hand with an improvised trench catapult and 'jam-tin' bombs with some degree of trepidation and here was his first introduction to what he called the Garland Gun. This was actually an improvised trench mortar invented by Herbert Garland, a pre-war metallurgist and superintendent of laboratories at the Cairo Citadel, in response to demands for an effective short-range, high-trajectory weapon designed specifically for trench warfare. It consisted of a smoothbore steel barrel fixed at 45 degrees to a solid wooden base and fired various improvised and home-made 'jam-tin' grenades which the men had had to resort to due to the then lack of a standard 'bomb' or hand grenade in sufficient quantities.

The loss of 26-year-old Able Seaman Richard Winship was obviously felt keenly by Kelly. Winship had felt it his duty to leave behind his wife Eleanor and his job as a furnace man in Darlington to enlist in the Durham Light Infantry on 2 September 1914. Transferring to the RNVR a week later he joined the Hood Battalion and sailed with it for Gallipoli. Wounded in the chest by shrapnel on the opening day of the Second Battle of Krithia on 6 May, 1915, he had been evacuated to hospital in Malta, returning to the peninsula three weeks later only to be picked off by a Turkish sniper at the advanced barricade in the British front line. Winship was originally buried on the battlefield in a small cemetery in Communication Trench B close to a position named Twelve Tree Copse to the west of the main Sedd el Bahr–Krithia road but his grave was lost. He is now remembered on the Helles Memorial.

Saturday, 28 August 1915 – Hood Battalion support trench behind Worcester Flat

A Hood officer carried out a reconnaissance on the night Friday/Saturday by crawling out alone to a Turkish trench 40 yards away where they knew digging had been going on. He first of all came [upon] what he was sure was a man asleep and whom [he thought] it was imperative to deal with if he wished to carry his investigations further. Having decided he couldn't murder him in cold blood he reached down to take him prisoner and found it was a corpse! The rest of the trench only contained dead bodies.

On his way back he was nearly attacked by one of his own men with a pickaxe. His little adventure was strictly against orders, but, like other forbidden things, as it was successfully carried out, he got nothing but praise from the authorities. The Drake [Battalion] scouts further down the line to the right were also sent out and found the first Turkish trench empty. B Company were relieved in the firing line at 2.00pm and moved down to the support trench. I did some work on my new violin sonata in G Major.

**Monday, 30 August 1915 – Hood Battalion, base camp near
Sedd el Bahr**

We were relieved in the trenches by Howe Battalion at 4.45pm and got back to camp about 6.30pm. I had a bath before dinner and enjoyed some wine the quartermaster had procured from Tenedos. It was a kind of a rough port in taste and a little strong but very enjoyable. It came in a lovely great bottle in a basket with handles.

**Friday, 3 September 1915 – Hood Battalion, base camp near
Sedd el Bahr**

I felt rather ill and depressed and found Philip Kershaw and [Lieutenant Reginald] Bickley of Drake Battalion in a similar mood. I met them at Sedd el Bahr where I went to bathe at 6.00pm and on the walk back we all agreed that [the higher command] are over working the RND men. We are only two depleted brigades and are doing the work of a division. It is not the higher ratings who suffer but the rank and file who are incessantly sent out on working parties both in the trenches and down in the rest camp. The sick list is constantly being added to.

During the month of August 1915, one company of the Hood, of which the average strength was about 130 men, had 102 men invalided off the peninsula with dysentery. Of those who were left practically all of them, like Kelly, were suffering to a greater or lesser extent from illness brought on as a result of the heat and unsanitary conditions.

**Tuesday, 7 September 1915 – Hood Battalion firing line,
'New Cut' – 400 yards to the right of Gully Ravine**

We left for the firing line at 1.00pm and I had rather a scramble to move off in time with my company. I was in a mood in which I couldn't summon up any energy to do anything and I suddenly realised half-an-hour before we moved off that my company was taking over a sector of the firing line and I had given no instructions to my platoon officers. All came right, however. We have a fairly easy line to deal with except for a barricade in a sap out towards the Turks from which bombs are exchanged. My catapult bombers were taken away from the barricade, and the Turks were unchecked from throwing about 20 at us during the night, without doing any harm. At midnight the whole of our line held by the RND fired off five rounds rapid just to worry the enemy.

Tuesday, 9 September 1915 – in support to A Company, 'Chelmsford Street', east of Gully Ravine

Another busy day receiving and carrying out orders. B Company were relieved out of the firing line at 3.00pm by A Company who made a mistake in the arrangements and clashed with us. I went out in front of the firing line B Company had occupied yesterday to fix some barbed wire at 8.30pm. Two engineers, ten men from B Company and Sub Lieutenant Morrison and I were out three-quarters-of-an-hour or so. Things were quiet except for one or two shots which may have been attracted by the tinkling of cans and wire. The Turkish trenches were about 120 yards away except for the left flank where they were only 50. Our task was to thread some coils of French rolling wire with two fresh coils of barbed wire – of about 30 yards each – and we all got in without mishap. A similar party from Drake to the right unfortunately lost two killed: Sub Lieutenant [Edward Henry Swinburne Bligh – shot through the head] and a man [Able Seaman Bertram Bizzell – chest].

Sunday, 12 September, 1915 – Hood Battalion, firing line in front of 'Hampshire Cut'

Patrick came up to my dugout at 7.45am on his liaison rounds and brought me the first news of Charles Lister's death, a day or so after he went away wounded from these trenches on 24 August.

The news came as a knock-out blow as I had been completely reassured by news we had had quite early, to the effect that he had been operated on successfully and that the wound was serious but not dangerous. I was very fond of Charles and his loss is as great a blow as

Rupert Brooke's. He was the most individual man I have ever known, I think, and his sense of humour was exquisite. There was something wonderfully fine and refined about him and he was completely unselfish. As an intellect too, he was remarkable.

One of my officers, James Morrison, got his face slightly cut by the pieces of glass from a broken periscope and I took his watches, 7.30–10.00pm and 12 midnight till 2.00am in the 'Southern Barricade'. One of our own bombs which, owing to the catapult not working right, burst just outside the barricade, set alight to the sandbags and I had a little excitement trying to put it out. I was afraid my whole barricade would tumble down, once the bags had burnt! Afterwards I tried to put the Turkish barricade in a similar predicament by firing Very lights at it, but their sandbags are too few and far between.

Lieutenant, The Honourable Charles Alfred Lister had been evacuated from the peninsula after receiving severe abdominal wounds, which Kelly had recorded in his diary, but had died four days later aboard the hospital ship Gascon. He was the second son of Thomas, 4th Lord Ribblesdale, who had been Lord in Waiting to Queen Victoria, and Lady Charlotte Monckton Lister, sister of Mrs Asquith, the prime minister's wife.

Educated, like Kelly, at Eton and Balliol Oxford, Lister had served in the diplomatic service and had been on the staff of the British Embassy in Constantinople prior to August 1914. Obtaining special permission he had joined the army in the autumn of 1914 and by February 1915 was in Gallipoli acting as interpreter on HMT Franconia attached as staff interpreter to the RND. He had applied for a transfer to the Hood Battalion in April 1915 to be amongst his great friends, 'Cleg' Kelly, Rupert Brooke, cousin Arthur Asquith, Patrick Shaw-Stewart and Bernard Freyberg. Mentioned posthumously in Sir Ian Hamilton's despatch of 22 September 1915, Charles Lister now lies in East Mudros Military Cemetery on the Greek island of Lemnos.

Monday, 13 September, 1915 – Hood Battalion, Chelmsford
Street, same trench as we occupied on 9 and 10 September
I finished reading Moliere's *Les Precieuses Ridicules* in the morning. It is
the first of his plays I have read, and I enjoyed it a good deal. I began
Shakespeare's *Antony & Cleopatra*, which, oddly enough, I have never
read. We were relieved by A Company in the firing line at 2.00pm. A
slack day.

Thursday, 16 September, 1915 – General Headquarters, Imbros
I was busy with company work during the morning. At lunchtime a desire
came over me to accompany Ock Asquith on a holiday to Imbros, so I at
once set about getting a leave and by 2.15pm had got permission from
General Mercer and DHQ. We caught the trawler leaving about 4.00pm
reaching Imbros about 6.00pm. Ock had telegraphed to [Lieutenant
Colonel] Robin [Robert Vere] Buxton [Eton, Oxford, Imperial Camel
Corps] who met us and fixed us up in GHQ in a tent. We dined in the
intelligence officers' mess and enjoyed a clean table and glasses and
other luxuries. Allright, who rowed in the Eton eight 1904 and 1905
and 3rd Trinity Grand Crew 1906, was also staying with Robin Buxton.
There were about 14 of us at dinner altogether, including the Italian
liaison officer. It blew very hard during the night. I had a new violin
sonata in my head in B Minor.

Imbros was a key staging post and the location – on the Bay of Kephalos –
of the General Headquarters of General Sir Ian Hamilton's MEF from the
end of May 1915. In addition to an extensive encampment of bell tents and
marquees which housed all the administrative arms of GHQ, Imbros boasted
a field hospital, Royal Naval Air Service airfield and stores.

Friday, 17 September 1915 – 'The Londons', Panagia, Imbros
It was blowing a gale, which I was afraid might ruin the day, as we
started from GHQ for Panagia at 10.00am. We crossed to K Beach in a
motor boat and there Arthur Asquith and myself made enquiries about

Charles Lister's grave from the APM [Assistant Provost Marshal]. It was a considerable surprise to us after what we have heard from Patrick Shaw-Stewart, to find he had not been buried on the island – that is to say if the APM's burial records could be trusted.

We accordingly set out for Panagia on foot – our kit following on animals with our two servants. It was a wholly delightful walk and we were both delighted at being free and in such lovely surroundings. We walked on to Kastro and after a delightful bathe on a beach behind which there was a river with bullrushes, we climbed up to Kastro and found an ancient Greek fountain (rather a lovely piece of work) and columns which might have once formed part of a small temple. At dinner we made the acquaintance of the governor of the island, a tiresome bore who was intent upon letting us know he was accustomed to better things than the restaurant table cloths and dinner-service. His French was almost unintelligible but voluble. We paid Lieutenant Thompson a visit afterwards and found two officers – one of them Stocks of the RND – within. He is a kind of resident for the island, and we had some interesting talk about the Balkan situation.

Arthur Asquith later reflected on Kelly's mood that day. 'FSK drank in the air in the hills and vented the exuberance of his joy of life in bursts of speech, peals of laughter and the curious animal noises of physical delight; habitual to him and not to be described'. It was not the first time that his friends had remarked on this; Rupert Brooke once describing Kelly's 'whinny' of a laugh coming from his tent in Egypt 'sending the ghosts of Antony and the gypsy scudding away across the sand'.

Saturday, 18 September 1915 – The Londons, Panagia, Imbros

Ock and I spent the day making an expedition to Skinudi, some three hours away, where we got an excellent lunch from a French-speaking Greek. The village is not very interesting, but the journey there lay through lovely country and we were both very happy. We rode most of the way. Lieutenant Thompson, Stocks and a younger officer dined with us at John Christo's!!

Sunday, 19 September 1915 – The Londons, Panagia, Imbros

We spent the morning shopping and getting such articles as we thought would be useful for the mess. George Lloyd and Robin Buxton rode out for lunch with us. Later in the afternoon, Asquith and I walked to Kastro and had a bathe. We bought some fish that had just been caught. There was a delightful street organ playing on our return to Panagia, playing a fascinating dance tune like Bizet – always on the same drone bass – and men were dancing to it. The barrel organ was quite small and its tone was far from unpleasant.

Monday, 20 September 1915 – Hood Battalion, new base camp, just north of DHQ, Cape Helles

Arthur Asquith and I left Panagia at 4.45am, after considerable delay in waking up the men and three horses we had ordered to take our luggage to K beach, Kephalo. It was very windy. We just caught the trawler and travelled over to Cape Helles with General Mercer and Commodore King. We found our camp had been changed. I rode up to the firing line with Freyberg and Mark Egerton at 2.00pm to see the sector we are taking over on Wednesday.

Sunday, 26 September 1915 – Hood Battalion, 'Putney Post'

Patrick Stewart-Shaw brought up a number of *Times* broad sheets with him. They are a revival of the old broadsheets and give purple passages and extracts from well-known authors for the purpose of supplying reading matter for the troops. [An officer] was round at midday rubbing in misapplied axioms from the drill book into every officer he saw. He has woolly hair and his brains are like cotton wool.

Monday, 27 September 1915 – Hood Battalion, Putney, same trench

A nice, slack day in which I had time for reading. The weather was warmer. News came of a big push in France [at Loos near Lens] in which 20,000 were taken. To fête the French we all raised three cheers during stand-to-arms at 7.00 pm and the guns fired several rounds. The Turks evidently thought it was the prelude to an attack as a very lively fire was opened and continued for a quarter of an hour or so. It seems the Russians are doing better.

Monday, 4 October 1915 – Hood Battalion, base camp near DHQ, Cape Helles

Two of our officers provided a great luxury for dinner, in the share of seven fish of about three-quarters-of-a-pound each, which they had bombed. Freyberg and Egerton dined in our mess. We now have a cook who is somewhat of an artist and I felt quite proud of the menu – soup, fried fish, fried steak and onions, jelly and stewed prunes and savoury (gentlemen's relish on toast), Vermouth, French red wine, beer, orange curaçao and coffee! I was rather hung up with the first movement of my violin sonata and had to give the matter some hard thought to get the details right.

Tuesday, 5 October 1915 – Hood Battalion, base camp near DHQ, Cape Helles

Major Peel lent me Belloc's fascinating analysis of the figures relating to the losses of Germany and Austria for the first year of the war, his estimate of their total number of men available for active service and their rate of wastage – published in *Land & Water* [of] 4 September. This convinced me that they must be somewhere about the turning of the tide when their reserves will be unequal to reinforcing their various fronts. In the afternoon came news of heavy German reverses on the Eastern Front, which were very gratifying. The telegram also contained the news of the 48-hour Russian ultimatum to Bulgaria. Altogether, it is a very exciting period, in great contrast to the peaceful conditions on our own front.

**Thursday, 7 October 1915 – Hood Battalion support trench,
Worcester Flat, about 500 yards from Krithia**

I finished reading Racine's *Andromaque* and enjoyed it more than I expected. My [B Company] headquarters are placed so that I have a lovely view of the tail end of the peninsula, of Rabbit Island, Tenedos and the Dardanelles. The twice-daily stand-to-arms are made very much pleasanter than they would otherwise be by the lovely sunrises and sunsets. A War Office telegram from France gave news that was somewhat an anti-climax after the [earlier] good news [regarding the fighting at Loos].

**Saturday, 9 October 1915 – Hood Battalion, support trench,
Worcester Flat, about 500 yards from Krithia**

It was a fine warm day, the morning of which we spent in feverish preparation for a threatened visit to our lines of the C-in-C, Sir Ian Hamilton. Everyone, from the Army Corps general down, was anxious for the show those under him would make and one of the most ludicrous orders we received was a command that trenches must be fully manned. As I am holding the support line of 400 yards with about 80 rifles I felt inclined to indent for a few hundred men, fully equipped! The visit never came off.

**Sunday, 10 October 1915 – Hood Battalion, support trench,
Worcester Flat, about 500 yards from Krithia**

A nice, slack day in which I spent some hours reading Tourgeneff's *Fumée*. The C-in-C paid us his postponed visit and my part of the line was filled out with headquarters orderlies etc sent up for the occasion!

**Monday, 11 October 1915 – Hood Battalion, support trench,
Worcester Flat, about 500 yards from Krithia**

I am making use of all the spare time I get in the trenches (which this week is practically the whole day) by pegging away at French. I am experiencing quite the same sort of keenness as I went through when I started working hard at music at Frankfurt. I read each paragraph of whatever book I am reading about six times in the hopes of picking up the words and the flow of the sentences. It is splendid having such a good opportunity and, as there is nothing I can do for my men, who are employed most of the day on fatigues, I can enjoy myself with a good conscience. We had a fairly heavy shower at 2.00pm which left the air nice and fresh. I noted the time the sun took to rise after stand-to-arms – about two-and-a-quarter minutes.

In Frankfurt, Kelly had studied music for five years at the Dr Hoch Konservatorium.

Tuesday, 12 October 1915 – Hood Battalion, support trench, Worcester Flat, about 500 yards from Krithia

One of my officers, Ivan Heald, is distinctly good company and we have a good many interests, mostly literary, in common. This morning we had an interesting talk after breakfast, during which he quoted me sonnets of Wordsworth and Yeats and sang me a few Irish folk songs.

I heard and saw what I took to be a flight of cranes half-a-mile or so away. Their cries sounded delightful in the fresh morning sunshine. One is very lucky to be campaigning in such lovely surroundings.

Another good letter from Logan Pearsall Smith came after breakfast, quoting a phrase of Henry James as to America's behaviour during the war, describing it as 'stretching out its great flat face to be slapped again'! I read more of *Fumée*.

Ivan Heald had been a columnist on the staff of the Daily Express *before the war, specialising in ironic and humorous pieces. He was 'fearless, witty, adventurous and unbuttoned', according to Arthur Asquith, who later became his commanding officer in the Hood. Asquith also recalled that 'the only part of the ritual of soldering which [Heald] could abide was paying the men' and that Kelly's view of his fellow company officer was 'divided between respect for Heald's qualities and enjoyment of his mind on the one side and extreme irritation at his unexemplary sloppiness in details of dress and discipline.'*

Monday, 18 October 1915 – Hood Battalion, base camp near DHQ, Cape Helles

I went up to our new winter camp area with Freyberg, Asquith and Egerton after breakfast and we discussed the arrangement of the various dugouts. On our way back, Egerton and I saw two more triangles of what looked like flighting storks, wending their way south, and the air was full of their rich cackle. On reaching the end of the peninsula they seemed to make across to Asia instead of continuing on their course. I slept from 2.00pm till teatime and then went on with the first movement of my violin sonata.

Thursday, 21 October 1915 – Hood Battalion, firing line from 'Union Street' to Sap 6

It was rather cold and at night a strong north-easterly wind made it extremely cold.

Friday, 22 October 1915 – Hood Battalion, firing line from Sap 6 to halfway between Union Street and Sap 7

It was a most disagreeable day for, in addition to the strong cold wind that was blowing, the rain began about midday and lasted intermittently through the night. I am feeling very stiff, very tired, sleepy and full of weariness – the symptoms, so Molesworth the doctor informed me, of jaundice in its early stages. It has been very prevalent amongst officers and men.

Freyberg did me a great act of kindness in pretending he wanted to spend a couple of nights in the firing line and ordering me to take his place at headquarters. As his dugout was [well] built it is about as safe and comfortable as anything one could desire with the existing materials and I had a very welcome long night's rest tucked in Freyberg's sleeping bag. I felt considerably better the next morning. We heard of Greece's craven refusal to come to Serbia's aid.

Sunday, 24 October 1915 – Hood Battalion, firing line from Sap 6 to half way between 'Union Street' and Sap 7

It was a cold dull day. Egerton and I divide the night in two for watches in the firing line. This doesn't entail one's being awake all that time but obliges one to make three or four rounds to see that officers and men are alert. A corpse – or what probably was a corpse – was burning brightly in the early hours of the morning.

Reports of burning corpses, apparently as a result of spontaneous combustion, abounded on the peninsula. The gases released during the process of decomposition bloated the blackened bodies of the dead lying out in no man's land and particularly their abdomens. It has been suggested that the corpses were set alight when their bodies and ammunition pouches were struck by bullets or shell fragments so exploding the cartridges and igniting the gases released.

Kelly's fellow officer Ivan Heald was convinced he witnessed such a phenomenon, telling his mother in a letter home in September 1915 that the dead bodies 'set alight in some mysterious way and at night you can see them blazing in front of the parapet and all their ammunition exploding like squibs and sending up sparks'.

As gruesome a spectacle as this immolation must have been, the one great advantage was that the corpses no longer gave off the overpowering stench which caused almost everyone in their vicinity to be violently sick as Kelly had recorded in mid-July 1915.

Friday, 29 October 1915 – Hood Battalion base camp near DHQ, Cape Helles

I went on to Sedd el Bahr, looked up Patrick Shaw-Stewart, who was not at home and then bathed. On walking back, I was struck with the excellent preparations the French have made for the winter. They have tackled the problem in a far more practical spirit than we have.

A French general was showing three ladies about Sedd el Bahr and very unfamiliar their figures seemed. Considerable interest in their presence was manifested by the various officers and privates whom they passed.

Saturday, 30 October 1915 – Hood Battalion, base camp near DHQ, Cape Helles

I spent the morning in walking up to 'Trotman Road', our fire trench of 4 June, with Leonard Cockey, who was the only Hood officer who returned alive from the Turkish trench [that day], inspecting the place he had got out and the part of the Turkish trench he was in. The firing line is at present some 500 yards in advance of the then Turkish trench so we could inspect the ground without much difficulty. What struck me was the absurd distance – some 400 yards – our men had to cover before they could assault the enemy's trench.

Monday, 1 November 1915 – Hood Battalion, RND winter camp, just north of X Beach, about one mile north-east of Tekke Burnu [Cape Tekke]

C and D Companies moved into our new camp in the morning and by the end of the day practically the whole battalion was established in its winter quarters. Things, however, are far from having settled down. We were digging officers' messes, kitchens and the quartermaster's store all day long and we shall need a full week after returning from the trenches next week to get things shipshape. We have got a very nice site on top of the cliff with a view over the sea to Imbros and it seems to be ideal, if somewhat draughty.

Tuesday, 2 November 1915 – Hood Battalion, RND winter camp, just north of X Beach, about one mile north-east of Tekke Burnu

A busy day in the new camp, most of which I spent in superintending the erection of the dugout for A and C Companies' mess. We have sufficient sandbags for the walls but at present our roof consists of an inadequate tarpaulin and a tent, through the joins of which the first rain will probably find its way. We are promised corrugated iron for roofs – when it arrives.

I lunched with Patrick Shaw-Stewart in a French headquarters mess in the fortress at Sedd el Bahr. I arrived late and found myself entirely among French officers and away from Patrick Shaw-Stewart and Arthur Asquith, who also was lunching with him. It was the first occasion on which I have been cast on my own resources without a chance of reverting to English and I was not altogether dissatisfied with the way I got on.

Wednesday, 3 November 1915 – Worcester Flat support to firing line

I spent the morning preparing for the trenches, for which we set out about 2.00pm. Two platoons of B Company occupy Worcester Barricade and two platoons Worcester Flat from Sap 5 to Sap 6. Attached we have 34 men and two officers of the 2nd/4th London (Regiment) for 48 hours for instruction in the trenches. The extra officers were useful for watches as I was obliged to maintain one officer in the barricade and one in Worcester Flat the whole night through.

Worcester Barricade is somewhat of a white elephant at present, as there are places for only about two men to fire, the remainder listening and bombing if necessary. The Turkish trench is about 15 yards away there. General Paris's idea is to sap a T-head [trench extending into no man's land in the shape of a capital T] and make room for six bombing stations. I made about three tours of my lines during the course of the night.

Friday, 5 November 1915 – Worcester Flat support to firing line

I spent most of the day trying to work out the number of men available in B Company for fatigues on the basis of an eight-hour day, after men had been told off for sentry duty at the rate of one man in four by night and one in eight by day – and leaving sufficient men detailed for fetching water and food. I found my brain worked somewhat heavily at the unwanted mathematical problem.

Early in the morning there was a strafe of the trenches opposite our lines with batteries, trench mortars and a 'Dumezil'. Worcester Barricade, in which I have two platoons, was practically cleared of men except for a few lookouts and a bombing party in case of emergency and Morrison and I set up near the end of the barricade with our revolvers. The Turks didn't reply, but some of our own shells and bombs fell pretty close to the barricade, one from a 3.7 [-inch] mortar knocking in the top of it. This happened while I ran back in Worcester Flat giving the word to carry on after stand-to-arms. One Dumezil fell just outside the barricade but as one could see them in the air one had ample time to take cover in case they came too near the trench.

The platoon of Territorials I have attached was relieved by another platoon.

Dumezil was a generic name for a 240mm heavy trench mortar of the type originally designed by the French company Dumezil Battignoles in 1915. Kelly mentions 'trench mortars' in the same sentence as the Dumezil to draw a distinction between trench mortars of smaller calibre and the large calibre, heavy mortar capable of causing substantial damage to trenches and dugouts.

Saturday, 6 November 1915 – Worcester Flat support to firing line
Three additional catapults were sent up to Worcester Barricade, bringing the total up to five. The general is bent upon keeping the Turks busy but, as there are only positions for two catapults, the three had to be laid aside. During my visits to the barricade at night I was struck by the loud creaking that accompanies their winding up, giving ample time for all Turks within range to get well under cover. It is as if the catapult were protesting against the treatment it is undergoing, like a camel being loaded.

Arthur Asquith has a fascinating project of our both getting off to Athens next Thursday for the inside of a week. Patrick Shaw-Stewart was up in the trenches and said he thought he could arrange boats if we can get leave.

Monday, 8 November 1915 – Worcester Flat support to firing line
I had words with Heald after the morning stand-to-arms, about his slovenliness in dress. He is of a bohemian temperament – a great source of interest as a companion and in the mess and does his work as an officer fairly well and keenly – but there is some substratum of labour rant in him which chafes at small pomps of discipline and makes him casual in lots of ways. When this side of him appears he becomes like a pouting and sulky child.

Edward Nelson, who recently left us to [command] Nelson Battalion, paid me a visit in my headquarters in the morning while Egerton was with me. He passed on what he said was a well-founded rumour that a new army was coming out to relieve us all here at the new year.

The new B Company officer talks far too much.

Thursday, 11 November 1915 – Hood Battalion, RND winter camp, just north of X Beach near Tekke Burnu
It was a windy day. Arthur Asquith went off with Patrick Shaw-Stewart to Athens, where they will spend 24 hours. Asquith had kindly put in for me too, but GHQ wouldn't allow the 'friend'. As a consolation, Shaw-Stewart sent me Edward Marsh's manuscript of his memoir on Rupert Brooke. I began it in the afternoon with great eagerness.

Friday, 12 November 1915 – Hood Battalion, RND Winter Camp, just north of X Beach, near Tekke Burnu
I spent a large part of the day reading Marsh's memoir of Rupert Brooke and finished it at 11.30pm. It consists mostly of extracts from his letters and there is an almost excessive self-effacement on the part of Marsh. The letters are fascinating and I long to get at a larger selection of them. He [Brooke] seems to have passed through rather a silly and slightly self-conscious phase when he was younger – a side of his character of which I saw no trace during my acquaintance with him and I was interested to read of the marked change which Edward Marsh said came over him some two to three years ago – when he came to the conclusion that goodness in

people was the only thing that mattered. There are one or two delightful things about Denis [Browne], like his power of making friends.

Freyberg dined in our mess and we had out the Chinese lanterns one of us had got in Tenedos or Imbros.

A staunch patron of the arts and supporter of the Georgian School of poets Edward Marsh became Rupert Brooke's literary executor, editing and publishing Brooke's Collected Poems with a Memoir – *the manuscript of which Kelly read in less than two days – in 1918.*

Monday, 15 November 1915 – Hood Battalion, RND winter camp, just north of X Beach, near Tekke Burnu

I walked up to a piece of high ground just behind the Eski Line with Egerton to see a trench taken by the 42nd Division between Krithia Nullah and the [Krithia] Vineyard at 3.00pm. Everything happened according to programme and to time. A big explosion demolished the Turkish trench at 3.00pm and an assaulting party of some 150 to 200 men left our trench to occupy it. The Turks didn't seem to realise what was happening as our men were halfway there before a shot was fired and even then the rifle fire was weak for several minutes. None of our men fell as far as I could see. The artillery of both sides was active for half an hour or so afterwards. We looked down on the scene from a distance of nearly a mile through glasses.

I dined in the 2nd Echelon, DHQ, with Major George Peel [APM of the RND], who surprised me by letting out he was a New College man and had been president of the union in Belloc's day. He admires his work in *Land & Water* very much. During dinner there was a thunderstorm with a very strong wind and a torrential downpour. On getting back to camp I found all the men bailing out their dugouts with no prospect of any dry ground to sleep on. The rain had got through my roof and wet all my bed things. I managed, however, to spend a fairly comfortable night in a greatcoat, a blanket I borrowed from Egerton and a Burberry.

Wednesday, 17 November 1915 – Hood Battalion, firing line between Sap 6 and Worcester Flat Barricade

We left camp for the trenches at 1.15pm and, on account of the flooding of some of the trenches, we were obliged to take a new route after 'Fusilier Street', part of which led through a narrow howitzer trench which was difficult to negotiate with our gear on. There was the usual discomfort on arrival in the trenches, numbers of matters to attend to and constant messages interrupting one. To add to the discomfort, it came on to rain in torrents for an hour or more about 7.30pm and in places the trench was several inches deep in water.

Saturday, 20 November 1915 – Hood Battalion, firing line between Sap 6 and Worcester Flat Barricade

I had a visitor in the shape of the padre – [the Reverend Richard] Close – while we were having lunch. He works under the Archbishop of York in peace time and talked with the ardour of a disciple of his great qualities and abilities. A man – one of the advanced bombing class – was shot in Sap 30 just before he came in and I remember feeling the incongruity of the complete absence of feeling with which I went up to see him and then returned to finish my lunch.

Sunday, 21 November 1915 – Hood Battalion, firing line between Sap 6 and Worcester Flat Barricade

Heald showed me a cutting from the *Westminster* which contained the following:

EPIGRAMS AFTER THE GREEK

Lieut Charles Lister (Gallipoli)
At home in youth's hot flush, friend of the folk
I was, and spokesman of their plight
Who now far off, beneath a warrior's cloak,
Lie slain for every people's right.

Lieut Rupert Brooke (Lemnos)
Thou wert to England's living Helicon
A star of dawn as bright as swiftly shed;
And now at sudden eve, with life undone,
Thy loveliness is light unto the dead.

Shane Leslie

I had a good many people coming to see me in my dugout throughout the day and I spent my spare time in preparing the report on pushing forward the barricade in Sap 30, which [Brigadier General] Mercer asked for.

The Turks shelled our trenches to the right of Krithia Nullah about 4.00pm when it was drizzling and beginning to get dark and, after half-an-hour's bombardment or thereabouts, they attacked the 52nd Division and the Drake and Nelson Battalions on our right. The attack seems to have been a complete failure, the attackers being all mown down before they had got over their own barbed wire. I felt somewhat uneasy being [officer commanding the] firing line but there was no movement in front of our line and no shells.

Monday, 22 November 1915 – Hood Battalion, firing line between Worcester Flat Barricade and Sap 30

It was a dour, cold day during which all my time was taken with my duties.

At the evening stand-to-arms, Freyberg and I found the officer in charge of the company attached to us in the firing line and his [fellow] officers perturbed about a hollow sound that was distinctly audible in the neighbourhood of his dugout. Mines and electric drills were mentioned and I was to find a miner and send him along to give his views. Just as I was leaving the anxious company in the dugout I spied an empty rum-jar on the parados [rear of the trench] out of their sight. By moving it about I at once saw it was the cause of the noise and it made a somewhat ludicrous ending to the gathering when I handed it in to them.

Thursday, 25 November 1915 – Hood Battalion, RND winter camp, just north of X Beach, near Tekke Burnu

Another cold, cheerless day, with a northerly wind. As I could not move about easily, owing to my ankle, I took the opportunity of reading three numbers of *Land & Water*, which I procured from one of the [forward observation officers] of the 92nd Battery [RFA]. Belloc seems to me to be doing the country a really valuable service in his insistence on a sane and unbiased study of the numbers of the enemy and our side, and their respective reserves of manpower, as the best criterion of judgment for the future. His healthy optimism is most heartening and reassuring after the panic-mongering of *The Times*. My cold is rather a nuisance.

Sunday, 28 November 1915 – Hood Battalion, RND winter camp, just north of X Beach, near Tekke Burnu

I was obliged to leave my dugout about 3.00am when I found it was sleeting. The north wind blew a gale all day and it was bitterly cold. It was sleeting nearly all day. I worked a little at the slow movement of my G Major violin sonata. I heard several days later that one of these nights there were 20 degrees of frost.

Wednesday, 1 December 1915 – Hood Battalion, firing line between Saps R and U

It was a keen and frosty night: clear, still and very cold. We heard 15 Royal Marines Light Infantry men had been laid out with frostbitten feet the previous week and one of them (this man, I think, a Howe) was so stiff with cold that he had to be lifted down from the parapet in the position in which his limbs had become benumbed and carried away on a stretcher. There are, in consequence, stringent rules as to the daily inspection of men's feet by platoon officers, who have to see the feet rubbed and socks changed. I have 40 men in the firing line and 14 in support.

Thursday, 2 December 1915 – Hood Battalion, firing line between Saps R and U

I had a pretty busy day – the afternoon being spent in making arrangements to dig a sap 40 yards long in front of my part of the firing line out towards the Turkish trench which is here about 120 yards away. I had a party of 36 – 18 from B Company – out from 6.15pm till midnight. It was a very still, starlit night, but except for numerous Very lights and the much brighter French flares, we were completely unmolested.

Sunday, 5 December 1915 – Hood Battalion, firing line between Saps R and U

General Mercer was round our lines in the morning and I accompanied him along the line. We did more digging in the open from 7.00pm till 11.30pm – a party of 20 men digging the next stretch of Sap T, 20 yards in length.

Before sending anyone out I crawled out nearly 40 yards in the direction the sap was to be laid to make sure there were no surprises and before turning in at 8.00pm I crawled out 30 yards or more in the direction the next turn will have to be dug.

Freyberg came in while I was at tea with Morrison after stand-to-arms and began unfolding a project he had formed of crawling out to the Turkish trench with Arthur Asquith. He was like an excited schoolboy and had no object in view as far as I would make out other than the thirst for adventure. I argued him out of it. But about 8.30pm he came in while Asquith was in my dugout and told us he'd been about 30 yards in front of A Company's wire but found it too light to go further.

Monday, 6 December 1915 – Hood Battalion, firing line between Saps R and U

Our company cooks are in 'S' communication trench and when I passed them in the dark during the morning stand-to-arms their fires, the cluster of black dixies on them and their lit-up faces made an effect quite like a Dutch picture. Egerton passed on a piece of official news he had had from one of the padres – to the effect that 250,000 Russians were marching through Roumania and that the latter was coming in on the Allies' side. I felt half credulous at first, but as the night wore on and there was no confirmation of it I began to doubt its authenticity.

Gallipoli was now competing for men and resources with another 'sideshow' front which had opened up in Salonika, in addition to the ever voracious demands of the Western Front., the key theatre for many senior soldiers and politicians. This was where the bulk of the German Field Army had to be fought to a standstill.

For the British, the pressures exerted by their failure to make any real impact on the German defences at Loos in September and October 1915 had simply reinforced the fact that other campaigns were draining vital troops and guns from the only front that really mattered. All three battlefields at Gallipoli – Helles, Anzac and Suvla – were now effectively locked down with no victory in sight and with 'General Winter' now adding to the misery of the men holding the trenches, assailing them with biting northerly winds, sleet and frost, senior military figures in London had already begun to think the unthinkable. General Sir Ian Hamilton had been replaced as Commander-in-Chief by General Sir Charles Monro, a confirmed 'Westerner', on 14 October and the subject of a planned evacuation in two stages; Suvla and Anzac first followed by Helles, had already been discussed. In preparation for this some units were to be moved from the junction with the French on the eastern side of the peninsula and, when the French duly departed, the RND would slide into the gap. Kelly's Hood would find itself holding a different sector with responsibility for the front line overlooking the depths of a deep ravine – the Kereves Dere – which ran into the Dardanelles.

Tuesday, 7 December 1915 – Hood Battalion, firing line between Saps R and U

Great excitement was caused among company commanders in the middle of the day by a hasty summons to battalion headquarters, where

Freyberg showed us a brigade order to the effect that the usual relief would not take place the following day, but that we would be relieved on Thursday by the 87th Brigade, who are next to the French on the right. Freyberg was convinced the news signalled an evacuation of the peninsula – a conviction largely inspired by the hope that the affair would entail critical fighting, in which Hood would conduct a glorious rearguard action!

I thought it might mean the relief of the RND by fresh troops but, if subsequent information turns out to be correct, it appears the French have had so many men affected by the recent cold snap that they want us to take over some of their line. The 87th Brigade is not numerous enough to do this, hence their change with the RND. The order as to relief was accompanied by instructions to stop all work on the forward saps and to make the front line as secure as possible, so that there was plenty of food for speculation. Also, Sketchley, [the general staff officer 2] knew nothing about the change as to relief when he was in my company's lines at midday – hence it must have been altered very suddenly.

Our trench was bombarded a little – a traverse next to a machine gun being blown into the trench. I began the day by 'telling off' an officer – a lumpy man with a thick skin – for sitting down during stand-to-arms. 'Telling off' of officers is not easy in these conditions as one can't get them sufficiently far away from their men to be able to raise one's voice. This particular scene took place down S communication trench.

Thursday, 9 December 1915 – Hood Battalion, firing line between Saps R and U

There had been much talk of a couple of Turks having been seen and shot in the open the night before and as some of my men vouched they saw a man moving not far from the left and of Sap Q, 60 or 70 yards in front of the firing line – I thought he might be severely wounded and that it would be charitable to get him in. The report of his being seen came at the beginning of the evening stand-to-arms. I located what they pointed out while it was still light and immediately stand-to-arms was over I crawled out (about 20 yards from the end of the sap) and explored several bodies, only to find they must have been there since August or earlier.

Monday, 13 December 1915 – Hood Battalion, rest camp, X Beach, north-east of Tekke Burnu

It was another mild day. The tie for the final of the RND cup between Hood and Anson was played off at 2.00pm and resulted in a 5–0 win for Anson. I did a little work at the slow movement of my violin sonata in G Major after tea. Freyberg is experiencing a great wave of energy in his determination to bring the battalion to a greater state of efficiency and some toes have already been trodden on.

Thursday, 16 December 1915 – Hood Battalion, rest camp, X Beach, north-east of Tekke Burnu

I began the morning with a bathe just below the camp. I wrote several letters and before dinner I did a little work at my G Major violin sonata (2nd movement). I very nearly came to an end at 10.00am; I was talking with Heald when a shell pitched in a dugout occupied by officers' servants about 35 yards away. We went along to lend assistance to a few men who were wounded and, as we stood there, a second shell pitched and exploded a couple of yards away from me, covering my face with earth which stung a good deal. I only received a scratch on my neck.

Saturday, 18 December 1915 – Hood Battalion, new camp in French area, high ground half-a-mile north-east of Sedd el Bahr

We spent the day moving camp. Luckily, it is a misty day, though warm and sunny, and we could move in the open without danger of drawing shell fire. Our new camp has just been vacated by the French and some of its lines are covered with *tôle ondulée* [corrugated iron]. Others, however, are uncovered and my company has been unlucky in getting these. The French do not make use of sandbags but make walls out of stones and clay.

Our officers' quarters are splendid, but they have unfortunately excited the cupidity of officers of less fortunate battalions and in consequence we have had to 'lend' a third of them to Marines. I've a very safe little underground room to myself. I walked into Sedd el Bahr about dusk and saw Patrick Shaw-Stewart, who gave me some tea and rat-eaten currant loaf, the un-nibbled portions of which were very good.

Sunday, 19 December 1915 – Hood Battalion, new camp in French area, high ground half-a-mile north-east of Sedd el Bahr

I heard that they had carried out a successful evacuation of Suvla last night and that Anzac was to be evacuated tonight. There is much speculation as to whether we shall evacuate this end of the peninsula. My feeling is that we ought to stay. Oddly enough, I dreamt last night that a French officer told me the whole of the forces were leaving here – not, however, for good but to give everyone a fortnight's holiday. In vain I protested it would be unwise to throw away nine months' work if we were going to return and should have to make the landing over again. He assured me all arrangements had been made for returning and anticipated no difficulty! I worked at the slow movement of my G Major violin sonata after tea.

The evacuations of Anzac and Suvla were a triumph of meticulous military organisation and perfect planning – the only success of a failed campaign. A little over 83,000 men, 4,695 animals and 186 guns were evacuated from under the very noses of the Turks and not a single man, beast or gun was lost to enemy action. In a few days the Turks would realise that there was no-one left to fight at Anzac and Suvla but Kelly would still be engaged on the Helles battlefield and the decision to evacuate the base of the peninsula would not be confirmed until 27 December 1915. Now forewarned, the Turks would soon be wondering if anything else was afoot and with the extra manpower released from holding the line at Anzac and Suvla, they might develop plans of their own. Kelly and the men holding the Helles front now stood alone.

**Monday, 20 December 1915 – Hood Battalion, new camp in
French area, high ground half-a-mile north-east of Sedd el Bahr**

We are all observing one of our officers who is making an unnecessary
display of alleged rheumatism or some similar complaint in the leg. The
doctor says he has been importuning him to send him to hospital. We
have had several similar cases and the temper of the battalion is against
letting another one slip through its fingers.

**Tuesday, 21 December 1915 – Hood Battalion, new camp in
French Area, high ground half-a-mile north-east of Sedd el Bahr**

A south wind had sprung up during the night and it was blowing pretty
hard all the morning. Rain came about midday and a very heavy shower
washed out all uncovered lines. B Company's lines were very wet and
I got leave to shift them to unoccupied covered lines belonging to
the Londons: [London Regiment], who do not come down from the
trenches till tomorrow. I spent nearly my whole day writing down the
last movement of my G Major violin sonata.

**Wednesday, 22 December 1915 – Hood Battalion,
support trenches, right sector, facing Kereves Dere**

I spent the whole day packing and preparing for the trenches – a more
formidable job than in our last camp, as all gear has to be stored so as
to leave the dugouts clear for Nelson officers. C and D Companies went
up to the trenches early on Tuesday morning and A and B followed at
5.30pm today.

We reached the 'Ligne de Repli' [trench] about 9.30pm, after such
an uncomfortable tramp through flooded trenches that it was quite
amusing. In some places, one found it difficult to extract one's feet from
thick, clay mud; in others one waded along canals a foot to 18 inches
deep and, every now and then, one forced one's feet through a foot deep
of what looked like porridge. It made quite a pleasant sloppy noise!

One platoon, in whose lines I spent the night, is in close support to
the firing line, another is in support 200 yards or so in rear and the other

two platoons are with their officer [Sub Lieutenant Thomas] Barrow Green in the Ligne de Repli about 20 minutes' walk back from the first support line. I was lucky in getting an excellent hot stew of bully beef, potatoes and lentils in battalion headquarters with Freyberg.

The men have been served out with thigh gumboots, about 20 pairs to a company and, in addition, we had the loan of those belonging to the Nelson Battalion. I was very glad to have procured a pair. I got to bed about 1.30pm and made a round of the firing and support lines at 3.30pm.

Freyberg told me the officer who gave everyone the impression of exaggerating his ills to avoid coming up to the trenches had been put under arrest for turning in on his watch. I hope an example may be made of him.

Friday, 24 December, 1915 – Hood Battalion, support trenches, right sector, facing Kereves Dere

We had a peaceful morning but about 12 o'clock several shells began to pitch near my dugout. Just as Heald and I were finishing lunch a severe bombardment of our line began and lasted for about 45 minutes. We sat in comparative safety except for the chance of a direct hit, but there must have been some 24 shells or more which sent the ground clattering over our tin roof. We were under the impression they must be searching for some position just in rear of us and we did not realise the shells were falling as thickly along the rest of our support line.

I ventured out, however, after about 25 minutes of it and found my support line spattered all over with earth and the parapet blown in in five places. Luckily it is thinly held and only one of my men was wounded, A C Company PO – [Charles] Winter – was killed and another man wounded. Hawke [Battalion] lost about 14 killed and wounded, so I heard. There were no big shells as far as I could judge by the bursts – most of them being 12- or 18-pounders.

This bombardment interrupted rather an amusing little conversation Heald and I had at lunch about things which are generally voted trivial or unimportant, but which really are a considerable source of pleasure – the kinds of things which Rupert Brooke indicates in his poem 'I am so great a lover' [The Great Lover] – the 'male kiss' of a blanket, the touch of fur, etc. I instanced the stroking of a dog one likes and the smell, like newly mown hay, of an Aberdeen terrier's ruffle. This encouraged Heald to own up to something he had hitherto felt half-ashamed to confess – a liking for the atmosphere a cat produces when she is curled up asleep. He also confessed to a secret indulgence in stroking his eyelids with the backs of her paws!

Saturday, 25 December (Christmas Day)1915 – Hood Battalion, support trenches, right sector, facing Kereves Dere
We all expected an attack with a preliminary bombardment – on what grounds I do not know. But we were prepared throughout the day and stood-to-arms from 5.00pm till moonrise at 9.00pm without firing a shot, in the hopes of inducing the Turks to attack us. We were unsuccessful in this and wrong in our previous expectations so that we enjoyed a lovely still, sunny day in peace.

My Christmas expressions of goodwill to the men at morning stand-to-arms must have seemed so unwonted that many of the men were some moments in realising I was not accusing them of some breach of discipline or absence of gear. Our cook supplied us with an excellent Christmas lunch which I ate with Heald and [Sub Lieutenant Herbert] Donaldson and a dozen of port, which arrived very conveniently from an unknown donor, enlivened our meal and gave me the opportunity to send Christmas gifts to the other company and headquarters, messes. I suspect [brother-in-law] Joe [Kelly] must have sent it as it came from Malta.

Possibly under its influence, Heald and I hurried off to Freyberg in the afternoon to make him carry out a suggestion he had made of sniping an unexploded 6-inch shell that was lying out in the open a little way from his headquarters. We each had a few shots at it in an upright position but as they did not penetrate the casing I arranged the shell with its fuse pointing towards us. At about the fourth shot the thing went off with a tremendous burst just as I was preparing to have a shot myself and I discovered a splinter had gone through my cap. We felt exactly like schoolboys. It was 15 yards away but we had a good buttress of sandbags from behind which to fire.

General Paris and Sketchley had just left [Freyberg's] headquarters when we went out bent on mischief. They assured us there was no chance of our trying to evacuate this end of the peninsula!

Sunday, 26 December, 1915 – Hood Battalion, support trenches, right sector, facing Kereves Dere

An uneventful day except for a certain amount of shelling. A good many were passing over my dugout before lunch and I went out to see how my men were faring. All the fire however, seemed to be concentrated on a point behind my dugout and when I came back I found one shell had pitched quite close and sent a lot of earth into the entrance of my quarters.

An orderly came to tell Heald and me that Freyberg wanted to see us and we immediately suspected he had found another shell to snipe. It was a 6-inch and Heald and I had to carry it some 50 yards along the trench to the place we fired at the one the day before. We placed it out in the open with its fuse towards us, a rise in the ground making a background to stop misses and then started shooting at it in turns – each putting 10/- into the pool for whoever first got it. It was at a distance of about 25 yards and we had each fired about six shots before I got it. It made about double the noise our yesterday's shell had made and twice as big a hole. Arthur Asquith adopted a croaking attitude as to the silliness of it.

Later in the afternoon Freyberg announced he had found another dud – a Dumezil – which I expect will be the end of us.

Orders came up for complete silence between 8.00pm and 10.00pm - no sniping. It looks as though something might be toward, especially as we were told we should probably be taking over more of the French line.

Tuesday, 28 December 1915 – Hood Battalion support trenches, right sector, facing Kereves Dere

It was a nice sunny day. Our lines were shelled pretty badly again and our Sergeant Major, CPO [Robert] Walker, recently my CPO in B Company, was literally blown to pieces in a communication trench. He was a very good man and I felt sorry at his loss. He was conducting a party of POs and a CPO from Nelson Battalion round our trenches and of those the CPO and POs were also knocked out.

Later in the day three more D Company men were wounded by a shell in a dugout. Yesterday they lost ten to one shell. I had just passed Walker and his party of Nelson POs – I was returning from a tour of the French lines to our right with Egerton – and wondered, on hearing a terrific burst 40 yards back, whether they had been hit by it.

The French lines run along the south side of Kereves Dere – in one place crossing it to a listening post – down to the sea. On the left there is a Turkish trench perched on our side of Kereves Dere right on top with a very steep slope behind it and it seems as though we could quite easily push it over the cliff.

Further to the right the French enjoy complete immunity, the Turks never firing at them. It is lovely scenery – a valley with steep sides – ending at the top in precipitous rocks and on one's right a delightful little sandy bay with olive trees. It was more like a ramble along mountain paths than a visit to trenches we may occupy, one was constantly climbing down to picturesque listening posts and one got quite used to being completely exposed to view from the other side of the valley. There was only one place – a bridge across the tiny stream in the bottom of the valley – where we were told it was advisable to pass quickly on account of a machine gun being trained on it. Both Egerton and I thought that an enterprising Turkish sniper might have shot dozens of Frenchmen. It is true the few Turkish trenches one sees are overlooked and probably unoccupied, but there is a whole countryside in which snipers might be concealed.

We returned along the Ligne de Repli. We met no French officers in their lines but I passed a good many remarks to sergeants and men.

I got ideas for third and fourth movements to my B Minor violin sonata, No. 2.

According to Kelly, CPO Robert Walker had taken the full force of the shell that struck him and so there was no body left to bury. He had enlisted in the RNVR in January 1908 and had joined the Hood in late August 1914. Promoted to CPO on 13 September 1915, he had only received his promotion to battalion sergeant major 11 days before his death. Kelly had clearly recognised and valued his qualities as a senior non-commissioned officer (NCO) and others had too, for he had received a certificate commending his 'zeal and devotion to duty' from General Paris on 20 April, just prior to the Gallipoli landings.

Walker had already been wounded during the campaign, receiving a bullet wound to the scalp on 6 June 1915 which had kept him off the peninsula until the end of July. He was posthumously Mentioned in Despatches 'for distinguished and gallant service' in July 1916. Today he is remembered on the Helles Memorial to the Missing along with CPO Thomas McLaughlin of the Nelson Battalion, one of the men Walker was showing around the trenches and who died with him that day.

Wednesday, 29 December 1915 – Hood Battalion, rest camp, half-a-mile north of Sedd el Bahr

I read a certain amount of Tourgenoff's *Fumée* in the morning and at night waiting for the Nelson [Battalion] to relieve us. The whole of the afternoon I spent talking to Freyberg who came to see me in my dugout. The Nelson Battalion were very late in relieving us and I did not get away with my men till 11.30pm. The mud in the 'Boyau Nord No. 2' [trench] down which we came was like glue and very thick glue too. We didn't reach camp till 2.00am. We left the trenches at 'Pointe d'Eau' and came the rest of the way over the open.

In the morning we were officially told that the VIII Army Corps was to be relieved by the IX Army Corps and we were ordered to inform all ranks. Freyberg has been convinced for some weeks that we would evacuate this end of the peninsula and there was something suspicious about this bald announcement that made one feel he was probably right. The men, so my observer said, would not believe they were going at last.

With the decision taken to evacuate Helles on 27 December there was no time to lose. With two fronts now abandoned the Turks were on the alert. But the front line at Helles – where no man's land was very narrow in several places – was some four miles from the beaches at the tip of the peninsula where any evacuation would take place. The withdrawal would have to be conducted in stages and if the Turks got wind of such a plan and attacked at that time a disaster would ensue.

An elaborate deception plan would have to be put in place to fool the Turks into believing the British were staying put at Helles: ruses would have to be employed and demonstrations made to make it appear as though trenches were fully manned, obstacles would have to be erected, trenches barricaded with barbed wire and trip mines laid. Kelly was keenly aware that something was afoot.

Friday, 31 December 1915 – Hood Battalion, rest camp, north of Sedd el Bahr

Every sign seems to point to an evacuation – suspicious notices coming round as to all officers' gear having to be ready at a moment's notice and parties being sent to the trenches to take stock of the main communications and to block all trenches leading off them.

I spent the morning and afternoon working at the last movement of my G Major violin sonata and had the satisfaction of finishing it at tea time. It has been rather a race against time as I was anxious to get it packed up and sent off with my gear – which might, for all I know, be called for at any moment. The gear left in the evening and I had put my manuscripts in the top of my tin box, but Freyberg very considerately suggested I should put them in the orderly room strong box, which is going off in charge of two men. So there they went, the violin sonata and a red book containing the E Minor piece I wrote at the Crystal Palace, two organ preludes, a setting of C Smart's 'He Sang of God, the

Mighty Source of All Things' and a revision of my early song, 'Rough Wind, that Moanest Loud'. I am not displeased with the violin sonata, but its ideas are neither as distinguished nor as original as I should like.

Perhaps distinction and originality are more likely qualities in forms in which one is most accustomed to write. I am still serving my apprenticeship in sonata form but in lyric form I feel I have every now and then said something good and original, for example my monographs in E Flat Major, B Minor, C Minor and my studies in F Major and D Minor. I had no time to put in phrasing, nor expression marks and the indications of tempo are of the scantiest.

As the officers' gear was being piled on limbers there were the first rustlings of a north wind, which seemed by the thick clouds it was bringing, to prelude the breakup of the still, warm weather we have been enjoying. I am filled with foreboding as to our safety if we really are carrying out an evacuation. A really bad spell of weather might mean a disaster. As I write the wind is increasing.

Saturday, 1 January 1916 – Hood Battalion, firing line [points] A12 to O16, about 1,000 yards from the mouth of Kereves Dere

There is an air of mystery about everything and I don't know what the men think. The officers of course have all made up their minds we shall one night walk out of the firing line on to V Beach.

I shot a vulture which must have been hit in the wing by a bullet. It came down in our camp and as it couldn't fly I put an end to it with my revolver.

Sunday, 2 January 1916 – Hood Battalion, firing line, A12 to O16

A busy day attending to a number of orders – nothing definitive – as to the impending evacuation. I have the impression that a great deal of thought has been given to the problem. I filled in the entrance to a number of trenches leading out of my line, which might mislead men when the hour arrives. Egerton is our adjutant and I felt confident the arrangements as far as our battalion is concerned will be as good as possible.

Our line is a dangerous one. Last night two B Company men were killed by rifle bullets and half an hour ago (1.45pm) another man has been hit and Heald says he does not think he will live. Rifle fire is to die down after midnight to a complete cessation at 1.00am. Everyone is obviously somewhat nervous as to the impending evacuation. After Suvla and Anzac the Turks must be on the look out. This morning an enemy aeroplane flew very low over our firing line regardless of rifle fire.

Able Seamen Harry Mitchell and David Huish were the victims Kelly referred to, shot during the night of 2/3 January 1916. Both were buried by the Reverend Richard Close in trench B9 just behind the Hood front line. After the war their remains were moved to Redoubt Cemetery.

Monday, 3 January 1916 – Hood Battalion, firing line, A12 to O16 facing Kereves Dere

We spent the day up till evening stand-to-arms under the impression that the night might prove to be the last but one of the evacuation – Y night – and making our arrangements according to orders. There was a company commanders' meeting at 10.30am at which Egerton had time to read out the newly arrived orders from divisional headquarters as to numbers in the firing line, supports, pickets, etc with his own allocation of our men accordingly.

At stand-to-arms we heard the DHQ instructions were a wash out, that the wind had interfered with the embarkation and that everything would probably be delayed some days. It was a clear night and the wind dropped completely – which I hope may make things easier. There were no instructions as to a period of silence. I wasted the afternoon on making a fresh list of part of B Company that was to be left in the firing line on the last night.

Tuesday, 4 January 1916 – Hood Battalion, firing line, A12 to O16 facing Kereves Dere

A dull still day. We had a good many shells into our lines in the afternoon – 'whizz bangs', larger shells, and late in the afternoon some howitzer shells that lighted into our lines at a very high angle. Some of them were 'duds' but Egerton and I had an uncomfortable quarter of an hour in my dugout while half-a-dozen or more shells seemed to burst close overhead. The earth clattered on to the tin roof, but luckily no pieces. Two A Company officers who were not many yards in rear of my dugout in the support line, were wounded in the head.

There was a test of control stations – of which I am in charge of No. 4 – at 8.00pm; a party from the Nelson Battalion marched down through them as [they would] on the last night and being progressively reported to DHQ from each. Just after they had left a strong northerly wind sprang up and filled me with uneasiness as to the embarkation of men and stores which I understand is proceeding every night.

Wednesday, 5 January 1916 – Hood Battalion, firing line, A12 to O16 facing Kereves Dere

The wind, which promised to cause trouble on the beaches, dropped completely throughout the day, and it was a lovely, still night. 11.30pm till 5.00am were the hours of silence and as I made some rounds I found the stillness tense. Some sentries declared they heard the Turks mending their parapet and patting the sandbags. They must have been very quiet about it for their trench is only about 60 yards away. There was a thrilling feeling of both armies being on the watch like cats for indications of the other's movements – they to find out whether we were leaving the trenches, we to catch any patrols in the open and shoot them.

There were two further tests of the control stations which exist for informing DHQ of the progress of all parties left in the firing line on their way to the rendezvous on the last night. There were, however, no definite instructions as to what anyone was to do and the thing was somewhat of a fiasco.

It has been cold and I revelled in a charcoal burner that was sent up for us. We sat round it in our dugout and almost worshipped the black metal with the sight of red coke and the occasional fairy sparks of the charcoal.

Thursday, 6 January 1916 – Hood Battalion, firing line, A12 to O16 facing Kereves Dere

Another day spent in making preparations for evacuation. General Paris and Sketchley paid me a visit in the morning to discuss No. 4 control station and picket at O16. We had a rehearsal of the former with parties going through at 6.00pm but DHQ had forgotten to inform the brigade signallers and the telephones were not working! We learnt a few useful things, however. No date yet fixed for Y and Z nights. It was a still, sunny day and we were all wondering why they were delaying.

Friday, 7 January, 1916 – Hood Battalion, firing line, A12 to O16 facing Kereves Dere

I spent some of the morning at battalion headquarters receiving orders and comparing my company roll with that of the adjutant. Fresh orders from DHQ seemed to be coming in every hour and Appendix E had just come cancelling all previous allocations of troops. In it, or in one of the appendices, a staff officer had forgotten the Hood machine guns and thus was out in his numbers by 25 in reckoning the number of men we should have left on the final night of the evacuation. When taxed by Freyberg he hit upon the delightful excuse that he had made a mistake in the dark! As though it were like picking up the wrong pair of boots!

It was Y night and at 7.30pm A Company trooped back to the Ligne de Repli leaving us with only 225 men all told. As I went the rounds and back by empty support trenches it felt like walking on thin ice.

The hours of silence were from 11.30pm till 5.00am in which there was no sniping. My officers and men said they heard the Turks busy with their parapet. One of them was seen in the open near [point] O16 and shot at. In the early part of the afternoon there was a heavy bombardment of our lines for about three-quarters-of-an-hour, during which I lay in the safest position I could find in the big dugout I share with Heald, while any number of 'whizz-bangs' burst in the neighbourhood. Freyberg was with us part of the time. We heard in the evening that Turks had attacked part of the 13th [Western] Division at Fusilier Bluff and were repulsed.

Saturday, 8 January 1916 – Hood Battalion, HMS *Bulldog* TBD [Torpedo Boat Destroyer], voyage from Cape Helles to Mudros

The day passed uneventfully though we were all apprehensive of an afternoon bombardment and attack. Our aeroplanes were up at dawn and seem to have kept the Taubes [literally 'doves' – German manufactured aircraft] off most of the day. If a good watch had been kept, the emptiness of our support and reserve trenches must have been very apparent and it seemed difficult to believe our intentions were not known to the Turks. They shelled our lines a little in the afternoon.

I took up my post at No. 4 Control Station at 7.00pm with my two signallers PO Lucas and LS Croft and a few yards away I placed my picket consisting of PO John Rayment and Able Seamen Thomas Goulden and John Peddie of my original platoon, in a bomb-proof shelter in the firing line with loop holes commanding the firing line to the right and left, the parapet in front and the support line to the right.

I had handed over B Company to Ivan Heald, my second-in-command, in the morning and he made all the arrangements for silently withdrawing the men into the support line at 11.30pm and marching them off past my control station at O 14 down the Boyau Nord No. 2.

As OC No.4 station I was in direct telephonic communication with DHQ and had to pass out (a) Heald and Donaldson and 62 men of B Company, (b) Freyberg and two orderlies and finally announce that (c) I was withdrawing my picket and signallers after detaching the telephone and cutting the wire.

Everything went without incident except that the time Egerton had obtained from DHQ in the afternoon as being official was five minutes in advance of the time I got on ringing up the [staff officer] Sketchley about 8.00pm. The result was that I had to report Heald's party as having passed me at 11.42pm, three minutes too early, and the Napoleonic reply came to stop the party! Useless to try to do so, but Freyberg insisted on my telephoning to say they had been stopped. Sketchley had rung me up at 10.30pm telling me to call him up at 11.45pm when all the parties were clear, but as he was receiving all the messages from the other control stations I couldn't get him. Things went on like this till 11.55pm when Freyberg insisted on my sending a message to the operator at the other end to say I was withdrawing.

Once started we got through the different control stations very quickly and arrived at the RND rendezvous at the foot of 'Caesar's Spur' after about 50 minutes from Point d'Eau.

About half-a-mile behind the firing line, we came over the open and I felt relieved when at last we were clear of the overthrows of the unsuspecting Turkish snipers – who carried on in their usual desultory fashion until all our troops were clear of the peninsula. We were some time – perhaps three quarters of an hour – on V Beach in a long line of column of route which moved slowly up the jetty leading to the sunken ships. A sort of sentinel shell from Asia came once every quarter-of-an-hour but luckily those I heard were duds and did no damage.

We were hustled – 750 of us – onto a destroyer by breezy naval officers and we all felt very much relieved at being clear of shell fire. A south-westerly wind sprung up about midnight and our destroyer was bumping against the sunken ship from which we embarked in rather an alarming manner.

We had quite a roughish passage. The men were packed all over the deck and the officers crammed into the wardroom. There was a brigadier and some 52nd Division officers, but they were mostly [of] Howe Battalion. Colonel C was as usual inimitable. He'd not been on board half an hour before he was asking his adjutant – whom he treats like a valet – to try and find him a bunk. He also made use of me to impress our neighbours with the fact that he had been on the peninsula since the beginning: 'You know, Kelly, you and I are very lucky to get out of that'. I couldn't help feeling that the gods help those who help themselves and probably likewise that they look after those who look after themselves!

Everyone seems to have got clear of the peninsula without mishap except for one man shot in the leg by an overthrow and one other slight casualty. It was a pretty smart piece of work. I heard that when everyone had left and certain pre-arranged explosions took place on the beach, the Turks set to deluging the communication trenches and the beaches with shells! It was a dismal ending, however, to an expedition which set out to take Constantinople.

There was an excellent VIII Army Corps Christmas card of a bulldog with legs planted on warships and mouth tugging at the foot of the Gallipoli Peninsula shaped like a leg, with the words 'Pulling our Weight'. The name of our destroyer and the course she was steering suggested that it was the other end of the bulldog with which the Turk's foot was now in contact. I felt it a mistake not hanging on, though I was ready enough that the task should fall to some other division.

ISLAND DUTY

JANUARY 1916–FEBRUARY 1916

'No small wave of cosy satisfaction'

As the Bulldog *butted its way west across the Aegean and the coastline of Cape Helles receded into the distance, Kelly was left to reflect on leaving the peninsula with mixed feelings. The Gallipoli campaign was over. In spite of an understandable feeling of relief at being safely off the peninsula at last and in spite of the 'triumph' of the exquisitely planned and executed evacuation – arguably the finest calculated 'retreat' in British military and naval history – his emotions were tempered by the knowledge that with their final, irrevocable exit the British had been driven out by a tenacious and determined foe intent on protecting their homeland against foreign invaders.*

Kelly would never return, yet a man of his heightened sensitivities could not but have pondered on the high price in both blood and treasure of the nine-month campaign and to remember those of his comrades in the Hood and the rest of the RND who had paid the ultimate price. Out of some 16,000 men who had fought with the division during the campaign, just over 7,000 had been killed and wounded and of those almost 2,500 would never leave the peninsula.

Those men, men like Kelly's former commanding officer, Lieutenant Colonel Arnold Quilter, his great friend Denis Browne and his trusted CPO Robert Walker, are commemorated today in six cemeteries in the Helles area or, for those like Denis Browne and Robert Walker who have no known grave, on the vast Memorial to the Missing at Cape Helles, which bears the names of more the 20,000 men from Britain, Australia and India.

He could not know what lay ahead for him and his battalion but even as the Bulldog steamed towards Lemnos in order that the RND could patch itself up and begin to count the terrible cost of its eastern adventure, the division was facing an existential crisis. The very survival of this 'mongrel' unit – sailors of the navy fighting on land alongside the soldiers of the army – hung in the balance as the Admiralty and the War Office began to cross swords over the eventual fate of the RND. Would the Admiralty still want to administer a division which had, for many months, been attached to the army; would the army want to take responsibility for an essentially naval unit?

With its fate hanging in the balance the RND began to be broken up over the next few months; the 1st Royal Naval Brigade, including Kelly's Hood, back under the command of Admiral Sir John de Robeck, was split into penny packets for policing and garrison duties on the islands of Lemnos, Imbros and Tenedos while the 2nd Brigade was despatched to the Salonika front. Whatever his final destination or the future of his battalion, Kelly, like every other hardened Gallipoli veteran, hoped and prayed for a lengthy and much-needed spell of home leave.

Sunday, 9 January 1916 – Hood Battalion, south camp, west of Mudros Bay, Lemnos

We reached Mudros Bay about 8.00am and were trans-shipped direct on to the SS *Minneapolis*, where we got breakfast and lunch. We got orders – all the RND officers and men – to disembark after lunch and we were landed from a tug at south pier. From here to our camp it was about a two-and-a-half mile march. Freyberg, Asquith and Egerton had not arrived so for the time being I was CO. The RND camp is pitched near the west shore of Mudros Bay, looking out to sea.

Tuesday, 11 January 1916 – Hood Battalion, south camp, west of Mudros Bay, Lemnos

I fell in the company at 10.30am and made it slope arms [rifle sloped over the left shoulder] – rather an unfamiliar occupation after all these months – and then they were allotted tents. There is a new draft of seven officers and over 200 men.

News of ten days leave in England was rumoured and battalions were asked to submit 15 per cent of their officers. We all felt the allowance to be very mean for officers who have been some six to eight months on the peninsula and there was considerable ill feeling against DHQ when it was said that was all they had asked for. Nothing too was said about leave for the men and several of us felt so strongly about the latter omission that we held an officers' meeting at which every one, except three recently promoted CPOs and one other, declared they would not apply for leave unless something were done for the men. Freyberg accordingly got hold of the other battalion commanders and got up an agitation to petition the general on the subject.

Wednesday, 12 January 1916 – Hood Battalion, south camp, west of Mudros Bay, Lemnos

We were [the] duty company so Heald and I got leave to go off to Kastro after lunch. It was rather further than we thought and we did not arrive there till 4.15pm, having started two and a half hours earlier. We went by the direct mule track over the mountains. It is a delightful town and we enjoyed exploring its streets and the old fortress on the headland in the remaining hour of daylight. On entering an orthodox church we both remembered our vows of candles while under shell fire a week or so ago. We accordingly had a dozen and lighted six and watched them with a queer mixture of irreverence and awe.

We had a nice dinner at a restaurant in a street a few steps off the sea front and while we dined it rained. Heald was for spending the night and returning in the early morning but as we had not asked for leave I insisted on returning. He was put out of humour by it and followed me somewhat unwillingly. It was cloudy but the rain had stopped. The way was difficult to find but I eventually reached camp at 11.30pm after experiencing some uncertainty as to where I was. I picked up two Howe men a couple of miles out of Kastro and one of them followed me home. Heald dawdled and we became separated.

Friday, 14 January 1916 – Hood Battalion, south camp, west of Mudros Bay, Lemnos

My gear arrived from the [Deputy Assistant Director Ordnance Services] undamaged and I was much relieved as the 29th Division officers were said to have lost theirs in the evacuation. I set out with Egerton and Asquith for Kastro about 3.30pm and on the way we had baths at Thermon (or some such name) where there are hot springs. We reached Kastro after a walk of some nine miles at 7.15pm and got rooms in the Restaurant Francais where Heald and I dined a few days ago. The dinner was excellent and after dinner we went round to see the four officers [of a picket stationed in Kastro].

Saturday, 15 January 1916 – Hood Battalion, south camp, west of Mudros Bay, Lemnos

A blizzard had come on during the night and continued all day. We spent the morning reading the *Weekly Times* in our hotel but at 2.30pm we were obliged to sally forth. We got very wet and in crossing one of the swollen streams I stumbled in well above the knees. I was much relieved on reaching camp to find the tent I share with Cockey was dry. The messes were all flooded. We heard the first batch of officers had gone home on leave on board the *Olympic*.

Sunday, 16 January 1916 – Hood Battalion, south camp, west of Mudros Bay, Lemnos

The rain, which had been incessant for nearly 36 hours, stopped at breakfast time but it was a dull day and the ground was very wet. I spent a large part of my time reading recent numbers of the *Weekly Times* and

Land & Water. The war is in the most interesting state just at present and the spring offensive on the part of the Allies is not so far distant.

Our camp looks towards a number of hospital ships at anchor in the mouth of Mudros Bay and at night their green and red lights make a nice if somewhat bizarre sight. At Helles there were no red lights and from the peninsula the delicate curved lines of green looked like something out of fairyland.

Tuesday, 18 January 1916 – Hood Battalion, south camp, west of Mudros Bay, Lemnos

On getting back to camp at sunset we heard there was going to be leave in England for men and we're wondering whether our refusing leave has had anything to do with it.

Thursday, 20 January 1916 – Hood Battalion, HMT *Princess Alberta*, Mudros Bay, Lemnos

We were all up early and the usual fuss and discomfort of preparing to move was accentuated by the transport turning up at 8.00am two hours in advance of the stipulated time. A and B Companies and most of headquarters left camp between midday and 1.00pm and we spent the rest of the afternoon at north pier loading our gear on to lighters. We were all on the *Princess Alberta,* a ship of about 1,300 tons, by 5.30pm with the prospect of a provisionless night before us.

Freyberg and I made several attempts to get a motor boat to convey ourselves, Heald, Cockey and a medical officer called Walker, to and from the [troopship] *Aragon* [to find a meal]. Both the attempts we made on shore, firstly from a captain in the RN in charge of the naval boat slip, and secondly from a lieutenant in charge of the motor boats, were fruitless, but we finally induced a midshipman in charge of a steam pinnace alongside the *Princess Alberta,* to take us off. He did so with reluctance and was eventually 'told off' on the *Aragon* for having done so.

Dinner proved a more difficult task than the obtaining of a boat, and after two rebuffs – first from a supercilious, bespectacled young adjutant, who looked as if he had no intention of seeing any active service, and secondly from the captain RN of the ship to whom he sent me – I thought it advisable to beat a temporary retreat and hold a council of war with Freyberg and the others.

Apparently there were strict orders against any dinner being served to anyone other than the officers living on the ship and their friends and it was apparent from our reception that there had been considerable difficulty in enforcing the rule in the past. By this time dinner had begun and we felt ourselves to be the objects of considerable interest – seated as we were with cocktails, at the unlaid centre table of the saloon.

The rest of the campaign was conducted by Freyberg. The captain I had interviewed skipped the responsibility on to Romilly [Rombulow] Pearse, a Royal Marines Light Infantry colonel, as senior RND officer on the ship, and as he was very good natured, he was quickly won over to our cause and promised to get us the signed chits, without which the second steward would not give us dinner.

The bleary-eyed little adjutant had further difficulties in store and arranged a series of spiteful obstacles, such as presenting a chit for dinner which was not valid without the signature of the senior officer, and then when Romilly Pearse had signed it, insisting it must have the captain's signature. But he reckoned without a proper appreciation of Freyberg, who was quite equal to walking to and fro across the saloon and tackling first one authority and then another and we finally sat down to an excellent dinner with ill-concealed satisfaction over our victory.

The *Aragon*, to those on the peninsula, stood for a collection of useless staff officers, officers suffering from 'shock' and a number of supercilious underlings, like the adjutant, who bore a very intelligible hatred of others who knew their game of sticking to soft jobs. Whether this reputation was deserved or not I haven't an idea but we were sufficiently prejudiced to enjoy our triumph all the more in that our enemies were worthy of the greatest contempt. Freyberg managed to procure a launch for us at 9.30pm on which we embarked after

Heald and Cockey had danced a minuet in the light of the full moon on the deck.

Friday, 21 January 1916 – Hood Battalion, camp No. 2, southern shore of Tenedos

We left Mudros Bay about 7.00am and reached Tenedos about midday. A French motor boat met us and we dropped anchor off a sandy beach on the southern shore. The rest of the day was spent in landing stores and getting them up to the camp 600 yards or so inland, where the French had kindly left their tents standing for us.

Freyberg, Egerton and I were motored round the island in a Ford car belonging to the French. I was delighted with the island. The general impression I got was one of nice varied cultivation, stretches of heather, a few fir woods, isolated fig trees and pleasant little valleys running down to white sandy beaches. We interviewed the French governor, in which I had to act as interpreter and lunched afterwards at a restaurant in Tenedos.

Sunday, 23 January 1916 – Hood Battalion, camp No. 2, southern shore of Tenedos

I walked with Hedderwick to Tenedos, where we lunched with Freyberg. We spent the afternoon in a couple of shops making ourselves objectionable about the high prices they were asking for wines and groceries. As we may be here for some months we thought it as well to tackle the question of prices straight off. We also arranged to buy some red wine (106 litres at 53/-) from the French.

Monday, 24 January 1916 – Hood Battalion, camp No. 2, southern shore of Tenedos

Cockey, Heald and I spent a very happy morning visiting the western picket post. We passed one or two delicious little woods – with crooked little trees not more than 12 to 15 feet in height – and the soil mostly consisted of white sand with a profusion of nice shrubs. We went as far as the lighthouse and returned along the shore looking for possible landing places capable of being made use of by a raiding flotilla of caiques from Asia. We returned to a late lunch of bully beef, boiled potatoes, a kind of pumpkin vegetable marrow and some excellent sherry we procured in Lemnos.

Heald showed me a ballad he had written on the evacuation at tea-time and I spent from then till dinner-time putting a tune to it. When I sang it to him he was disappointed with it and quite rightly. We sang a lot of folk songs after dinner.

Ivan Heald had been one of the last to leave the forward British trenches with Kelly on 8 January 1916. His ballad was heavy with remembrance of the men they had left behind:

EVACUATION

So quietly we left our trench
  That night, yet this I know –
As we stole down to Sedd el Bahr
  Our dead mates heard us go.

As I came down the Boyau Nord
  A dead hand touched my sleeve,
A dead hand from the parapet
  Reached out and plucked my sleeve.

'Oh what is toward, O mate o' mine,
  That ye pass with muffled tread,
And there comes no guard for the firing trench,
  The trench won by your dead?'

The dawn was springing on the hills,
  'Twas time to put to sea
But all along the Boyau Nord
  A dead voice followed me:

'Oh little I thought,' a voice did say,
  'That ever a lad of the Tyne
Would leave me lone in the cold trench side,
  And him a mate of mine.'

We sailed away from Sedd el Bahr,
  We are sailing home on leave,
But this I know – through all the years
  Dead hands will pluck my sleeve.

Tuesday, 25 January 1916 – Hood Battalion, camp No. 2, southern shore of Tenedos

I tried to write some letters amid interruptions. In the afternoon I went for a walk with Egerton to North Post and we bathed. It was a lovely sunny afternoon but the water was cold. I began making another tune for Heald's ballad 'Evacuation' on the walk back.

Thursday, 27 January 1916 – SS *Malgache*, voyage to Mytilene

The governor of [Tenedos] and some other French officers came to lunch at our camp and afterwards somewhat of a ceremony was made of exploding a bomb a German aeroplane had dropped a few nights back and which had failed to explode. The governor lit a five-minute fuse himself and we all withdrew to a very safe distance. Cockey and I were given leave to go to Mytilene [modern-day Lesbos] for a few days to try and procure a piano and we accordingly embarked on a small French cargo steamer at South Bay and travelled with some of the mechanics from the French aviation camp.

Friday, 28 January 1916 – annex of Hotel de la Grande Bretagne, Mytilene

We reached Iera Harbour about 7.00am and came to anchor half-a-mile or so beyond the narrow entrance. We were lucky enough to find a one-horsed vehicle into which we put our belongings, and we set out thus for Mytilene.

I was delighted with the olive groves and the lovely stretch of inland water, and not less so when we got on to the ridge from which we saw the town of Mytilene beneath us. It has a fascinating little port round which the houses cluster and there was a considerable air of bustle on the quays. I heard afterwards that the crowd was unusual; being the result of the influx of refugees from Asia.

We enjoyed a fairly good lunch at the hotel and then spent the afternoon shopping with a Greek we found at the consulate office. About 5.30pm, we went out to call on Mrs Heathcote Smith, the wife of the British Consul, at her house on the south side of the town, a mile away from our hotel. At her house we met James Aristarchi, a delightful old Greek, who is a very cultivated man and very pro-English. During our stay he was invaluable to us in helping us get a piano and whatever else we required.

Saturday, 29 January 1916 – annex of Hotel de la Grande Bretagne, Mytilene

We breakfasted with Aristarchi and his wife at their house and he gave us information about what there was to see in the island. We told him we were in search of a piano and he accompanied us into Mytilene and made enquiries about that and our other requirements. There is no music shop in the town but it appeared there were pianos in private houses for which one could bargain.

In the afternoon he procured us a friend of his named Peter Keaia – who had been in England for a course of engineering – to show us the aqueduct at Morea and the site of the theatre about the town, where there was literally not a piece of marble to be seen, and Potamos' chair, a piece of late Greek work (marble) that was not of any artistic interest. I had some tea with Mrs Heathcote Smith and played to her the E Minor symphony among other things. I had not touched a piano since July, but I was not so much at sea as I expected to be.

Sunday, 30 January 1916 – annex of Hotel de la Grande Bretagne, Mytilene

Cockey and I drove out with some of the French aviation officers in a tumble down Ford Car we hired, to Thermae, 10 kilometres north of Mytilene on the shore, where they have their aviation ground. It was a lovely day and we had a beautiful view of Asia with snow-capped mountains in the background.

We went up flying after lunch. A sous-officer took me up and we flew over Mytilene and back. It was my first flight and I was delighted. I had the sensation of going quite slowly, though we actually must have been travelling 50 to 60 miles an hour, and I experienced no sense of insecurity until we descended in a spiral movement which made me giddy.

Some of the officers went up after we had all finished flying and made some very steep spiral turns. I was delighted with them personally. They were very good company, had delightful manners and made the impression of being very efficient in their work. On the morning of our arrival at Mytilene they had paid a visit in their planes *'pour épater les bourgeois'* [shock the middle class] and they skimmed the housetops like so many performing dogs. Cockey and I had to walk half the way back because our old rattletrap of a motor had a puncture.

Monday, 31 January 1916 – annex of Hotel de la Grande Bretagne, Mytilene

We had a Turkish bath in a hamam [hammam] to which Aristarchi took us not far from the Turkish fort. The hot rooms had some well-worn marble fountains which might well have been late Greek work. It was quite clean and very enjoyable; two real Turkish masseurs adding to the interest. We had the bath to ourselves. We lunched with Aristarchi and met a man called Worcester from the consulate.

In the afternoon Aristarchi took me to call at a house where a piano was to be had. It belonged to a family called Papadopoulos of whom we saw the mother and daughter, to the latter of whom it belonged. Aristarchi paid a great many compliments and generally got the atmosphere prepared for broaching the subject, and then when our business had been made clear I had to play a few pieces, one of them being Beethoven's *Sonata Pathetique* for which Mademoiselle specially asked and produced the music. She did not seem to me very anxious to part with her piano, but it was agreed that we should leave them to think it over.

In the course of a day or two they agreed to let us have it for 50 'Napoleons' [French 20 - franc gold coin]. It had seen 12 years' service, but on the other hand they were not anxious to part with it and the only other piano, from the Palace Hotel, was available at a sum of 150 lira and an upright, too!

Wednesday, 2 February 1916 – annex of Hotel de la Grande Bretagne, Mytilene

We returned to lunch on the [British monitor, a small warship] M22 where [our group was] Lieutenant Commander Piercey, Lieutenant Commander Wilkinson from the [Torpedo Boat Destroyer] *Ribble*, Lieutenant Marston (of M22) and the doctor, Wade, who was anxious to exchange for a time into the RND for variety. It was a tiny little wardroom, the ship not being much more than 500 tons. Her draught was only 7 feet and she carried one 9.2-inch gun and a 12-pounder. It was very jolly seeing something of the navy. [HMS] *Canopus* was coaling and all the officers had their coaling clothes on.

We dined with Worcester and 'Charley' Hatkinson, both from the consulate, at the Pantorichon Restaurant. Afterwards the former took us into a Greek cafe where there was a band of violin, cello, cembalo [harpsichord] and a cornet, to which men danced Greek dances. The most persistent dancer was a boatman whose natural enthusiasm was considerably heightened by the drinks his friends kept standing him. It was not long before he was aware of the interest we were taking in the performance and presently we were brought liqueurs, which he had stood us. Before we had left he was sitting down beside Hatkinson and myself, clicking glasses.

The raucous intrusion of the cornet rather spoilt most of the dance, but one dance, in which it was silent, went to my head like wine and we made them repeat it several times. It was the most delightful experience. The people in the cafe – all men – were drawn from the lowest classes and it appeared that the dancing was supplied by those who felt like doing a turn. One of the dancers was a sailor from the Greek navy and though he danced better than the other two dancers, his face showed not a trace of enthusiasm. All the time there was a terrible din from the rest of the customers. This dance had the same kind of intoxicating effect on me that, for example, Bizet has.

Friday, 4 February 4 1916 – Hood Battalion, Paraskevi Camp, Tenedos

After a great deal of trouble as to what boat we should get back in – one of the Greek steamboat companies asking 75 francs for each person with 70 francs for the piano – we hired an open motor boat about 36 feet long called the *Dewv*. It had a broad beam and was said to be a good sea boat. The price, 400 francs, was enormous but we had the pleasure of having the boat to ourselves – Cockey, [Sub Lieutenant Garnet] Orphan, my servant and myself – and the convenience of just taking the piano with us from pier to pier. We were supplied with an excellent lunch with bottles of Demestica wine and one bottle of sherry and as it was a fine day with a slight following wind we thoroughly enjoyed ourselves.

We left at 9.50am and reached Tenedos harbour about 4.30pm. We were met by Freyberg, Heald and the doctor, Molesworth, and the piano reached camp a short while after we did.

We are in Paraskevi camp now, where things promise to be very comfortable. I was in a tent for the night with Cockey and it rained a good deal. I played a certain amount after dinner.

Our trip to Mytilene was a delightful little chapter in the war. I liked the people we met very much – Mr Heathcote Smith and James Aristarchi – and the sight of so many olive trees was a pleasant change after the bareness of most of the islands around here. We were introduced and fell victims to an excellent local dish – yaoult [yoghurt] or some such name, a sort of cream cheese one eats with milk. It was about the only good food we got in the restaurants, where neither the food nor the wine was good.

Saturday, 5 February 1916 – Hood Battalion, Paraskevi Camp, Tenedos

It was a wet day and I postponed visiting my outposts at North, South and West Posts where nearly the whole of B Company is at present.

I played for about an hour or more in the morning in the headquarters bell tent a number of pieces, including my Monographs Nos. 13 and 24 and my E Minor piece. Some of the officers seem to be musical and attentive.

After dinner I played for an hour-and-a-half mostly pieces by Chopin, but also Schumann's *Études Symphoniques*. Freyberg, Cockey, Molesworth, [Sub Lieutenant Gerald] Tamplin, [Sub Lieutenant Laurence] Callingham and Richards, the engineer officer living with us, were among my audience. Freyberg turned down the lamp and there was silence and attention – the first occasion in an officers' mess when I have enjoyed these essentials.

Sunday, 6 February 1916 – Hood Battalion, Paraskevi Camp, Tenedos

Our camp promises to be very comfortable. There are enough wooden huts left by the French to accommodate two companies and the officers and their messes will be housed in some small buildings that are grouped round a marble fountain which supplies us with all our drinking water. There is even a small underground chapel with two pillars which, if one scraped off the whitewash, might turn out to be the remains of an earlier building. The huts are well sheltered in a little valley which leads in a few hundred yards down to a beach where we can bathe when the weather becomes warmer. In addition to our officers' messes we have a room which will do for a wardroom in which we are placing the piano. There are trees dotted about the fountain, and buildings and the sound of the running water and the shade should make it very delightful when the weather becomes hot.

I walked out to South Post in the afternoon and made the senior officer, [Sub Lieutenant Leslie] Holland, take me round two of his sentry groups. I went on to Tenedos to make some purchases and only reached camp about 6.45pm. There was a wedding going on in Tenedos and a very pretty effect was made by a number of the guests joining hands and moving round in a circle – one lilt back to every two or three forward. I played among other things Beethoven's 'Sonata in A Flat Major' Op. 26, Chopin's 'Barcarolle', my monographs Nos. 13–18 and 'Waltz Pageant' after dinner.

Egerton returned from Mudros, where he has been a few days.

Tuesday, 8 February 1916 – Hood Battalion, Paraskevi Camp, Tenedos

I rode out to the West Post in the morning with a fellow officer and found all the rifles in one of the sentry groups in a filthy condition.

We had a great dispute on the way as to the rights and wrongs of the behaviour of the British naval officer in command of the *Baralong* in shooting the crew of the German submarine – if such really turns out to be the truth. He maintained retaliation was the only method of putting an end to their behaviour – by inspiring a wholesome fear of the consequences attaching to their policy of sinking unarmed merchantmen without warning. This seemed to me the identical justification the Germans put forward for their frightfulness.

I slept from 3.30pm till 6.30pm. A Company left Paraskevi Camp for the castle and [Second Lieutenant William] Milton and I joined the headquarters mess until C and D Companies arrive from Mudros.

The summary execution of the crew of a German submarine by a British naval officer turned out to be true. On 19, August 1915, the Q Ship, HMS

Baralong, *raked the German submarine U-27, with gunfire and sank it. The captain of the* Baralong, *Lieutenant Godfrey Herbert RN, ordered that all 12 survivors of the German submarine – some whilst climbing up the lifeboat falls of a nearby merchantman and others after they had been taken aboard – be shot out of hand. All 37 crew were killed. In spite of the British Admiralty's efforts to suppress it, news of the incident inevitably leaked and reached Germany, whose government called the shootings 'cowardly murder'. This first 'Baralong incident' – she was involved in two – was undoubtedly a war crime which was never prosecuted and served to fuel already heightened feelings of animosity and reprisal in the war at sea.*

Wednesday, 9 February 1916 – Hood Battalion, Paraskevi Camp, Tenedos

I spent the afternoon pulling the piano to bits with Sergeant Blake of the engineers, who had been recommended for the job of adjusting the dampers on the strength of his having made the gramophone work!

I played through my violin sonata in G Major from the music (for the first time) after dinner and was tolerably well satisfied with it. The form of the first movement seems to be good. Egerton sat by me and listened to it.

Friday, 11 February 1916 – Hood Battalion, Paraskevi Camp, Tenedos

I spent most of the morning recalling Bach's *Italian Concerto* as I had done the day before with the A Minor organ fugue. I was enjoying myself in a similar manner with Beethoven's *Sonata Pathétique* before dinner when I was summoned to the orderly room and sent off to the wireless station near the French aviation ground about two-and-a-half miles away, to send a code message off.

The annoying part of it was that if I had not been over-energetic in visiting the North as well as the West Post in the afternoon I should have been left in peace, but having brought back news of a submarine having been seen there, I just had an hour's respite while Egerton was wrestling with the task of putting the news into code for transmission to Imbros.

I had a bathe in the afternoon between West and North Posts. There was a southerly gale blowing and we had some heavy rain in the night again. When I got back I was taken up to interview the Serbian who keeps the canteen. The sergeant major and a sentry had both been shot at – the one in the middle of the day, and the other late at night and we had sentries out on watch. The Serbian was said to have told such a ridiculous story about his having seen the shot fired by a man with a face like a dog, that his house was being watched. Egerton and I were sent up to search it for any firearms, but we decided to put a sentry on it and postpone the search for a better light.

Tuesday, 15 February 1916 – Hood Battalion, Paraskevi Camp, Tenedos

I had to go out to the Camp des Zouaves at 8.00am to arrange relieving the French guard over the wireless. I rode out and on my way back along the beach I saw a steamer of some 2,000 tons lying off Paraskevi Camp. My first guess as to her business was that she might be bringing the rest of the battalion (C and D Companies) from Mudros, but she turned out to be the yacht of Admiral de Robeck who was expected to visit the island at this time, whom Freyberg and Egerton had gone into Tenedos to meet.

As his boat grounded about six feet or more from the beach and I was trying to get men to place stepping stones in the water, the admiral airily seized a long boathook and very deftly vaulted on shore without so much as touching the water – a feat I admire all the more when one of the commanders, trying to follow suit, broke the boathook and fell in. After Freyberg had arrived he motored the admiral in to see the French governor and I went to act as interpreter. We were only in there 20 minutes or so and on arriving back at Paraskevi the admiral embarked again. I was delighted with his charm and geniality. He also struck me as being clever and well-informed. The French governor left Tenedos at 10.00pm but there are still a few French left here.

I walked out to the aviation ground with Egerton in the afternoon to show a sentry group, sent out by A Company from the castle, to their posts. I spent a couple of hours tuning the piano before dinner and found it was not an easy task. I played a certain amount after dinner. Heald arrived back from Mytilene just as I was stopping. I played him and Freyberg Chopin's 'Nocturne in F Major' before turning in.

Saturday, 19 February 1916 – Hood Battalion, Paraskevi Camp, Tenedos

I found my first opportunity for using the booklets of folk songs which I had printed a year ago. Heald and I collected some 15 men from B Company, at 3.15pm and we sang 'Green Grow the Rushes, O!', 'The Mermaid', 'The Wraggle Taggle Gypsies, O!', 'The Girl I left Behind Me', 'What to do with a Drunken Sailor' and 'A Roving'. We did several of them twice through, and 'Green Grow the Rushes, O!' three times. I played Chopin's C Minor waltz and Grieg's 'Morgenstimmung' before the company dispersed; but the piano was badly out of tune.

One of the men lingered on after the rest had gone and I played him Chopin's E nocturne, Mendelssohn's 'Spring Song' and Rachmaninoff's C Minor prelude. Later on I played Brahms' 'Variations on an Original Theme', my 'Elegy in Memoriam Rupert Brooke' and the 'Volga Boating Song' to Heald. The piano is giving a great deal of trouble by getting out of tune constantly. I tuned it twice today and it was quickly out of tune again.

Sunday, 20 February 1916 – Hood Battalion, Paraskevi Camp, Tenedos

I rode into Tenedos at 3.00pm and had a Turkish bath in the hamam which the battalion has hired and been heating. Practically all the men have had a good wash – their first for several months, in many cases. I rode out to Paraskevi with Freyberg after dark.

Monday, 21 February 1916 – Hood Battalion, Paraskevi Camp, Tenedos

News came that leave had been granted to the men and we hailed it as a great victory. Thirty seven go from the battalion. It was a wet day and though I was to start on leave the following day I felt depressed – probably owing to my repeated failures with the piano. Freyberg left for Mudros.

Wednesday, 23 February 1916 – Hood Battalion, 27th General Hospital, Mudros, Lemnos

A party of Hawkes and Drakes arrived on board at 10.15am or so and at 11.00am we left for Mudros. It was a very calm sea and a sunny day. I ready *Daisy Miller* by Henry James – the first of his books I have ever read. We reached Mudros at 4.30pm but were not landed till sunset. We found the rest of the battalion had just moved into new huts and things were far from comfortable. My three-dozen of champagne had at last turned up – the wine I thought would cheer us up at Christmas! No arrangements had been made for the Hawke and Drake drafts that came with us and we had to fix them up to our lines.

Saturday, 26 February 1916 – HMT *Olympic*, Mudros

There was a parade at 8.00am at which the Hood flag was hoisted. The piano had arrived from Tenedos the night before and as it was not so atrociously out of tune as it had been there (I am at a loss to know why) I played Chopin's F Major – impromptu; Mendelessohn's 'Scherzo a Capriccio', 'Spring Song' and 'Venetian Gondollied'; Chopin's Op. 10 Nos. 9, 3, 12; Op. 25 No. 1, his étude (posthumous); E nocturne; Beethoven's *Sonata Pathétique* and *Moonlight Sonata*; my studies Nos. 1, 2, 4, 5, 6; Schumann's *Études Symphoniques*; my Monographs Nos. 13–18; Rachmaninoff's Prelude and my 'Elegy on Rupert Brooke for String Orchestra'.

I had orders to see the leave party of 38 men on to the *Olympic* and I marched them off from camp with the band at 2.00pm. We were all aboard and settled by 4.30pm. Unlike the staffs of the other transports of which I've had experience the stewards on board this ship are extremely obliging and every consideration seems to be given to avoid tiresome regulations. I have a large two-berthed cabin on A Deck (the top deck, with the exception of the boat deck) and as I turned in I had the lines from the 'Wraggle Taggle Gypsies' running in my head:

'Last night you slept in a goose-feather bed/With the sheets turned down so bravely, oh!'

I could hear a shower of rain pattering on the deck above, and to know that my roof was secure and that I need have no anxiety as to pools forming and dripping through the joins in waterproof sheets – was the source of no small wave of cosy satisfaction. The champagne, too, is excellent.

HOME

MARCH 1916–MAY 1916

*'I seem to have gone up 21 lbs
in a couple of months'*

*W*e *can only imagine what thoughts were going through Kelly's mind
when, after eight months of trial and tribulation, death and disease
on the Gallipoli Peninsula, and relatively relaxed weeks of duty on the Aegean
islands behind him, he finally crossed the threshold of 29 Queen Anne Street
in London.*

*We will never know whether he found the transition from Gallipoli veteran
to temporary civilian especially traumatic but what is most striking about
Kelly's diary entries when back home in England is the apparent ease with
which he slipped back into the habits of his old life. There are no apparent
signs of a sense of displacement or detachment, despite being at war for the
best part of a year. It may seem surprising that Kelly and the RND ended up
having nine weeks of leave and indeed they themselves must have regarded it
as fortunate, but nevertheless necessary given the hardships they had had to
endure at Gallipoli.*

*Kelly's time was spent mostly in London, at his flat in Queen Anne Street,
but there were also visits back home to Bisham Grange to see his beloved sister
Maisie and her new husband, Joe Kelly.*

His entries for this period of home leave remind us once more of the rarefied social circles in which he moved, dining with the prime minister at Downing Street and meeting Sir Ian Hamilton, the ex-Commander-in-Chief of the MEF under whom he had served at Gallipoli, the composer Sir Hubert Parry and Ivor Novello, writer of the hugely popular patriotic Great War ballad 'Keep the Home Fires Burning'. Jelly d'Arányi features once more in Kelly's life, but characteristically he gives no hint as to any of his feelings towards her or any other aspect of his personal life.

Importantly, leave offered Kelly the opportunity to continue working on his music, particularly on the 'Elegy for Strings in Memoriam Rupert Brooke', but also the violin sonata he worked on in Gallipoli and a piano sonata in F Minor which dated back to 1909. The diary does perhaps betray some of Kelly's insecurities about his compositions, as he sought both advice and approval of the 'Elegy' in particular.

It was clearly a hugely enjoyable period for Frederick Kelly – a much-needed break from 'soldiering' and a reminder of his civilian life but it could not last. One day short of a year since Kelly had first set foot on Gallipoli, the telephone rang while he was at Bisham Grange. It was his CO Bernard Freyberg with the news that the RND was going to war again.

Saturday, 4 March 1916 – Bisham Grange, Marlow

I reached 29 Queen Anne Street at 12.15pm and received a very warm welcome from Leonard Borwick who had placed myrtle outside my door with a note containing the words: 'To dear Cleg, with a deep joy and thankfulness, from Len'. I felt much touched. He had also placed the reproduction of Sargent's drawing of me on my piano and surrounded it with tricolor.

Archibald Borwick [Leonard's brother] was at home on leave – dressed in a kilt. He is an officer in some Scotch regiment [the Queen's Own Cameron Highlanders]. It was not long before Felix Warre had put in an appearance and he stayed to lunch with the Borwicks and myself. Leonard looked pale and a little overworked – possibly the result of his night watches as special constable and his munition work. Felix Warre's arm was in a sling from his wound in France.

My room gave me all the satisfaction I had been hoping and it was a joy to see the great deep Hammershøi [painting] again. Poor Hammershøi is dead, so I heard, and the question immediately presented itself as to the best steps to take towards securing the twin picture to my own. It has been in my room since the beginning of the war when Ethel Nettleship [daughter of the painter Jack Nettleship] asked me to take charge of it.

I caught the 4.05pm train to Maidenhead, where I was met by Maisie and Joe, the first time I had seen them together since their marriage. They struck me as being very pleased with each other. Lady Vansittart-Neale, Mr and Mrs Farrer and Mary Ethel Long-Innes came in to tea. The Grange, as usually happens, after long periods of absence, contained several new bits of furniture and an interesting portrait of a lady which looks like a Sir Joshua [Reynolds]. After dinner I played Maisie my 'Elegy on Rupert Brooke' and she sang a number of folk songs and among them rather an interesting Polish patriotic song or some such name by Chopin. I sang 'Green Grow the Rushes, O!' – which encouraged Joe to give utterance in an enormous sea-dog kind of voice to some songs of the sea. It was a very happy homecoming – though neither Blackie nor Wattle were quite sure they had ever seen me before. The river was up to the edge of the garden.

Vilhelm Hammershøi was a Danish artist. Born 1864, died 13 February 1916.

Monday, 6 March 1916 – 29 Queen Anne Street, London

I got back to a late tea with Leonard Borwick and Golden – to whom I played my 'Elegy on Rupert Brooke'. Leonard seemed to thoroughly feel all that the music should express and he had no criticism to offer except that the addition of a harp might just sweeten the solemnity without detracting from the elegiac character. I had considered its addition to the score when writing it and felt that as it would play such a small part I should not do amiss to make myself independent of it – putting it in, if desirable, later on. He has a very keen sense of humour and a nice sense of the value of words in discussing such matters.

I dined with Felix Warre and his wife – the first time I have seen them since their marriage – in a house they have taken for three months at 8 Neville Street, Onslow Square. Jelly [d'Arányi] was there and I brought my 'Violin Sonata in G Major' and we played it after dinner. She read it extremely well and I felt far from disappointed with it. This was the first time I have tried it with a violin. Felix thought the first movement somewhat classically conventional but was enthusiastic over the second and last movements. Jelly also played my flute serenade – which sounds quite well on the violin. I played my 'Elegy on Rupert Brooke', the Greek dance I heard and took down at Mytilene and – while Felix was looking for a taxi – Ravel's 'Ondine'.

Tuesday, 7 March 1916 – 29 Queen Anne Street, London

It snowed most of the day. I dined at 10 Downing Street with the Prime Minister, Mrs Asquith, Lady Horner, 'Bongie' [Maurice Bonham Carter the prime minister's Chief Secretary] and his wife (the first time I have seen them since their marriage) and Lady Gwendolen somebody, Bernard Freyberg, Ock Asquith and Patrick Shaw-Stewart. The prime minster, whose two sole hatreds – so Ock told me afterwards – are music and dogs, paid a few amused visits to our neighbouring room during dummy hands [card game] and I heard stage whispers to Violet Bonham Carter, such as 'Is this really good?' On this last visit I was in the middle of my 'Elegy' and I had just an impression of a slight rebuff administered by Mrs Bonham Carter, who, as a great friend of Rupert, was keenly interested – at all events the amused whispers ceased and there was complete silence for the remainder of the piece.

Friday, 10 March 1916 – 29 Queen Anne Street, London

I spent the morning reading Joe's records of the *Dublin*, which interested me a good deal. Maisie says he holds the record for the number of torpedoes fired at him – 15 – of which, fortunately, only one struck his ship.

I travelled up to town by the 2.10pm train and did a little shopping before meeting Jelly d'Arányi at 29 Queen Anne Street to rehearse my 'Violin Sonata in G Major'. We went through it pretty carefully and when it came to performing it in the evening at the Bonham Carters (Dorset House) it went extremely well. She really plays wonderfully well. Violet Bonham Carter had asked Adila [Jelly d'Arányi's sister], Jelly, Hugh Godley and Fachiri (Adila's husband) to come and play quartets and I was a later addition to the original programme. There were about a dozen people there besides the players, half of them invited by me – the Felix Warres, Edmond Warre and Logan Pearsall Smith. Among the rest of the audience were Walter and Dorothy James and Reggie Rowe, who has spent nine months in France at the front since I last saw him.

I arrived during the first movement of Beethoven's G Major quartet 18, after which Jelly and I played my violin sonata. We then played the beloved Dvořák quintet and I ended the programme by playing four studies in F Major, B Minor and D Minor. Bongie and Ock sang 'Green Grow the Rushes, O!'

Monday, 13 March 1916 – 29 Queen Anne Street, London

I dined with Mrs and Mrs Fowler – friends of Jelly d'Arányi – at 26 Gilbert Street. [Jelly] was dining there, too and after dinner Williams, the cellist – who returned recently from Ruhleben concentration camp – his wife, Golden, Fachiri and Adila and a few other friends – including Langley, the once famous boy singer at Eton – came in.

Jelly played Brahms' C Major trio with the Williamses then followed my violin sonata and Schubert's B Flat trio – which I played and brought the programme to an end.

The Fowlers seemed to be delightful people. The house contained many good things – not the least beautiful being a small animal like a lemur, which they called a 'bush baby' and which inhabited a book shelf and darted about like a mongoose. Its movements were like [composer] Domenico Scarlatti.

Wednesday, 15 March 1916 – 29 Queen Anne Street, London

Edward Marsh and Percy Lubbock dined with Leonard Borwick and myself and after dinner Edmond Lancelot Warre joined us.

Leonard played Moszkowski's Waltzes Op. 8 *vierhändig* [duet] with me and then he played a number of pieces by Palmgren. I played my 'Elegy on Rupert Brooke' and after Leonard had gone off to make shells, Bach's A Minor organ fugue, *Italian Concerto*, Chopin's 'Barcarolle', Dvořák's *'Auf der alten Burg'*, Debussy's 'La Fille aux Cheveux de Lin', Chopin's E Minor nocturne Op. 48 No. 1, Mendelssohn's E Minor scherzo Op. 16 and 'Spring Song'. I was glad to find Leonard had a considerably heightened opinion of my 'Elegy' – especially as he was very appreciative after a first performance.

In the morning Maisie came and Jelly d'Arányi played my violin sonata to her, Golden and Leonard. The latter, as usual hit the right nail on the head in sizing it up as a good solid bit of work – with just the implied criticism with which I heartily concur – that there is room for more originality in form and idea.

Jelly d'Arányi came into Frederick Kelly's life as a 15-year-old on 19 March 1909 at a musical party at Haslemere and she remained a significant friend and musical associate for the rest of his life. Born in Budapest in May 1893, she was an accomplished violinist who counted Bela Bartok amongst her acquaintances. Despite some reports suggesting that Kelly and d'Arányi were engaged, any romantic feelings she may have held for him do not appear to have been reciprocated. Although frequently mentioned in his diaries, Kelly never reveals any deeper feelings towards her other than brotherly regard. Jelly d'Arányi did not marry and for the rest of her life she is said to have kept a photograph of Kelly on her piano.

The violin sonata which d'Arányi played to Maisie in March 1916, and to which Kelly referred so frequently in his diary, was thought to be lost but came to light in 2010 thanks to the dogged detective work of Australian music scholar Chris Latham. Kelly had written down at least three versions of the sonata, one of which was in the possession of Jelly d'Arányi. Latham, the former director of the Canberra International Music Festival, traced the great-niece of d'Arányi to Florence and discovered that she had kept a copy – written in Kelly's hand – of what has now become known as the 'Gallipoli Sonata'.

Tuesday, 21 March 1916 – 29 Queen Anne Street, London

I spent the day reading Rupert Brooke's *Letters from America* – which I found full of fresh metaphor, ripe judgment and exquisite humour. What a satisfaction it is to find that each new piece of work of his that I come across intensifies my admiration of him – and to think that at first I feared to look at his poetry for fear that in it I should find blemishes that I could not see in him as a man!

Wednesday, 22 March 1916 – 29 Queen Anne Street, London

I spent most of the afternoon wrestling with Henry James' Intro-duction to Rupert Brooke's *Letters from America*. It has some true things to say, but wrapt in what a lumbering great muddle of obscurely expressed images. It is like a man trying to undo a tangle and finding himself obliged to pass through great bunches of string in following out the thread.

Sunday, 26 March 1916 – 29 Queen Anne Street, London

I finished reading *Antony & Cleopatra*. I had my leg swathed in bandages and could not do more than get into a dressing gown. I spent the afternoon writing letters and going through accounts – except for half-an-hour or so when Leonard came in and we played Mozart's two fantasias in F Minor which he ranks with the very biggest things of Beethoven. Under the influence of their poignancy and greatness of conception I felt I agreed with him. It seems as though the influence of the big things of Handel and Bach had brought him into a bigger world – in which he perhaps might have been as great. To feel that he died on the verge of entering into a new inheritance makes of his death an added tragedy. We were both struck by the incredible clarity of the part writing.

Tuesday, 28 March 1916 – 29 Queen Anne Street, London

I had a short dinner at Paganis [Great Portland Street] where I saw Sir Hubert Parry and from there went to a meeting at Queen's Hall organised in furtherance of the Fight for Right movement. I was attracted [to the meeting] by new compositions by Parry [and] Elgar, written for the occasion and sung by a choir with organ accompaniment. These turned out to be the usual worthless stuff of which most *pieces d'occasion* are made.

The poet laureate was in the chair and the other speakers were Miss Evelyn Underhill, W A Appleton (General Secretary of the Federation of Trades Unions), Monsieur de Leval, the Belgian lawyers who tried to save nurse [Edith] Cavell, and J W Williams. The latter somewhat marred a speech, full of enthusiasm, by declaring: 'It was Byron who said, "There is a tide in the affairs of men".' The meeting was not well attended and I wasn't aware of much enthusiasm. I went down to find Robert Bridges afterwards and he walked with me to my rooms. I played him my 'Elegy on Rupert Brooke' which he seemed to like, though he did not comment further than to say it was very solemn. He did not stay more than half-an-hour.

What Kelly dismissed as 'worthless stuff' was the first public performance – by a choir of 300 conducted by Walford Davies – of 'Jerusalem', Sir Hubert Parry's famous setting of Blake's poem 'And Did Those Feet in Ancient Time'. Robert Bridges, the poet laureate had sent Parry the poem and was of the opinion that Parry should write 'music that an audience could take up and join in'.

The Fight for Right movement was the brainchild of Francis Younghusband, an imperialist, British Army officer and explorer whose life later became suffused with mysticism and spirituality. A year after the outbreak of war he published a letter in the Daily Telegraph *in which he claimed that humankind was not just fighting a material war but was engaged in a spiritual conflict – a war he called the 'fight for right'. Younghusband's ideas and aims chimed with the thoughts of several public figures in society, literary and musical circles and within weeks he began to hold meetings. The movement was to wither away over the next 18 months or so as it met with opposition from more jingoistic quarters and Sir Hubert Parry went so far as to withdraw the use of 'Jerusalem' during its gatherings.*

Wednesday, 29 March 1916 – 29 Queen Anne Street, London

Robert Bridges came again at 11.00am and spent an hour-and-a-half in my room. After he had been with me some 20 minutes Arthur Asquith came and after him Leonard Borwick came in to meet Bridges. [Bridges] interested me very much in what he had to say. He began by talking of his anthology, *The Spirit of Man*, which was published a few months back and he let fall incidentally some interesting expressions of opinion on literary subjects. Speaking of Shakespeare's sonnets he said that sex hardly entered into them. Of Shelley and Keats he remarked that few people realised what ordered and logical thought there was in their poems. He incidentally declared Keats to have the greater mind of the two – which I didn't agree with.

He showed us a poem of Fontaine in his anthology *'Mon Petit Fils Qui n'as Encore Rien Vu' [My Little Son Has Seen Nothing Yet]* and said that one could not find its equal (of poetry in the same vein) in the whole of English literature. I ventured to suggest Blake, but he wouldn't admit Blake to have the requisite perfection of diction. He also called another French poem to our attention *'Oisive Jeunesse' ['Idle Youth']*, which I did not grasp quite so readily as the other. I showed him Heald's poem 'Evacuation' and he thought it very good – though he had one or two criticisms to make.

After Leonard and Asquith had gone I asked him his opinion of Hammershøi's 'Interior with the Table and a Flower Pot on it, the Spinet Beloved with the Open Door to the Right of it'. He looked at it for a considerable time but said it meant nothing to him. He criticised all the straight lines in it.

Leonard came back from the Minerva munition works to lunch and we spent the afternoon finishing our household accounts. I sang him 'Green Grow the Rushes, O!' which he didn't know. He liked it and approved of my harmonies to it. I walked to Novello in Wardour Street after tea and looked through some part-songs for men's voices with a view to taking some out to teach the men in the Hood Battalion. The shop closed before I had got a quarter way through a large bound collection of them, but I was allowed to take it away with me and I spent an hour after dinner, finishing it. I played a few of Chopin's Nocturnes before writing my diary.

Friday, 31 March 1916 – 29 Queen Anne Street, London

I went to the exhibition of the Barbizon School at Tooth's again at 10.45am with Leonard with the object of taking another look at the Oudinot picture that attracted my attention yesterday. It disappointed me on a second inspection – a certain flatness and soft sentiment being noticeable. We went from Tooth's to a house in Montagu Square where there was an exhibition of Fordin's drawings. They were all of the war, the intention being to bring home the enormity of German methods of conducting it. The irony was very penetrating and the drawing itself excellent.

I lunched with Mrs Fowler, Adila Fachiri, Jelly d'Arányi and another lady at Claridge's and at 2.45pm we went to Sunderland House (Curzon Street) where Jelly was taking part in a charity concert. She played my flute serenade, in which I accompanied her. Muriel Foster, Gervase Oliver, McInnes and [actress] Irene Vanbrugh were among the performers, but, as is usual at such shows, there was not much enjoyment to be had owing to the whispering and the press of people. I made [French-born composer] Maude Valerie White's acquaintance and found her quite delightful, and Miss Heald, who was there reporting for the *Daily Sketch* came in and saw me.

I went to tea with the Felix Warres to meet Sir Ian and Lady Hamilton and to play them my 'Elegy on Rupert Brooke'. Henry Warre was also there and later on Vereker Hamilton [Scottish military artist and Felix Warre's brother-in-law]. I played Mendelssohn's E Minor scherzo, a major characteristic piece and Debussy's 'La Fille aux Cheveux de Lin' and 'Mouvement' after Sir Ian and Lady Hamilton had gone.

Sir Ian has a delightful Aberdeen terrier that was strutting up and down by his car as I arrived.

Sunday, 9 April 1916 – 29 Queen Anne Street, London

Mr and Mrs Felix Warre called for me at 11.30am and we spent a delightful hour-and-a-quarter at the zoo. I saw for the first time a bird eating a spider, a creature about five inches long, with thick fleshy limbs and thick body, covered with long hairs and a giant centipede. The mountain sheep were giving a delightful exhibition of how to get round impossible pieces of rock, with the minimum of effort.

Leonard and I dined at home. Archibald Borwick put in an appearance, having got a few days leave from his soldiering.

Tuesday, 11 April 1916 – 29 Queen Anne Street, London

I called for Ock Asquith at the Automobile Club at 3.45pm and we went to 139 Picadilly, where a number of poets were reciting their works for a war charity.

Mr Augustine Birrell, the cabinet minister, was in the chair, and the poets were W B Yeats, Sir Henry Newbolt, Mrs Margaret L Woods, William Henry Davies, Owen Seaman, Walter de la Mare, Maurice Hewlitt, Hilaire Belloc, Emile Cammaerts and Laurence Binyon. Henry Ainley [the actor] showed a great lack of comprehension of the spirit of Rupert Brooke's *1914* sonnets and '[The Old Vicarage,] Grantchester', which he recited.

The two whose reading impressed me as being that of true poets, were Yeats and Davies – Yeats' manner conveying, perhaps, a touch of self-satisfaction, but Davies, on the other hand, looking like an unconscious humble little animal that could not be anything else than just itself. His poems he recited were 'Birds', 'The Moon', 'Dreams of the Sea' and 'Love's Silent Hour', to which he added a few encores. Yeats recited 'The Hosting of the Sidhe' 'The Song of Wandering Angus', 'Innisfree' and 'The Fiddler of Dooney'.

Belloc's poem 'The Dons' was very funny.

Friday, 14 April 1916 – 29 Queen Anne Street, London

I began writing down my F Minor piano sonata and the ideas of which date back to about 1909. I don't feel they are very fresh and there is just a suspicion of academic workmanship which damps my enthusiasm a little at the outset – still, the work is well constructed, and it may attain salvation in the progress of being set down.

Saturday, 15 April 1916 – 29 Queen Anne Street, London

Seeing the advertisement of a performance at the Aldwych Theatre of *The Magic Flute*, by [Sir Thomas] Beecham, I read it up in Dent's *Mozart's Operas* and went for myself. I was much interested, and found that a proper understanding of the story made a great deal of difference to my enjoyment. I was struck with the solemnity of the music dealing with the priests and initiation into the brotherhood, as to which Dent has something to say.

Wednesday, 19 April 1916 – 29 Queen Anne Street, London

Frank Bridge and his wife dined with Leonard and myself, and we made him play us his three poems for piano and his 'Lament for String Orchestra'. I played him his Arabesque – which I had spent an hour or so of the afternoon in learning. His work made a better impression upon both of us than it did when I ran through the same things with Leonard a day or two before. It seems one can never do justice to new music on a first hearing. Harmonically it all seems vinegar and one finds too, that things which at first hearing seem trivial, like the Arabesque, acquire some body and stability later on.

As a close friend of Arthur Asquith, Kelly also visited the country residence of the Asquith family – the Wharf, Sutton Courteney near Abingdon in Oxfordshire – during his extensive period of home leave. Arthur Asquith's father had chosen the village as the perfect site for his country retreat in 1912 and built it a year later. His wife Margot converted the old barn directly on the river which served for accommodation for the many guests which attended her weekend house parties.

Before the war it had also been a meeting place of what those of its members called 'the Coterie' and others called the 'Corrupt Coterie'; the children of wealthy, political and artistic figures – centred on the Asquiths – who prided themselves on living life to the full and often to excess. Charles Lister and Patrick Shaw-Stewart had both been associated with the Coterie as were drama critic Alan Parsons and his wife Viola, the daughter of the famed Victorian actor and theatre manager Sir Herbert Beerbohm Tree. The Asquiths stayed in the village after Ock's father had resigned as prime minister. Herbert Asquith is buried in the churchyard of All Saints.

Saturday, 22 April 1916 – The Wharf, Sutton Courteney

During the course of the day I ran through a certain number of songs with Viola Parsons including my songs 'March' and 'Music, when Soft Voices Die'. After tea we went completely through the 4th Act of Verdi's *Otello*. Verdi seems to me to resemble Handel in that great beauty – and something approaching to sheer greatness – seems to triumph over an absence of critical revision, which few other composers of equal powers could tolerate, an absence of criticism, not as to dramatic construction, but as to actual themes and harmony.

I finished reading a volume of W H Davies' poems *Foliage* before breakfast. I was delighted with the first few, but they quickly palled, as they all expressed the same idea. There was something tiresome about the insistence on the delights (and self-satisfaction) of the simple rural pleasures which the poet contrasts with his limited conception of the life of towns and affairs.

Monday, 24 April 1916 – 29, Queen Anne Street, London

I called for Viola Parsons at 29 Welbeck Street at 7.50pm and after trying through the songs she was going to sing after dinner we set out for the Moulin d'Or in Soho (Deane Street) where we dined with Edward Marsh, Ivor Novello, Lady Juliet Duff – a niece of Sir Hubert Parry – and W H Davies – the 'super-tramp' [he published *The Autobiography of a Super-Tramp* in 1908]. I played my 'Elegy on Rupert Brooke' and Mendelssohn's E Minor scherzo. Viola Parsons sang Denis Browne's two songs 'Salathiel' and 'Gratiana' – both of which I like enormously. I liked Davies a good deal; he is very simple and genuine. I was interested to hear him say he thought the lines out of Marlow's *Faustus*, 'Was this the face that launched a thousand ships?', superior to any passage in Shakespeare.

Wednesday, 26 April 1916 – Bisham Grange, Marlow

On sifting my music to pack up I came across the manuscript of my studies which I had left with Schott to get copied. The copy was worthless as it was so inaccurate but I had decided not to make a fuss about it when Schott told me it was an old Belgian who was in want of work. On looking at the manuscript, however, I found the copyist had treated it as though it were pupil's work – had made pencil marks freely and in some places had made alterations in the text. I accordingly hurried off to Schott and vented my anger on Mr Volkert, who at last prevailed on me to let him make the copyist rub out his marks and after restoring the text to what it was, make his copy of it conform. I really felt very angry. Perhaps the most outrageous interference was the correction of one of my cadences to the E Major study. Mr Volkert told me the old man had written a harmony book as though that made it any better!

I have been egging on Leonard Borwick to make an anthology of English pianoforte pieces, and it was perhaps owing to this, as well as to my curiosity to try and find the tune Denis Browne has used in his song 'Gratiana', that we took out his Elizabethan *Virginal Book* after breakfast and spent an hour sampling its contents. I found one or two pieces – mostly by Byrd – that might do for performance.

I caught the 5.15pm train to Maidenhead and sailed before dinner – for the first time for over 18 months. It has become warm and the spring has already begun to push out. I ran through my F Minor piano sonata after dinner. There is an earthy smell about the garden.

Saturday, 29 April 1916 – Bisham Grange, Marlow
I heard from Freyberg by telephone in the morning that we are to return to Mudros next Saturday. The RND is having battalions added to it of which there is to be a second Hood Battalion commanded by Arthur Asquith with myself as second-in-command, and perhaps in a month we shall be in France. There was a fairly strong wind blowing up the river.

It had been a delightful leave for Kelly but Freyberg's call meant that his time at home was coming to an end. While he and others had been recharging their batteries in England, the Hood Battalion had continued with its garrison duties on the islands of the Aegean but at last it seemed that progress had been made as to the future of the RND.

Although the admiralty was of the opinion that the RND should be broken up – and some men had already left to serve at sea – Vice Admiral Sir John de Robeck, the commander of the Eastern Mediterranean Squadron was keen to see the RND kept intact, especially as it had been reinforced and was up to strength for the first time in many months. He firmly believed that the men had 'fought magnificently' on the battlefield and that its esprit de corps was second to none.

On 16 April 1916 the division's war diarist remarked that it had been 'placed under the Army Act' and that a telegram had been received from Sir John, informing the senior officers of the RND that it 'would be transferred to [the] Army'.

As Kelly had been told, a new battalion was to be raised to bring the division up to war establishment. This would be known as the 2nd Hood

Battalion. There were also plans afoot to relieve the RND from their island duties. All arrangements for English leave were therefore cancelled and all parties – including Kelly who was looking forward enormously to assuming his role as second-in-command of the 2nd Hood – were ordered to return to their battalions.

Friday, 5 May 1916 – P&O Express, Boulogne to Marseilles

I left at 8.30am and reached Charing Cross at 9.00am after stopping at the Union Club on the way. There were about a dozen RND officers, including Major Sketchley, Major [Reginald Dawson] Lough, Bernard Freyberg, Arthur Asquith and Edward Nelson – with whom I shared a berth. [Author] Robert Townsend Warner came to see me off. Mrs Asquith, who came to see Asquith off, had brought a bottle of eau de cologne each for him, Freyberg and myself. I felt she was a dear, kind-hearted soul when she embraced all three of us just as the train was leaving.

It was a calm passage. Our train didn't leave Boulogne till 7.00pm and Freyberg, Asquith, Nelson and I took a drive to Wimereux. We've had great luck in actually getting about nine weeks' leave in a ten days' leave – the delay being due to our being on leave while they were deciding to turn the RND over to the army.

Saturday, 6 May 1916 – Hotel Splendide, Marseilles

We reached Marseilles at 4.00pm and as the ship was going to be coaled during the night, Freyberg, Nelson, Asquith and I went to the Hotel Splendide where we got a good dinner and some divine claret – Chateau Lafite 1900, I think it was. We wandered out afterwards and had some supper in a restaurant. The town seemed to have an enormous number of people in the streets.

When we got back to the hotel we found Freyberg who was shortly engaged in a very congenial occupation – that of putting down a young officer who had not seen any active service, but who was ready to discuss and criticise the recent operations in Mesopotamia.

Arthur Asquith later recalled this occasion, offering a glimpse of Kelly's obvious enjoyment in exploring ideas. 'After enjoying the dinner and the wine with his usual wholehearted and infectious enthusiasm FSK initiated and became enthralled in a discussion as to whether, if we eschewed such creature comforts and lived with Franciscan austerity, our senses might not be quickened to keener appreciations and our imaginations to higher flights.'

Monday, 8 May 1916 – P&O SS *Medina*, voyage to Malta from Marseilles

It was a nice warm day, most of which I spent playing bridge. A swallow flew into the smoking room about 6.00pm in an exhausted condition and the movements of a black cat which happened to be there at the time quite took my attention off bridge. It had all its movements completely under control except for an involuntary spasm of its lips that laid bare its teeth. It made a very thorough reconnaissance of the position, but all to no avail and the bird, after some perilous adventures, at last blundered out of the porthole.

Tuesday, 9 May 1916 – Hotel Great Britain, Valletta

We reached Malta about 5.00pm coming to anchor in the outer harbour. It was typical of the prevailing contradiction of orders one is carrying out that we heard the RND were already leaving Malta and that we were to take the first available boat back to Marseilles from here. Freyberg and I weighed at the club, our respective weights being 15 stone 7 pounds and 15 stone. I seem to have gone up 21 pounds in a couple of months.

Even taking into account his socialising and good living during his three-month home leave, Kelly's weight in May 1916 seems a little on the heavy side for a man whose rowing weight at the height of his powers in 1908 was 12 stone 1 pound. Kelly had, after all, served on Gallipoli for many months, sharing the dangers and privations of his men and suffering from various stomach illnesses, jaundice, battle fatigue, as well as being wounded. His weight was probably nearer 13 stone.

Wednesday, 10 May 1916 – Hotel Great Britain, Valletta

At 4.00pm I visited St John's Cathedral, in which the pavement is the most noticeable thing, and the museum, and I walked around the highest ramparts of Valletta and then out to the botanical gardens. After tea I went for a walk with Asquith and Freyberg to the same ramparts overlooking the harbour and then we went down to bathe in the outer harbour (Marsa Muscette). We walked back through the deep ravine that encloses Valletta. I felt very proud of the British Empire during my sight-seeing. It is so unostentatious and yet so solid.

Thursday, 11 May 1916 – HMS *Isonzo*, voyage from Malta to Taranto

I bathed with Freyberg before breakfast and at 9.00am he, Asquith and I embarked on board the *Isonzo* – formerly P&O SS *Isis*. We left Malta about 11.00am. Apparently the RND has left or is leaving Lemnos so we are being sent back to back to Marseilles via Taranto and overland. It is a nice little trip for the 20 officers and 11 men involved!

WESTERN FRONT

MAY 1916–OCTOBER 1916

*'Life seems suddenly to have ceased
to be an eternity'*

*W*hile Kelly and his party continued to wend their way back through Europe on their 'nice little trip', the rest of the RND was also on the move.

Between 7 and 16 May 1916 the bulk of the division left Mudros, the Hood being amongst the last to leave on the 16th aboard the troop ship Ionian. Although Kelly was now technically second-in-command of a newly-formed 2nd Hood Battalion under Arthur Asquith, he and his new CO were yet to set eyes on any of their rank and file as they were travelling independently of their new command. In fact the question of how the men were to be divided up between Asquith's 2nd Hood and that of Bernard Freyberg's 1st Hood had not yet been arranged. That discussion would take place once the men were mustered again at their final destination and the general feeling was that that destination would be France.

Kelly's great rail journey terminated at the important rail hub of Pont-Remy – four miles south-east of Abbeville on the banks of the River Somme – several days ahead of the men. It proved a fortunate hiatus, giving Kelly and his fellow officers ample time to get acquainted with the area in order to reconnoitre, at some leisure, the villages where the battalions would assemble, identifying suitable billets and services.

THE LOST OLYMPIAN OF THE SOMME

While Kelly had been fighting the Turks in Gallipoli the British Army on the Western Front had been taking on an ever increasing share of the burden in the struggle against the Germans. With the armies under his command responsible for holding four-fifths of the 475-mile line in the west, General Joseph Joffre, the French Commander-in-Chief, had continued to badger the British into taking on a greater role in holding the Allied trenches.

As the months wore on and more British divisions had crossed to France, so the British Army had continued to slide southward, initially assuming responsibility for the line amongst the slag heaps and pit headstocks of the French coalfield from Cuinchy southward to opposite Lens and then, in the late summer of 1915, a further 15 miles from the village of Hebuterne down to Curlu on the rolling chalk landscape of the Somme.

But the British had not simply been 'holding the line'. Kelly had fought in two bloody actions at Krithia in the summer of 1915 but in France and Flanders the British had been involved in several bitter battles on a far greater scale than any of those fought on the Gallipoli Peninsula. The defensive battle of Second Ypres (22 April to 25 May 1915) and the offensives at Aubers Ridge and Festubert in May and Loos in September and October the same year, had given rise to truly dreadful casualty lists; the British suffering enormous losses for little appreciable gain.

When the final reckoning came, the 'butcher's bill' of British Empire and Dominion forces for the fighting at Second Ypres, Aubers Ridge, Festubert and Loos – including its three diversionary actions – amounted to over 163,000 men of which some 30,000 were killed. The Western Front was the key battleground: this was where the German Army had to be beaten and, with the closure of the Gallipoli campaign, the men who had fought the Turks could now be used to fight the Germans. As soon as it had set foot in France the RND had come under the control of the army and Kelly – the proud sailor who had never fought at sea – would soon be pitched into a war of an entirely different tempo and intensity from that on the peninsula. Kelly was in the army now; there would have to be further training for him and his men. The only question was – on which sector would he fight?

Wednesday, 17 May 1916 – Cafe Restaurant du Nord (à Devereaux) Pont-Remy

We reached Pont-Remy about 6.30am where Newman, the Army Service Corps (ASC) officer, met us and showed us into billets. Freyberg, Asquith, Nelson and myself are housed in a small cafe which has the merit of being clean. We saw General Paris down at the station, later in the morning. I felt very reassured by the appearance of the country in which the RND will spend the next month or two. Pont-Remy is a village on the Somme with a faint resemblance to Bisham that is borne out by a fifteenth-century stone château. We walked about three-quarters-of-a-mile up to the Somme at 11.30am and bathed. The current was fairly rapid and the water a little muddy.

And so ends rather a singular episode of the war. To have spent 12 days travelling at the government's expense to Malta and back by Italy without any duties to perform, cannot have been a common war experience.

Thursday, 18 May 1916 – château belonging to M Emile Ponche, Pont-Remy

I was woken up early by the chirping of swallows who had built nests in the window and in one of the nests I could see the disputed comings and goings from my bed.

Freyberg, Asquith and I bathed before breakfast. Sketchley and Lough motored Asquith and myself into Abbeville about 10.00am and we lunched at the Tête de Boeuf, after doing some shopping. The square has a pleasing variety of old houses and parts of the cathedral are beautiful. We started to walk back to Pont-Remy about 4.00pm but got a lift in a passing cab about halfway. It was very warm and fine.

We were somewhat crowded in our cafe, Ock and Nelson sharing a room, so the former and I moved into a small château between the bridge and the railway station to sleep, though we returned to the cafe for our meals.

Sunday, 21 May 1916 – La Mairie [town hall], Citerne [14 miles south of Abbeville]

Asquith and I left Pont-Remy on a motor lorry at midday for Citerne, where we decided to put up at the Mairie temporarily. The mayor is a big, honest bourgeois and his wife and two pretty daughters gave Asquith and me a strong impression of sterling middle-class characteristics. Freyberg, who was also lodging with them, was out. They insisted on our accepting their hospitality for the time being, so we had our meals with them.

Freyberg arrived back after lunch, and we spent the afternoon inspecting the billets. They consisted mostly of barns and outhouses – many of which, owing to the pools of filthy water in the farm yards, were far from sanitary. Later in the evening, the mayor showed us three pieces of ground, where, if we got leave, we could erect tents.

The château is situated in a nice wood, which is in pleasant contrast to the ubiquitous cultivation. M le Curé [parish priest] came to dinner, and we spent a very hilarious evening – the cider and white wine which one drank at the same time completely conquering his reserve. I played a piece or two on a very deficient, upright piano.

Monday, 22 May 1916 – house belonging to a man called Tueur, Citerne

Freyberg, Asquith and I walked to Hallencourt at 8.00am to catch the general before he went out, and spent half an hour or so with him and Sketchley. We procured a car in which we visited Forceville [-en-Vimeau] and Wiry [au-Mont] – villages within a few kilometres of Citerne. It was originally intended to put the 1st and 2nd Hood Battalions into billets in Citerne, but on our pointing out the lack of room and water, Asquith and I were sent to look at Forceville and Neuville. Freyberg was to go into Pont-Remy to meet the first arrivals of the battalions – half of B Company – and he dropped Asquith and myself in Oisemont, where we lunched. We visited Neuville and Forceville on foot before returning to Citerne.

He and I moved into a nice, clean little billet, where a talkative woman is foraging for us, pending the arrival of the battalion and the institution of messes. The two officers in charge of the first draught were Ivan Heald and [Sub Lieutenant Harry] Gealer – who came out in a lorry with a few men in advance. Freyberg arrived with the rest of the men about 9.00pm after we had begun dinner. I played a few pieces again after dinner. It was nice seeing Heald again and hearing his news.

Wednesday, 24 May 1916 – chez Tueur, Citerne

There was nothing for me to do – the day being spent by Heald, Gealer and Callingham chalking up for billets for the remainder of the battalion, who were due to arrive after dark.

I spent part of the morning and afternoon in making notes on a War Office book entitled *Notes for Infantry Officers on Trench Warfare (March 1916)*. The battalion began arriving by companies about 9.30pm and got into their billets without any confusion. Cockey, [Sub Lieutenant James] Hilton, [Sub Lieutenant Charles] Markey and Callingham had supper with Ock and myself in our billet, and we sat up till 1.30am talking over the last three months we had not seen one another.

Thursday, 25 May 1916 – chez Tueur, Citerne

After dinner we paid a visit to the mayor and his family and then Freyberg, Asquith, Egerton and I met round a table and went through the delicate process of dividing up the battalion, so as to form the 2nd Hoods.

The procedure adopted was the alternate choice of officers (with whom went their platoons), the first choice resting on the spin of a coin. Ock won the toss and by this we were enabled to avoid having one or two obvious undesirables. It was an amusing little symposium – in which either side was much concerned to keep its counsel secret. Ock and I were at an advantage here, as we relapsed into French, which the others did not understand.

On the whole the division was a fair one – though, at the end, the intention of giving two platoons of each company to form the new battalion had to be set aside when it was found that owing to the choice of officers, Asquith's and Egerton's original platoons were separated from the original officers. Freyberg was loath to allow three platoons of two companies to go to one battalion to satisfy these motherly feelings, but these two old 'hens' clucked away to such an extent that at last the original arrangement was amended to allow of their keeping their respective 'chickens'.

Sunday, 28 May 1916 – 2nd Hood Battalion, chez Tueur, Citerne

A doctor – the dud of the division, so McCracken told us – arrived about 4.00am. As a new wing in the division, the 2nd Hood has attracted the attention of all who think there may be a chance of unloading into it everything they wish to get rid of. The brigadier, who in Mudros labelled '2nd Hood' all officers and men whom other units will not have, tried to adopt the congratulatory attitude with Asquith yesterday to make a sow's ear appear a silk purse; but there was a novel situation when the latter really thought it was meant as a joke and took it as such. Luckily the brigadier's train moved out of Abbeville at the same moment.

Monday, 29 May 1916 – 2nd Hood Battalion, chez Tueur, Citerne

My birthday: and I reflected that another 35 years will probably see me out. Life seems suddenly to have ceased to be an eternity and I must disillusion myself of the fiction that I am a young man with a whole career in front of me! At the same age Beethoven was writing his *Fifth Symphony* – a depressing comparison! I had a sudden attack, too, of something in the nature of lumbago while I was out riding and it was like the final wrench off the top of the fence into the territory of middle age.

Brigadier Philips called on us in the morning. He is not a gossiper, not a pessimist but likes to talk of sport, the war [and] our policy in India.

Above: Hood advance: The position known as the 'White House' was captured by the Hood battalion on 6 May 1915 – when this photograph was taken – during the first day of the Second Battle of Krithia. Lasting until 8 May, the offensive was the second attempt to seize the village of Krithia and the neighbouring hill of Achi Baba and resulted in an advance of the Allied line of between 400 to 600 yards. Bernard Freyberg holds the water bottle.

Below: Savoury smell of Turk: A typical communication trench on the Cape Helles front on Gallipoli. Note the boot of a half-buried Turk sticking out of the parapet. The stench of decomposing corpses induced involuntarily vomiting amongst the men and the millions of flies feeding on them then landing on food gave rise to widespread dysentery.

Catapult bomb: An officer of the RND, bearing a remarkable resemblance to Kelly, watches the flight of a catapult bomb fired from a trench called 'Plymouth Avenue'. The bomb was released by striking the catch of the catapult with the handle of an entrenching tool. Kelly was scathing in his criticism of these improvised weapons. *(Courtesy Australian War Memorial)*

bove: Helles Firing Line: A typical front line trench on the Krithia front held
y units of the RND in mid-summer 1915. Kelly worked and lived in conditions
xactly like these.

elow: Old French trench: The trenches on the extreme right of the French line
ver-looking the Kereves Dere ravine, taken over by the RND towards the end of
•ecember 1915. Kelly was surprised by the French use of stones – clearly visible
:re – and corrugated iron to make their defences and dugouts more secure. Kelly
ould be the last to leave these trenches during the final evacuation of the Helles
•ctor on 8 January 1916.

Above: Boneyard: Looking down on a view Kelly got to know all too well from the war-ravaged Lorette Spur towards Vimy Ridge in the distance and the ruined villages of Ablain St Nazaire (right) and Souchez (left). Note the wooden cross and two German pickelhaube helmets marking a German grave left and the twin pylons of colliery winding gear towards top left.

(Courtesy Édouard Roose, Northern France Regional Tourist Board)

Below: Lacerated earth: This is the very area and the very conditions in which Kelly's B Company of the Hood Battalion went into the attack on 13 November. Note the railway running horizontally across the centre of the photograph which locates the image. *(Courtesy Imperial War Museum)*

Advanced Posts: A trench map of the Somme battle-field astride the River Ancre. Kelly, in command of B Company of the Hood Battalion, was responsible for the sector immediately to the west of the river and railway having outposts (circled) in the valley where, due to the flooded ground, there could be no trenches. Three such outposts were at the ruined mill, (*bottom centre*) and at 'Picturedrome' and 'Lancashire' Posts near the railway. Kelly was killed in the boxed area in the third German line and his original burial place is marked with a † bottom centre left.

Final act: An oblique aerial photograph of the ground over which the Hood Battalion of the RND attacked on 13 November 1916. The three interconnected lines of German trenches which make up the first line position are heavily traversed and even from this angle appear formidable. Each was protected by a belt of barbed wire and machine guns in depth and with interlocking fields of fire. Kelly was killed on his first objective – the third German trench – in the area indicated. Compare with trench map.

Final resting place: Originally buried close to the Ancre in the village of Hamel, Kelly's body was eventually moved to Martinsart British Cemetery located on the edge of the village where he had taken his last 'good hot bath' two days before he was killed. Kelly lies in an unusual cemetery in that the graves are marked by headstones of Corsehill or Locharbriggs sandstone rather than the usual white stone or marble. The Australian flag was placed there by his great niece Carol Jones during a visit in the summer of 2012.

Beloved brother: The Bisham War Memorial, designed by sculptor Eric Gill and erected by Kelly's sister Maisie in his memory, also commemorates all those from Bisham who were killed. It stands today close to the entrance of Bisham Abbey National Sports Centre a few hundred yards from Kelly's riverside home of Bisham Grange.

JESU MY STRENGTH AND MY REDEEMER

ERECTED IN MEMORY OF A MOST BELOVED BROTHER LIEUT. COMMDR FREDERICK SEP-TIMUS KELLY D. S. C. HOOD BATTN R.N. NAVAL DIV. WHO FELL AT THE TAKING OF BEAU-COURT S. R.ANCRE AFTER SERVING THROUGHOUT THE GALLIPOLI CAMPAIGN

Though he is not opinionated, such phrases as 'of course, I'm a soldier' seem to indicate that he does see some imperial problems in a clearer light than politicians. On the whole I am very favourably impressed and his personality is sympathetic to me. I wonder whether he is impulsive in the sense of dealing out a good many orders which subsequently in the conversational turn of an interview become modified. Asquith thought he detected this.

Brigadier General Lewis Francis 'Chico' Philips, CMG, DSO of the Rifle Brigade, commanded the 189th Infantry Brigade of the newly-designated 63rd (Royal Naval) Division, from the summer of 1916 until the winter of 1917.

Thursday, 1 June 1916 – 2nd Hood Battalion, chez Tueur, Citerne

I had a pretty busy day. There was an officers' meeting at 9.00am in the mayor's house, where Freyberg explained the reasons for splitting the Hood in two to form a second Hood Battalion. He spoke very well and at some length. The rest of the day was spent in moving the two halves into different parts of the town and in getting the organisation of the 2nd Hoods into being. Asquith went into Abbeville for the day to arrange drawing transport so I was in charge of the 2nd Hood. The method of splitting up was to take two platoons from each company to form the nucleus of the 2nd Hood. In the latter battalion we only have 11 officers and are working under difficulties.

In spite of Kelly's extensive front line service at Gallipoli, he had not yet entered the line on the Western Front and so was still required to undergo further training. The army had a policy of extracting parties of officers and non-commissioned officers from its battalions and placing them into instructional establishments, well behind the front lines, in order to learn the latest techniques and tactics of trench warfare and the effective use of weaponry. The theory was that these men would then cascade their newly-gained knowledge to the rest of their units.

In early June a party consisting of Kelly, Sub Lieutenant John Bentham, Sub Lieutenant Ralph Chapman and 12 petty officers and leading seamen were packed off to Rouen for a fortnight's bombing course which fortuitously gave Kelly the opportunity to indulge his love of music, the arts and architecture. He was going back to school but he would certainly cause a stir among the 5–6,000 men at No. 2 Infantry Base Depot.

John Bentham kept a diary of his time in the Hood Battalion and he recalled that when the Hood men arrived at the camp – all bearing naval ranks and with Kelly sporting the naval privilege of a 'full set' – moustache and beard – nobody quite knew who or what they were. Regulations did not permit beards in the British Army. According to Bentham, Kelly was intent on insisting that the 'senior service' took precedence over the army on parade and ensured that the Hood contingent lined up behind the band to lead all parades off the parade ground, doubtless to the annoyance of army officers quietly seething behind. It was at Rouen that Bentham first heard Kelly play the piano and it is clear that he was in awe of his talented and cultured superior officer.

Tuesday, 6 June 1916 – No. 2 Infantry Base Depot camp, Rouen
I visited an exhibition of the facsimiles of Raemaekers cartoons and then went to the cathedral and church of St Ouen. The cartoons were better than I expected to find them though in the majority of them there is gross exaggeration. I enjoyed seeing the two churches again. The Church of St Ouen has a lovely middle tower and its only noticeable blemish was the west window – which is in horrible contrast to the quiet tones of the rest of the glass.

Wednesday, 7 June 1916 – No. 2 Infantry Base Depot camp, Rouen
In the afternoon I and my party of four men were told off to a Captain Kettlewell who took a large party of men for instruction in the relief of trenches. As this was over familiar to me he suggested I should attend a lecture and demonstration nearby of the assault of the enemy's trenches.

The subject matter of this lecture was new to me and filled us with enthusiasm. It is evidently the result of some careful thinking as to the best method of breaking through the enemy's lines.

A party of some 300 men – who first were lectured as to the principle of the assault – were divided up into assaulting party and supports. Each party was then divided into four equal portions in each of whose functions respectively were (from the right) bayonet men, bombers, men carrying horizontal ladders (for subsequent parties to cross trenches gained) and, finally, men with entrenching tools (spades and picks) to consolidate trenches occupied.

The chief point of the system is that each party of men is told off for a particular trench, beyond which they're not to go. The first party gains and occupies the first trench, the second the second, etc. Each party of men advanced from the right in double file at a quick march. On arriving at a specified point the bayonet men extended to the left, lay down and opened fire on the trench in front of them, while the next party – the bombers – extended behind them and threw their bombs into the trench. When they had done this the bayonet men charged and occupied the trench in front of them, the bombers following them in.

Saturday, 10 June 1916 – No. 2 Infantry Base Depot camp, Rouen
The Russian offensive in Galicia seems to be of real importance and I wondered whether it was the first step of the general offensive and the beginning of the end as far as the Germans are concerned.

Wednesday, 14 June 1916 – No. 2 Infantry Base Depot camp, Rouen
I went down in the mess car with Chapman, Bentham, Walmsley and Kettlewell to Haumesser's music shop at 5.30pm and I played to them for an hour or more on a stiff upright piano in a small, unventilated back room.

At 7.00pm, just as we were leaving, I found Andre Haumesser, the proprietor so it seems, and he played me a trio in three movements in F

Major. He played it in a very slapdash style, singing the string parts to the names of the notes. He seemed to have such an incredible technique in the diction required that my attention was rather distracted from the work itself. It didn't sound particularly odd until he came to quick passages, when I could hardly keep my countenance. There were some good themes in the work, but, like most French works of any length and especially their chamber music, there was a lack of form. Of its three movements the second, a staccato scherzo, struck us as the most direct. He told me Vincent d'Indy [a French composer and teacher] had seen it and liked it. I played him my combination of the 'Spring Song' and the 'Honeysuckle and the Bee', which he had heard me playing to the other officers and he was much tickled over it.

Thursday, 15 June 1916 – No. 2 Infantry Base Depot camp, Rouen

I dined with [Captain] P B Ackroyd at the Hotel de la Poste, and found him very good company. A propos of the newer officers of Kitchener's Army he told me of a friend of his in the Regular Army, who, on hauling up a newly-joined officer for ladling his gravy into his mouth with his knife, was completely nonplussed by being then asked how otherwise was he to get it in?

Like everyone else he has the highest admiration for the Guards whose returns to the 3rd Echelon are always the first in, and who never have to have an order repeated. He told me of a fine thing that occurred during the retreat from Mons, when some of the Coldstreams picked up all the greatcoats that had been discarded by a regiment of the line, marched with them for several hours in addition to all their own kit and presented them to their owners at the end of the day.

Friday, 16 June 1916 – journey from Rouen to Abbeville

We moved off from Rouen in a troop train at 3.45pm and travelled slowly but continuously to Abbeville which we reached at 1.30am the next morning.

Saturday, 17 June 1916 – 2nd Hood Battalion, Dieval, France
[22 miles west of Lens]

The 1st Hood arrived here yesterday and I saw Freyberg and others. I have a very comfortable billet by the church. It is very pretty country where we are in spite of its proximity to the coal fields. The French miners and colliers we passed on the road were very bizarre looking.

Tuesday, 20 June 1916 – 2nd Hood Battalion, Dieval

I spent most of the morning and the entire afternoon preparing a lecture on trench routine which I delivered to the officers and NCOs of the battalion at 6.00pm. It lasted about 50 minutes.

At 10.00am a Major Campbell, of some Scotch Regiment, came and lectured us on bayonet fighting – that is, a proportion of officers and men of the 1st and 2nd Hood and some Drakes. It was extremely good besides being very funny. He had an NCO with him to illustrate. The underlying idea was that two men could practise bayonet fighting by means of a long stick with a pad at the end of it. The men who held this would place the pad in various positions – indicating an enemy's back, stomach, etc. – for the bayonet man to attack. The lecturer certainly inspired great keenness.

Asquith, [Lieutenant Sidney] Fish and I dined with 'Cardy' Montagu in his billet. No news of the big Russian offensive on the northern half of the line which we were told had begun on 27 June. At midday I tried a couple of the battalion horses to choose one for myself.

'Cardy' was The Honourable Lionel Montagu. At Oxford he was thought to be as much a fixture of the racecourse as the conmen who tricked punters with three-card Monte (or three-card trick), hence the nickname Cardy. He had been the divisional records officer in Alexandria when Kelly was evacuated to hospital after being wounded on the Gallipoli Peninsula in May 1915 but had managed to make his way over to Cape Helles soon afterwards. According to Arthur Asquith, 'two well-shelled dumps [of stores] over which he presided were christened after him "Monte" and "Carlo"'.

Montagu was later wounded and awarded the DSO while serving with the Hood on the Somme for 'conspicuous gallantry and devotion to duty' when leading his company into an attack and capturing his objective, whilst on 14 November 1916 he single-handedly captured 50 prisoners during the final capture of Beaucourt-sur-Ancre by the RND. After the war he bought and named a racehorse Beaucourt in memory of the Hood's bloody battle.

Wednesday, 21 June 1916 – 2nd Hood Battalion, Dieval

[An officer] about whom there has been such trouble in the battalion, has at last got to a safe job having been made a permanent instructor. Freyberg appears to have had words with the general about him. It is a scandal that someone who has taken such pains to get out of danger should be allowed to slip into a soft job.

Sunday, 25 June 1916 – 2nd Hood Battalion, Dieval

We paraded at 9.00am and after sizing the companies, marched down to the parade ground on the main road where the 1st Hood were and we formed a square for inspection by General [Sir Henry Hughes] Wilson, commanding IV Corps. The occasion was the presentation of the *Croix de Guerre* to Leonard Cockey, [Surgeon Lieutenant Edward Gustave] Schlesinger and a Royal Army Medical Corps man by General Wilson. After the presentation and inspection we marched past in column of route.

I slept for a couple of hours or more after lunch and then we sorted my gear with a view to deciding what I should take with me if we are ordered up to the trenches suddenly. I have been composing a tune somewhat unconsciously most of the day. I went for a walk with Ock after dinner. There was a heavy bombardment going on during our walk and as I was getting to bed at 11.50pm.

Tuesday, 27 June 1916 – 2nd Hood Battalion, Dieval

Orders arrived from the brigade to say that the 300 officers and men from the 2nd Hood were to leave tomorrow for Coupigny [12 miles west of Lens] and we spent the rest of the afternoon and evening making the necessary arrangements.

The geography of the sector on which Kelly would fight the next phase of his war could not have been more different from his last. Here there were neither the atmospheric scents of sage and thyme, nor olive groves, nor the clear Aegean to bathe in but neither was there the all-pervading stench of decomposing human flesh, nor millions of flies, nor rampant gut-wrenching dysentery or typhoid. Not only was the terrain unlike anything Kelly had seen on Gallipoli it was also unlike any other front on which the British Army was fighting.

While the rear areas consisted of rough and hilly country intersected with valleys and streams, the stretch between Bruay and the front line in front of Lens, was characterised by tall chimneys belching thick, black smoke sprouting amongst towers of latticed iron girders supporting the winding gear of numerous collieries. Dotted here and there, disfiguring the landscape, numerous large, black pyramidal slag heaps (terrils) rose from the ground.

Kelly was in the very heart of France's coalfield – the 'Gallic Black Country' – a region of heavy industry where dour people lived in rows of cottages and mined an essential resource for the war effort. The Germans occupying Lens were already sitting on a large percentage of France's coal reserves and, when Kelly arrived in France, they were also masters of the tactically vital ground of the Vimy Ridge – the key to controlling access to the Douai Plain to the east and the coal basin of the Pas de Calais.

To the south-east of Lens the River Souchez flowed between chalk spurs to either side, separating the northern extremity of Vimy Ridge from the Lorette Spur to the west. It was to secure the ground of the Lorette Spur and Vimy Ridge and to preserve what was left of their coal industry that the French had fought so desperately in the Second Battle of Artois in May 1915. French troops under General Paul Maistre battled for two weeks – often hand-to-hand – in dreadful conditions to drive the Germans from heavily fortified positions on the Lorette Spur above the village of Ablain St Nazaire.

Driven off the ridge the Germans clung on to the village of Souchez and the

Vimy Ridge but were later forced out of Souchez, leaving the Lorette Spur as a mass grave for French and German alike. Even after Kelly had left, soldiers were still walking ankle deep in bones and equipment in some places while skulls bobbed up and down in the water of shell holes.

Now the tortured and shell-battered village of Souchez – a place which even locals felt was 'non bon' – was almost on the front line, squeezed into the valley floor between the shoulders of chalk to either side.

Wednesday, 28 June 1916 – 2nd Hood Detachment, Coupigny

The 300 officers and men, with myself in command, moved off in company with a similar party from the 1st Hood (and the 1st Hood band to play us out of Dieval) at 9.45am. The 2nd Hoods were in front so that the task of finding the way devolved upon me. It is extremely difficult on the maps they give us, to distinguish the main roads from the country tracks, but [apart from] Houdain, where, up a steep hill, an apparent main road was really a stony track with a gradient of about one-in-four and which necessitated a detour for the transport, we didn't get into difficulties.

Our route took us through Division, Houdain, Barlin and Hersin and we halted about one mile out of Houdain for a hot dinner from the field kitchens. We had several showers, but conditions were not bad for marching. The total distance covered must have been over 12 miles, but though the men were tired at the end we reached Coupigny with no stragglers.

Thursday, 29 June 1916 – 2nd Hood Detachment, Bois de Verdrel [1½ miles south of Coupigny]

As our party of 300 men had to be subdivided into parties for the Bois de Verdrel and Bouvigny, we had a fairly busy time in the morning reorganising. We left at about 2.20pm, myself, C and D Companies, with transport and most of the special duty men for Verdrel Wood and A and B Companies under Lieutenant Hilton for Bouvigny.

The Verdrel Camp is in the south-west side of the wood and we have enough tents and to spare after putting eight men in each tent. The tents have bottom boards, so we are fairly independent of the weather. An engineer lieutenant named Dodson rang me up in the afternoon as to our digging parties and at 8.30pm I set off with all available men (about 110). It was about an hour's march to Bouvigny wood, where a [Royal Engineers] guide was to have met us and from there on to the place where we were to work was about another three quarters of an hour.

The men were set to a task of digging narrow trenches six-foot deep – to be filled in again when the telephone wires have been buried at the bottom of them, and the confined space makes it uncomfortable work – especially since the rain sometimes renders the work more like ladling soup than digging. The sides, too, have a habit of falling in in places and the Drake spent considerable time, so Pollock told me, in digging two of their men out!

We were working not far from the edge of the Notre Dame de Lorette ridge and we had a fine display of German starlights and search lights – which betokened a welcome nervousness on the enemy's part. The firing line seemed to be about 3,000 yards away, but except for the lights things seemed very quiet. Further, however, and out of earshot the sky was a quick succession of flashes which I took to be those of a very heavy bombardment. We worked till 2.50am, part of the time in the rain, and got home at 4.50am the men getting a hot breakfast before turning in.

I fell foul of [a fellow officer] on the march there and strafed both him and his acting CPO. [He] is constitutionally slow, unpunctual and completely incapable of taking charge of men and pitching into him is rather like beating a sheep; not least so, too, in the complete absence of ill-feeling with which he puts up with it. Both Asquith and I can't help liking him, as he has many good qualities and when his interest is aroused he is capable of taking trouble – but one wishes one could find a job for him in which he need not be in charge of men.

There are a great many shell holes on the ridge and one was constantly in danger of taking a plunge into them in the dark. About 6.00pm I rode out to see that Hilton had settled down all right in Bouvigny.

Lieutenant Commander Henry Broadhurst Pollock of the Drake Battalion transferred to and commanded the Hood in 1918 and was awarded the DSO and Bar.

Friday, 30 June 1916 – 2nd Hood Detachment, Bois de Verdrel

In Coupigny I met E W Wilson. His battalion has been up in the trenches – attached to 47th Division and he told me that the state of the trenches and the arrangements as to the times for relieving were much worse than ours on the peninsula, but he had nothing but praise for the more important arrangements, such as trench raids, which he thought were the work of the best brains, whereas the others were left to anyone to make. I got the loan of a shrapnel-marked blanket from the hotel in which his headquarters were.

Saturday, 1 July 1916 – 2nd Hood Detachment, Bois de Verdrel

I had a busy day, in the morning making arrangements in camp and in the afternoon riding to Barlin and from here to Ranchicourt in search of pay for the men. Our troubles, in the RND never cease. Though we are now in the army we're the only division which is not allowed to draw pay through an army paymaster, not even our own corps, nor the division to which, for the moment, my 2nd Hood detachment is attached for victualling. My visits, therefore, to the 47th Division at Barlin and the IV Corps at Ranchicourt were fruitless, though I had a very pleasant ride.

Long before I got up in the morning there was a distant rumble from the south like a seething cauldron and when I got to 47th Division headquarters they showed me the telegrams to say that our big offensive had begun at 7.30am and had penetrated the German trenches on a 15-mile front.

What Kelly so eloquently described as the 'distant rumble from the south like a seething cauldron' had actually marked the start of what was to become one of the greatest battles in British military history. Even as Kelly had been going about his business in the camp that morning, some 25 miles due south of the Bois de Verdrel tens of thousands of British soldiers had already gone 'over the top' from their front line trenches, straggling over a distance of 18 miles and roughly resembling a capital letter 'L,' in a joint Anglo-French offensive astride the River Somme.

Yet by the time Kelly had mounted his horse to set out on his fruitless quest to find a means of paying his men, that great British Army had already suffered a catastrophic reverse. Of an almost incomprehensible total of 57,470 casualties, 19,240 men lay dead or dying in the grasses of no man's land on the open, sun-drenched ridges and spurs of Picardy or were dangling from the German barbed-wire entanglements. Most of them had fallen before breakfast had been finished in Britain.

What was supposed to have been a great Allied breakthrough – the Big Push – had been preceded by a seven-day artillery bombardment, the power and ferocity of which had never before been witnessed. But with the notable exception of significant success along the horizontal bar of the 'L', parallel to the river, and a few isolated finger holds in the first German line elsewhere, almost every other sector had suffered crushing defeat. 1 July 1916 remains the darkest day in British military history.

As dusk fell on the Somme battlefield on 1 July 1916, however, the true picture and scale of the disaster had yet to emerge. Kelly himself had been assured that the British had managed to penetrate the hardened crust of the German trenches on a 15-mile front but no-one yet knew the whole truth. Even British commanders on the spot, coping with a flurry of fragmentary reports and poring over uncertain situation maps, were not entirely sure what had happened. But they knew that casualties had been heavy; they knew that the Germans had beaten their battalions back on the northern sectors of the battlefield and they knew too that, despite the losses, continued German pressure on the French Army at Verdun meant that they would have to try again. The embattled French demanded nothing less. The British would have to fight on.

Sunday, 2 July 1916 – 2nd Hood Detachment, Bois de Verdrel

Another fairly fine day. There was still much rumble of guns to the south and late in the evening I heard the Third Army had been driven out of the positions they had gained the day before by a German counter-attack.

After dinner Markey and I rode out through the Bois de Bouvigny to see our parties at work digging. On the way out we noticed that on a front of about three miles to the north-east the trenches were a line of glowing red, too constant to be accounted for by shell-bursts, and we wondered whether it was a liquid-fire attack. Someone suggested later it was the fires the Germans light during a hostile gas attack (to drive the gas up).

The view one gets on the way to Bouvigny Wood is magnificent – especially at night, when the whole firing line is traced out in star shells. To see it stretching away into the dim distance and to reflect that, all along – the firing line, support and reserve trenches – have to be manned, made one realise what a vast upheaval this war is. It would be a wonderful sight to get a bird's eye view of Europe at night, with its various fronts all marked out with illuminations and shell-bursts. I enjoyed the ride very much and found Markey pleasant company. He is from Meath and the war interrupted his time at Trinity College, Dublin.

In the afternoon the RE major, Ker, who put in a complaint about the Drake's digging, came to complain of the little we had done. Pollock had warned me about him and when I found his charges were vague – as Pollock had found them – we came to words. He held up sundry regiments for our edification who worked 12 hours a day on fatigue work, but of course he must be very ingenuous to think this takes anyone in.

Wednesday, 5 July 1916 – Hood Battalion, Verdrel

We spent the morning in camp packing up and in making what use we could be of transport, before it went back to store after midday, to cart the things over to Verdrel. The two Hood Battalions, after a separate existence of some five or six weeks, were reunited in Verdrel about 5.00pm, the 1st Hood and 2nd Hood headquarters and a few hundred men marching from Dieval.

It came on to rain after lunch and when the two battalions arrived from Dieval it was pouring in tropical fashion and the street was 6 inches deep in water in places. The men arrived cheering. For the night we billeted as two battalions but the 1st and 2nd Hood have ceased to exist in name. Some bad blundering, of course, must have been committed somewhere. Apparently the reason for washing out the four new battalions is the fact that when figures really were examined it was found there would be insufficient men left in Blandford for divisional reinforcements. The 3rd Brigade is now, so we hear, to be composed of a brigade from Kitchener's Army. It is of course hard luck on the officers and men who will lose promotion. In our case three of four company commanders will be seconds-in-command of companies.

With insufficient men available from the RND's own reserves to maintain the strength of the four battalions in each of its three brigades, it was clear that drastic rationalisation and reorganisation would have to take place.

The RND was re-designated the 63rd (Royal Naval) Division, with the naval battalions forming the first two infantry brigades – the Howe and Anson Battalions and the 1st and 2nd Royal Marines making up the 188th Brigade and the Hood, Hawke, Drake and Nelson Battalions the 189th Brigade.

For the first time in the RND's history in came four battalions of the army – the 1st/1st Honourable Artillery Company (HAC), 4th Bedfordshire Regiment, 7th Royal Fusiliers and the 10th Royal Dublin Fusiliers – which together formed the 190th Infantry Brigade. Out went Kelly's 2nd Hood Battalion, the men to be reabsorbed into the 1st Hood Battalion under Bernard Freyberg. Kelly's promotion and his short reign as Asquith's deputy had come to an end.

Saturday, 8, July 1916 – Hood Battalion, Verdrel
In the afternoon I watched some wiring instruction given by Montagu and Davidson. Before going away Cardy and I had much amusement

walking through three of the entanglements which ostensibly afforded complete protection. It arose out of an argument as to the efficiency of one he had just constructed and which I succeeded in negotiating in the course of about half-a-minute.

Monday, 10 July 1916 – Hood Battalion, Verdrel

There is a grouse on among the men about not having any leave and the 6th Platoon was obviously not trying to march in step. It was a nice fine day. C and D Companies left for Coupigny en route for the trenches – for the first time.

Thursday, 13 July 1916 – Hood Battalion, Coupigny

A party of four officers, [Lieutenant Cyril] Edmondson (OC A Company), [Sub Lieutenant George] Davidson, [Sub Lieutenant Geoffrey] Dunn (a B Company officer) and myself were to have started off with Freyberg for the trenches on horseback at 7.00am but at the last moment our start was postponed till 8.20am.

We rode to Aix-Noulette where Freyberg and I saw the staff captain of the brigade whose sector we were to visit and at 10.00am the remainder of us started off for the trenches with a guide leaving 'Frisbury' [Freyberg] to settle a number of details as to the moving up of A and B Companies tomorrow night.

Our walk up to the battalion headquarters we had to report to in the trenches took us about an hour and I was rather agreeably impressed with the neat bottom boards of the communication trenches, though there was not much cover from shell fire to be found. The trenches, both in the firing and support lines were much inferior to those in the Gallipoli Peninsula – the firing line except in a few places having no fire step. Things were very quiet, but if the Germans had felt disposed to snipe we made excellent targets in a dozen turns of the trench.

The Drakes were in the sector I had to visit and Pollock and [Sub Lieutenant James] Turrell between them showed me and Dunn round. The wire was in a very poor condition as was also the parapet – sandbags being just heaped up with no apparent consideration as to whether they afforded cover from fire. The deep dugouts were a novelty to me but they struck me as being traps. I got back to lunch at Coupigny at 5.30pm very tired. I slept from 5.00pm till 7.00pm. A dozen supernumerary officers arrived making our numbers for the battalion up to 50.

We left Coupigny at 7.15pm with our field kitchen, which came as far as Aix-Noulette to give us a hot stew. At Aix-Noulette there were four guides who took the four platoons along, one to a company in reserve behind the Arras road and three to the front line. There was a good deal of delay in drawing our rations at 'French Dump' from the limber we had brought up. I eventually arrived – with all my platoon in advance – at battalion headquarters about 12.30am.

The officers [of the 20th Battalion, the London Regiment] and especially the colonel – Matthews – seem very nice. I am attached to C Company with a Captain Hutchison. I went round his lines and out to 'Solferino' [post] where there is a detached bombing section. The shallow trench leading to it had been badly treated by *minenwerfer* [literally mine thrower] in the afternoon and there was a party mending it. I was surprised at the way men exposed themselves in the full moon. Wire was being put out and the Boche was also working. In getting back from Solferino to C Company headquarters we passed through some disused trenches that were more like rock gardens than trenches.

'Frisbury' was Kelly's occasional nickname for his commanding officer and friend Bernard Freyberg and his anglicising a Teutonic-sounding name was a good example of Kelly's ready wit. Although Freyberg was widely known as 'Tiny' during his youth, his surname also gave rise to the nickname 'Fritz' on the part of some of his fellow officers – although not perhaps to his face!

Saturday, 15 July 1916 – Hood Battalion, B Company attached to 20th Londons, Souchez II sector

I didn't get to bed until after the morning stand-to-arms when I walked round C Company's lines with Hutchison. I spent the day in visiting my various officers and their platoons, each of which is attached to a company of the 20th Londons.

The line is an extremely confusing one. In trying to find my way to the bombing post at the end of 'Hun Walk' after midnight (16 July) I took a wrong turning and ended up in the Anson [sector] – who are on our left.

I was on watch from midnight till stand-to-arms and I walked out to inspect our wire, which is very poor. We had a party working at it. We had a considerable strafing in the afternoon from *minenwerfers* and 'heavies' (large shells), but as I could not be of any use to my scattered men I remained in security in the deep C Company dugout where I live with their officers.

The 20th had one officer wounded (White, of C Company) and four men (C Company) killed. There may have been other casualties.

Colonel Matthews explained to Hutchison, the Lewis gun officer and myself, the plans for tomorrow night's trench raid.

Sunday, 16 July 1916 – Hood Battalion, B Company attached to 20th Londons, Souchez II sector

I was very sleepy by the morning stand-to-arms having been up all night, but except for breakfast time I slept from 4.30am till lunch time.

It came on to 'rain' in the afternoon of Boche artillery and of 'minnie'. Our 'toffee-apples' [spherical trench mortar bombs] were also being thrown over to the enemy's lines and our shrapnel was active. As we were sitting in C Company officers' dugout, the whole ground gave a sudden lurch – timbers and all – which gave us the impression that a *minenwerfer* had pitched its shell almost on the top of our dugout. It turned out, as far as the insufficient evidence indicated, to have been a mine but no-one seemed to know where the explosion had taken place for certain. Other dugouts had the same impression of the explosion taking place just above them.

A trench raid on the part of the 20th Londons had been arranged for 11.30am, but half-an-hour beforehand was postponed till 1.00am.

Eighty men and two officers raided a portion of front trench opposite our right and seemed to have bombed some Germans in dugouts effectually for 20 minutes before returning with a loss of two or three wounded – wounds that seemed to have been inflicted by their own men.

The play opened with some bombs from a Stokes [mortar] gun, and our artillery, after first peppering the trench to be raided for a minute or so, put up an effective barricade on all trenches leading to it. Fritz replied and it was not safe to put one's head outside a dugout. At the end of an hour all was quiet again and a number of excited men with blackened faces were talking over events. The thing has been done in too much of a hurry and they seem to have had some confusion as they got into the trench.

Monday, 17 July 1916 – march from trenches to Bois de Bouvigny
Freyberg came up to the trenches about 4.00pm and told us we were to leave the trenches at 10.30pm. This was subsequently altered to 11.30pm to allow the 20th Londons to bring up a company to take our place and the actual relieving was not finally over till 1.00am when the last of my platoons left the trench.

At Aix-Noulette we found a field kitchen with hot tea that Freyberg had sent out to us and also a limber and two riding horses. The remainder of our march took us an hour and three quarters and we reached the camp at 4.45am. [I am] in a room with Egerton and McCracken. The 20th Londons were very good to us and their CO Colonel Matthews struck me as being particularly nice.

Wednesday, 19 July 1916 – Hood Battalion, Aix-Noulette,
B Company attached to RNDE [Royal Naval Division Engineers]
It was one of those days on which, with plenty of work already on one's hands, pieces of paper were being constantly presented to one from the orderly room asking for this or that man to be detailed to report to somewhere else; or else it was a sheaf of orders relating to gas attacks in which all ranks must be instructed prior to the orders

being passed on 'quickly' to the next company commander. My head was buzzing by 6.30pm when the battalion fell in to move off. A, C and D Companies went to the battalion's new sector, Souchez I, in the trenches, but B Company was detailed to be in reserve at Aix-Noulette. We are attached to the RNDE and supply as many night and day working parties as we can.

Aix-Noulette is in ruins from shell fire and the majority of B Company are billeted in cellars. It is a pretty village naturally and the broken walls give it quite the appearance of a ruined Egyptian temple in places. The B Company officers, Hilton, Dunn, Bentham, Markey, [Sub Lieutenant Donald Frank] Bailey and myself inhabit a house which has a roof on but is much damaged by rifle and shell fire.

Apprentice mining engineer James Curzon Hilton joined the RNVR as an ordinary seaman in September 1914. Commissioned as a sub lieutenant he was posted to the Hood in Gallipoli in August 1915 aged 20 and spent a total of 144 days on the peninsula, celebrating his 21st birthday two weeks after the evacuation. Promoted to lieutenant he was second-in-command of Kelly's B Company when they moved into the trenches on the Souchez sector.

Saturday, 22 July 1916 – Hood Battalion, Aix-Noulette, B Company attached to RNDE

I was fairly busy during the morning; in the afternoon I went up with Hilton to see the Souchez I sector which the battalion has just taken over. After having a talk with Freyberg I walked round the sector with Egerton. The lie of the ground makes it difficult to construct safe trenches, but many of the trenches could be made a great deal safer than they are. Half the time I seemed to be having an uninterrupted view of the German trenches; especially of those on the Vimy Ridge to our right. Freyberg showed me a very sound scheme he had submitted to the brigadier – Philips – for the defence of his sector. There is no doubt he has a natural genius for soldiering.

Conversation at dinner turned on the printed books of songs I had

had printed for the Hood Battalion, which reminded me that I had four copies of men's part songs in my bag. I accordingly got them out and we invited in the four stretcher-bearers – who are all bandsmen – to take a part. They were not very quick at reading but by dint of rehearsal we contrived to learn more or less the first verse of H Elliot Button's arrangement of 'Annie Laurie'.

Thursday, 27 July 1916 – Hood Battalion, Aix-Noulette, B Company attached to RNDE

A King's Royal Rifle Corps captain (a promoted NCO, so it seemed), who is attached to brigade headquarters came at 10.00am to help me take evidence for the prosecution in the charge sheet against one of my platoon petty officers, who was too drunk to report his platoon on parade on 20 July. I was advised that it would be difficult to prove he was drunk, as nothing was done on the spot; so we fell back on two other charges – those of being late for parade and of absenting himself without leave before parade was dismissed. The taking of evidence occupied all the morning. The men had baths in the afternoon and I took one during the officers' hour from 5.00pm till 6.00pm at Noulette Wood.

The stretcher bearers came in at 9.00pm and we had more part-singing in the officers' mess. I had a pretty busy day but managed to write some letters.

Friday, 28 July 1916 – Hood Battalion, Aix-Noulette, B Company attached to RNDE

I dined in the Hawke headquarters mess in Noulette wood. An article on public schools from the pen of Jerrold, their adjutant, was produced by Herbert (their assistant adjutant, as I gathered) and we spent the evening discussing his charges that too much attention is paid to athletics. Most of his charges seemed to me trained to meet the case of a small percentage of boys who don't like games. This was apparently his case at Westminster and the personal element seemed to me to enter into his criticisms a little too much.

Douglas Francis Jerrold was the great-grandson of the famous Victorian playwright and journalist Douglas William Jerrold. After attending Westminster School he won a scholarship to read modern history at New College, Oxford but in 1914 he abandoned his studies to join the RND and saw action with the Hawke Battalion in Gallipoli.

In November 1916 his left arm would be shattered in the RND's attack on Beaucourt-sur-Ancre but he survived to write the definitive history of the RND in the early 1920s, in addition to writing and editing other books and a magazine, the English Review. *Jerrold went on to build a career in publishing, eventually becoming the director of Eyre and Spottiswoode and then its chairman in 1945.*

Alan Patrick (A P) Herbert also attended New College Oxford after Winchester where, in his last year, he had begun to write for Punch *magazine. Another veteran of the peninsula, Herbert was wounded on the Western Front in 1917 and during his convalescence wrote* The Secret Battle, *the story of a Gallipoli veteran's nervous breakdown and execution for cowardice. Published to great acclaim in 1919 and a favourite of Field Marshal Bernard Montgomery, it is still seen by many as one of the finest novels of the First World War, one which Arthur Asquith thought 'should be a text book at Staff Colleges'.*

Saturday, 27 July 1916 – Hood Battalion, Aix-Noulette, B Company attached to RNDE

I had rather an interesting ride across the Lorette ridge – through the wood – on my way out to lunch with Hood headquarters at Ablain St Nazaire. It was a hot day. Their billets there are under observation from the enemy trenches and in consequence of the men having orders not to show themselves in the street, the village looked very deserted. It was of course in a state of ruin.

Monday, 31 July 1916 – Hood Battalion, Souchez I sector, left of Vimy Ridge

My company had all arrived in the trenches by 10.30pm but it was midnight before the Drakes were clear. I relieved a company commander called [Ernest] Constable. My company is split up between the Right Front and Right Reserve Lines – a few over being placed in Headquarters Line under Morrison.

I spent the remaining time till morning stand-to-arms in going round my line and in reconnoitring [the] 'Duck Walk' [track] back to battalion headquarters across the open – about 400 yards long – and going out with a patrol of two men who have to patrol from the right of my line to a bombing station down by the Souchez river – some 150 yards or more to the right and rear. It was quite a boyish experience to be challenged by them in a whisper and have to give the password. My dugout which I share with Markey and Dunn in the front line is very ill-ventilated and has a horrible mousey smell. It was a very hot day.

Tuesday, 1 August 1916 – Hood Battalion, Souchez I sector, left of Souchez river

Another very hot day. Like the usual first day of a spell in the trenches, I was chased from morning till night and had an edged correspondence with Egerton over forgotten returns as to direction of wind and a hundred other things concerning ourselves and the enemy which I had had no time to observe.

I dined with Freyberg, Egerton, Asquith, Montagu (assistant adjutant) and McCracken at Hood headquarters. Our dinner was somewhat spoilt by two officers coming in for advice as to Sketchley of DHQ who had insisted on going out by himself to reconnoitre disused trenches by the Souchez river and had not returned. After Asquith had set off to send out a search party we heard by telephone that he was safely back at 189th Brigade Headquarters.

I spent most of the night wiring to the right of 'Northumberland Avenue' behind the firing line and in dead ground. The ground is extraordinarily cut up by shell fire and I nearly sprained my ankle once. About midnight, however, Asquith said he had orders to post a listening party of my men at a post – the whereabouts of which he was the only officer who knew – to the right of my line down by Souchez river, so I accompanied him.

He took us back to C Company bombing station somewhat in rear as he did not know the direct route and we had a very arduous and somewhat painful crawl along the edge of the river through longish grass and a great many nettles – with frequent encounters with barbed and French concertina wire. A number of Boche lights made us constantly halt. Eventually we arrived at a delightful secluded bend in the little stream among long grass and we reconnoitred a direct way back to the right of my front line. I then went back to my wiring till stand-to-arms.

I could not face the mousey smell of my dugout, so after the 'carry on' I got out behind my line into a small shell crater to sleep till breakfast time. Our Stokes gun, however, woke me up at 6.00am and I didn't think it worthwhile waiting for possible reprisals.

Freyberg is like a child with a new toy over his direct control of the Stokes gun batteries at his disposal. Before dinner, at his headquarters, he insisted on my timing how long it took between his telephoning to the trench mortars and their first shot. They were, I thought, remarkably quick in getting off their first shot within a minute and a quarter. Freyberg is delightfully keen on strafing the enemy.

Thursday, 3 August 1916 – Hood Battalion, Souchez I sector, near Souchez river

Another hot sunny day – the usual trench routine. There are elaborate arrangements as to the immediate retaliation on the part of our artillery if the enemy sends over rifle grenades or mines – but at present our telephones are so faulty that a great deal of time elapses before the message gets through.

There was a little excitement about 1.00am (4 August) when Hilton reported that neither [the officer] nor the leading seaman who had posted a listening post on the right of our line on Souchez river, could find it again. When I got up there I found Freyberg and Asquith on the point of going to look for it; so I accompanied them. B, perhaps owing to his wearing glasses, seems to have a very faulty sense of direction in night work. When we had got back I sent him out with a compass to set to find the place again and he only reached our trench by being challenged by a sentry, while he was wandering along 20 yards away and parallel to it.

At 2.45pm I reconnoitred the ground to the right of the 'Kellett Line' as far as the C Company bombing station near the Souchez river with the view of reporting as to whether a continuation of the Kellett Line to the river would be advisable. The ground was not much cut up and except for the good stretch of wire from Company Trench to the bombing station it was pretty free of entanglement. There has been a single line of railway down there, but now the track is hardly recognisable.

One of my leading seamen was before the CO for the contents of a green envelope liable to censorship at the base. The envelope has a printed affidavit which he signed to the effect that there were nothing but personal matters inside and as the latter stated he was near Vimy Ridge and gave the name of his sector, the CO has put him through for court martial. What was more annoying than the indication of the part of the line he was in was the blood-curdling account of a life in which he gave no quarter and expected none, combined with an account of a raid of the German trench on the part of the 20th Londons and in which he had taken no part.

The Kellett Line was named after Brigadier – later Major General – R O Kellett, the commanding officer of the 99th Infantry Brigade from 1915 to 1917.

Friday, 4 August 1916 – Hood Battalion, Souchez I sector, right-front and support lines

A hot, sunny day with a certain amount of strafing on both sides. A Company, I am glad to say, gets all the 'minnies' – our side only suffering from the occasional rifle grenades. A platoon of the HAC

[Honourable Artillery Company] are attached to me for instruction and arrived in the Kellett Line about 10.30pm.

Saturday, 5 August 1916 – Hood Battalion, Souchez I sector, right-front and support lines

Another hot, sunny day. I spent most of the morning writing, as usual, the morning situation report, 'BM [Brigade Major] Daily Reports' and the trench log books. As a company commander in the trenches in France one seems to spend most of one's time writing reports of what one has not had time to observe.

Sunday, 6 August 1916 – Hood Battalion, B Company in 'Dugout Alley', Lorette Spur

It was a lovely still, sunny day and not so hot as it has recently been. Besides writing the usual reports I read about half of a delightful little book by G K Chesterton which consisted of some short sketches of Byron, Pope, Stevenson.

We were relieved by the Drake Battalion at 10.15pm; Turrell of C Company relieving my company. We moved up to reserve trenches on Lorette Spur and had some difficulty in finding our way as we relied merely on guides, whom Hilton had taken down the same afternoon.

The trenches were very familiar to me and it seems inevitable that we should have been in them again. At first it was odd to be 'standing-to-arms' without the contour of Achi Baba facing one. Souchez I Sector has lots of interesting features not the least interesting being the large unheld space of ground down by the river which gives admirable opportunities for scouting. The rats are a novelty, but serve a very useful purpose as scavengers. The mosquitoes are very tiresome.

Monday, 7 August 1916 – Hood Battalion, B Company in Dugout Alley, Lorette Spur

We didn't wake up till 11.30am and, as I had to be at battalion head-quarters in Ablain St Nazaire – 20 minutes' walk away, round the bottom of the Lorette Ridge – I only managed breakfast at 1.00pm. There was a company commanders' meeting at 2.00pm which lasted till 4.00pm.

The battalion is very much split up and we are all in trenches mostly about a mile behind the firing line. I had no time for anything but make arrangements as to working parties and guards. At the end of the company commanders' meeting a message marked 'very urgent' came to the CO asking for the number of horses required to make up to establishment and when shortly afterwards two officers from the 37th Division came to enquire as to billeting in Ablain St Nazaire I felt pretty certain we should shortly be on the move; all the more so when we heard the 37th Division had been moved out from the Somme offensive.

Tuesday, 8 August 1916 – Hood Battalion, B Company in Dugout Alley, Lorette Spur

A fine day. I spent the day mostly trying to reconcile the requirements as to working parties, and the number of men always to be in line as garrison with the order that marching must always be carried on during hours of darkness. I knew it was impossible, but I nevertheless went through the form of tying my head in knots. General Paris and the new GSO [General Staff Officer] 1 Aspinall passed through my lines at 11.00am.

Major General Paris had fretted as the future of his division hung in the balance after the evacuation from Gallipoli and had been overjoyed when the decision was made to keep it together, albeit being subsumed into the army structure.

Lieutenant Colonel Cecil Faber Aspinall had served on Sir Ian Hamilton's staff at GHQ during the Gallipoli campaign and was general staff officer 1 of the RND until his promotion to brigadier general, general staff of an army corps. He later changed his name to Aspinall-Oglander and wrote the British Official History of the Gallipoli campaign.

Wednesday, 9 August 1916 – Hood Battalion, B Company in Dugout Alley, Lorette Spur

On the way over to Ablain St Nazaire I saw one of our aeroplanes brought down over the enemy lines – a mile away – by two German aeroplanes at 4.55pm. It turned round like a leaf falling and didn't fall very fast. As it fell, the sausage balloon it had gone to attack rose again after its temporary prudence.

Friday, 11 August 1916 – Hood Battalion, B Company in Dugout Alley, Lorette Spur

Another day of somewhat harassing messages. I got muddled to the extent of putting one of them in my pocket, as to which I only convicted myself, after having walked into Ablain St Nazaire and convinced Egerton I had never received it. It was a bad ending to an otherwise triumphant discussion.

Saturday, 12 August 1916 – Hood Battalion, Souchez I sector

We had completed relief about 11.15pm. I went out to 'Souchez Station Guard' with Freyberg about midnight. It is a trench about 500 yards to the right of Company Trench and about 50 yards from the Souchez river with which it runs parallel. It is overlooked in the deep dugouts.

There was a heavy sound of mutual artillery strafing about two miles south at 2.25am and a number of red lights went up. It came on to rain about the same time.

Sunday, 13 August, 1916 – Hood Battalion, Souchez I sector

The only rest I got was from 5.00am till 9.45am; the usual unforeseen worries crowding in to a day in which I hoped to get in a little observation from the front line with a view to taking Markey out to somewhere near the German trenches after dark. This was knocked on the head firstly by a bright full moon, and secondly by preparations we had to make for VIENNA at 10.00pm, meaning that gas was going to be let off from the next sector but one on the left.

We took elaborate precautions against a possible change of wind so as to prevent ourselves being gassed, but at 10.00pm, just as Markey and I were listening for the issue of the gas and with a good view of the sector where it was to be released, the message BERLIN came through, meaning that the attack was postponed. The wind must have been too weak.

I had, in making preparations, to walk out to my men in Souchez Station Guard – a very warm undertaking, having, as one had to do, crouch down along an exposed trench in full view from Vimy Ridge. I was up all night till 3.00am.

Tuesday, 15 August 1916 – Hood Battalion, headquarters line, Souchez I sub-sector

CPO [Charles] Throsby, our excellent transport sergeant, was reported from hospital to have died from the wound he received a couple of nights ago at French Dump on the Arras road, where he had brought up rations after dark. As a result they have asked for my best platoon commander, Markey, as transport officer. As he is, in addition, an excellent companion, it is a great bore losing him.

The gas attack that was postponed from the night before last was to take place at 9.00pm but again the wind was not strong enough and the code word BERLIN came through. It was a wet day though it never rained heavily.

I took Collins, one of my officers, out to Souchez Station Guard and on from there to the right of the front line and back by Company Trench at 10.00pm. This escape into the open for 20 minutes walking or so is very refreshing after being in the trenches.

The papers that arrived announced [German General von] Bothmer's retreat from the Strypa [river in the Carpathians]. We are all wondering whether the war has got into a stage like the end of a game of patience, when portions of the enemy's forces will be gathered up like sequences of cards.

One of the results of Markey's going is that B Company mess loses a cook, Berryman, whose formula for answering all questions – 'Don't know, I'm sure' – has been causing us considerable amusement. His place is to be taken by an orderly called C who has been as persistent as a little begging dog to try to get himself established as an officer's servant or in the entourage of the mess. He is not unlike the White Rabbit in *Alice in Wonderland* – at all events, in the animal-like complete absence of humour. His persistence has shown itself in his always standing by to lend a hand in washing up or waiting. I had made up my mind not to give way, but in the absence of a cook, like in other difficulties, principle goes by the board. A few weeks back he nearly managed to slither from the post of B Company orderly at headquarters, into being sergeant major's cook, and it was to knock this on the head I withdrew him to be my own messenger.

Leicester-born 25-year-old CPO Charles Throsby died of his wounds on 14 August 1916 and is buried in Barlin Communal Cemetery Extension near Bethune in France.

Wednesday, 16 August 1916 – Hood Battalion, Headquarters Line, Souchez I sub-sector

Another rainy day, though again there were no heavy showers. There was a heavy bombardment of the enemy trenches in front of our own and the Hawke line – on my left – at 6.00pm for 20 minutes. I had an excellent view of the bursting shells from just outside my headquarters in the Headquarters Line. The sight of so many explosions and so much earth flying about was very exhilarating and especially the leisurely bustle of a big howitzer that made a noise like a motor bus. But I wondered how much damage they did other than knocking trenches about.

Thursday, 17 August 1916 – Hood Battalion, Headquarters Line, Souchez I sub-sector

[In going out on reconnaissance] I had no particular object in view, other than to give two NCOs a little experience and perhaps get close enough to the enemy trench to overhear something. On the right front of our line there is about 200 yards or more of no man's land with nice long grass and thistles for cover. I first of all visited the Listening Post down by the river, and from there went straight out for a distance of what seemed 100 yards. By this time the half moon was so clear and the evening so still, that I thought there was little chance of being able to approach within listening distance, without being heard. I accordingly turned to the left and made my way back.

About 40 yards on the way home we came across a shallow crater, with a shallow, overgrown sap leading back in the direction of the enemy's trench. I reconnoitred it for a few yards and then we came in without being challenged – though two sentries, whom I questioned, said they knew it was us! We were out about two hours and came back wet through about the knees. My revolver, too, was a mass of mud. It was rather amusing all in all, and at times I felt exactly like a tibbins [Kelly's name for a cat], as I felt for a place that wouldn't crackle before I put my hand down. I had a talk with Freyberg before going to bed – wrapped up in sandbags and newspapers.

Friday, 18 August 1916 – Hood Battalion, Headquarters Line, Souchez I sub-sector

During the evening stand-to-arms I found my thoughts turning to the set of organ preludes or Voluntaries, of which those in C Major ('Good King Wenceslas') and the one in E Flat are two. I got an idea for one in B Minor.

Saturday, 19 August 1916 – Hood Battalion, Bois de Noulette

We were relieved by the Drake after dark, but I came on to Bois de Noulette in advance with Egerton at 8.00pm. Freyberg arrived there soon after we did, full of the Somme offensive. He had spent the day motoring down to [the village of] Fricourt with General Philips and going over the ground of the first few days' fighting. It was extremely dark in Noulette woods, and the men were falling about on the slippery paths.

Monday, 21 August 1916 – Hood Battalion, Bois de Noulette

Freyberg had asked me to take the band, owing to our week in Bois de Noulette, and after listening to them a little in the morning, I arranged a practice for 2.30pm. We practised an arrangement of Rubinstein's *Faust* and 'Melody in F' and I found it rather amusing.

I was not in the best of humour at having to take a working party of 200 with two other officers, to bury a cable in trenches 6-feet deep, to the right of 'Ration Trench'. We set out at 7.30pm, started work at about 9.45pm and continued till 3.30am. It was very dark – especially when some very thick black clouds came over about 1.00am and gave us a heavy shower of rain. I got to bed about 5.30am.

Tuesday, 22 August 1916 – Hood Battalion, Bois de Noulette

I remained in bed till lunch-time, trying to rest after last night's working party. In the afternoon I walked out with McCracken, our MO [Medical Officer], to see B Company's 'battle line' in case of hostile attack. This is in the dugout line 'Bois 6', beyond the village of Noulette. We walked on beyond the dugouts, trying to find trenches in front – as the dugouts themselves do not constitute a defensive position. We came in for a Boche artillery strafe, and a 15-pounder 'pip-squeak' shell fell about ten feet from us, without exploding. The doctor actually saw it fall, and skid along, but I was busy with some excellent blackberries I had discovered. I carried it back about a mile, till I found an artillery officer in the Bois de Noulette to hand it over.

Saturday, 26 August 1916 – Hood Battalion, Souchez I sub-sector, right-front and support lines – headquarters in Kellett I dugout

I had been up all night and spent the latter half of the afternoon trying to make up for it. It was wet in showers.

About 11.45pm I took Bentham, PO Livingstone, LS John Joseph Robinson and a bomber called Coombe on patrol. I had told Bentham to explore the sap leading back toward the German trench, which I had come across on the night of 17 – 18 August, and I went out merely to guide him to the shallow crater some 70 yards out from which it started. I had some difficulty in finding it – as it was twice as far as the spot where, from the trench by daylight, I thought I had located it.

After Bentham had got back, Freyberg and Montagu were on their way round the lines and [Freyberg] – thinking [Bentham] had been out to place men at a new listening post, told him to show them where he had been. After passing their crater they began to have misgivings as to where they were being taken (they were both unarmed) and the final discovery that they were well on towards the German wire put them in a state of some perturbation! They at all events woke me up on their way back through Kellett Line to tell me about it. Bentham the next day assured me he had not taken them anything like as far as he'd been with his patrol!

Sunday, 27 August 1916 – Hood Battalion, Souchez I sub-sector, right-front and support lines – headquarters in Kellett I dugout

It rained most of the day and the trenches got into a nasty, muddy state.

[Sub Lieutenant Robert John] Hall took out a patrol of three men, PO Sanderson, LS Eves and a bomber, from 11.30pm to 1.00am. I was up in the line awaiting their return, and could trace their movements by the successive bursts of language as they encountered fresh pieces of barbed wire.

At 7.00pm there was a trench-mortar strafe, and the trench mortar [TM] officer greeted each burst with ecstatic cries of 'That's in the trench', 'There's another!' etc. The CO, Cardy Montagu and I were also looking with no greater facilities for observing the fall of shots, and I could discover very little evidence for the high percentage of hits. The Boche, on the other hand, treated 'Northumberland Avenue' and the left front line to three gorgeous rum-jars [heavy trench mortar shells], which it was a delight to watch. The unfortunate A Company were again busy all night trying to restore mud-heaps into the semblance of a trench. The intelligence, no doubt, will tell us all about the good effect with which our trench mortars bombarded the German trenches at [trench map reference] S. 2. d.

The TM Officer has found that the traverse in which Kellett I dugout is situated is the only good observation post in the line, and a telephone has been established to communicate with the cause of all A Company's trouble. As at each daily bombardment, some half-a-dozen eager heads (and some shoulders) are observable over the parapet above my company headquarters, I can only hope that the inevitable attention to the spot will be delayed until the Drake has relieved us.

Monday, 28 August 1916 – Hood Battalion, Souchez I sub-sector, right-front and support lines – headquarters in Kellett I dugout
Egerton came in with a brigade signal to the effect that Roumania had declared war on Austria and Italy on Germany. Our expectations as to the effect of Italy's intervention 15 months ago, were so falsified by subsequent events, that I hardly like to build too many hopes on the present addition to the Allies' numbers, but on the face of it, it does look as though it should call off half a million men to stop a new menace.

The brigade message ended 'Tell the Hun', so I accordingly told Dunn to see whether he could find a blackboard. He produced something after stand-to-arms, with dimensions of about $2\frac{1}{2}$ feet square, and some pieces of chalk, out of the side of the trench, and I proceeded to indite a message. There was not room, I found, for more than a few words – if one were to make sure of their being visible at a distance – and I finally could think of nothing better than 'RUMANIEN IST MIT UNS', which I chalked on in thick and, I think, legible type.

At 10.00pm I took Dunn, PO Crehin, Leading Seaman Wilson and Able Seaman C Smith out and after taking a line with a compass we made our way out from the Right Front Line (near Company Trench) and steered more or less a straight course for the Boche Trench. After some 125–150 yards, we came to the edge of a thick belt of wire, and as further progress seemed out of the question, Dunn screwed in the iron picket, and after he had withdrawn his men about 30 yards Crehin and I fixed the blackboard on to it and followed them. After getting back to the trench (where we met the CO and Sandilands, the brigade major, just on the point of visiting the Souchez river listening post) I had the satisfaction of seeing the white reserve side of the board showing up clearly in the light of a Boche star shell. I had a talk with the CO and brigade major from 1.00am to 2.15am in headquarters. We were about one-and-three-quarters-of-an-hour on patrol.

Tuesday, 29 August 1916 – Hood Battalion, Souchez I sub-sector, right-front and support lines – headquarters in Kellett I dugout
It was a very wet afternoon and the trenches in many places were ankle deep.

There was a TM strafe at 3.00pm and the artillery were to perform from 3.30pm till 5.00pm but much the most apparent result of the afternoon's work was that A Company's front trench and Northumberland Avenue looked like a ploughed field in the places where three rum-jars had come down on it. Another platoon of the [4th] Bedfords relieved the one attached to me at 11.00pm in a heavy shower, and it was extremely uncomfortable work placing them.

Wednesday, 30 August 1916 – Hood Battalion, Souchez I sub-sector, right-front and support lines – B Company headquarters in Kellett I dugout
Our front trench is subsiding and falling in, owing to the rain, and I think we shall have to decide whether we intend to hold it as a fire-trench or not, and put thorough repairs in hand accordingly. I have been going there the last few days, across the open over the Duck Walk – in preference to going through the mud in Company Trench. The papers were very welcome, with their corroboration of the news that Roumania had come in on our side.

Thursday, 31 August 1916 – Hood Battalion, Bois de Noulette, in huts
It was a fine day and everyone's spirits rose after the recent wet, muddy depression.

About 5.30pm Hall came down to say that a German sentry in their sap, opposite Sap 6, had been waving his hands and exchanging whistle calls with our bombers, and that they had both been showing themselves without any apprehension. He thought an invitation might be successful in bringing him in after dark. I accordingly went up, but neither our whistling, nor my 'Guten Abends' had any success. Someone said the artillery had put some shells into the sap in the meanwhile. I tried again at stand-to-arms, but without success.

I was relieved by B Company, Drake [Battalion], about 11.00pm.

Sub Lieutenant John Bentham noted that Kelly had also tried to woo the German sentry into coming across to the Hood's trenches by singing extracts from Wagner's Siegfried *– the German always carrying on 'where Kelly left off'– but all attempts to entice him had failed. Bentham claims that he and four men later crawled over to the sap one evening and found the German alone at which point they 'hastily put him to sleep, secured his papers, cap and badge, and returned'.*

Friday, 1 September 1916 – Hood Battalion, Bois de Noulette – in huts

We had a very late breakfast and no lunch and parade at 2.30pm. I took the band practice as soon as I had finished parade and we spent an hour working on Elgar's 'Pomp and Circumstance' military march, No. 1. I was surprised at how quickly they picked it up. We also practised Joyce's waltz 'Songe d'Automne'. There is something very appealing about this waltz and also about his other waltz 'Salome'. They're ideal dance music. I dined in headquarters with Freyberg, Egerton, Montagu and the doctor McCracken.

Saturday, 2 September 1916 – Hood Battalion, Bois de Noulette

I took band practice at 10.30am and we worked at Elgar's 'Pomp and Circumstance' No. 1 and Joyce's delightful waltz 'Salome'. Bailey played a rather inferior drum. I find it amusing conducting the band. There are about 18 players (cornets, tenors, horns, baritones, trombones, contrabass-tuba). The men are interesting and quickly improve when things are pointed out to them.

At 6.45pm I took about eight of the band and a couple of officers' servants out into the wood and we learnt H Elliot Button's setting for men's voices of 'Annie Laurie'. We're less at a disadvantage now that we were at Noulette as we have two real tenors.

Callingham came into our mess after dinner and he, Hall, Dunn and I had an interesting talk about Shakespeare and other subjects. The band was playing for the headquarters mess and the dreamy phrases of, Songe d'Automne, and 'Salome' transported one into very different surroundings. The air was still and one might have been listening in the more secluded parts of a garden to the sounds from an enchanted ballroom.

Sunday, 3 September 1916 – Hood Battalion, Bois de Noulette

I was interrupted at 11.00am when on the point of starting band practice by having to investigate a charge of stealing made by an old woman and daughter, who kept an estaminet, against one of my men, [Able Seaman George Henry] Simpson. I was obliged to go into Aix Noulette at 2.30pm with him and witnesses to go into the matter on the spot where the theft was alleged to have taken place. I couldn't see that there was evidence to hang a dog on, but the two women evidently felt that a gross miscarriage of justice was taking place and I finally left with no more agreement than was conveyed in the sullen answers to my questions – *'Que sais-je?'* ['What do I know?'] – there being no evidence as to accused having taken the money. *'Je sais que j'ai perdu mon argent. Quel est mon nom? Moi je suis honnete femme.'* ['I know that my money is gone. My name? I know I am an honest woman'.]

We had more part-singing at 6.30pm but there was a large attendance. I looked in at the headquarters mess after dinner and met the brigade major there. There was a discussion between him and Montagu as to the blame attaching respectively to the military and the politicians in the first year of the war. I took band practice at 11.00am and we practised *Faust*.

Although Kelly found no evidence against George Simpson on this occasion, the young labourer from Darlington had already fallen foul of military authority and by war's end he would boast a lengthy charge sheet and several serious wounds. Even at this point, though, Kelly must have known that in the person of George Simpson there were the makings of arguably one of the Hood's more 'colourful' characters.

There was no doubting Simpson's bravery – he was seriously wounded in the right thigh and admitted to hospital with gastro-enteritis during his service in Gallipoli, would be shot in both knees on 13 November 1916 during the attack on Beaucourt-sur-Ancre and gassed twice in 1918 whilst serving with a trench mortar battery – but it appears he could not stay out of trouble. His many misdemeanours – a range of offences 'prejudicial to good order and military discipline' which included going absent from parade, breaking out of a guard room, being in possession of someone else's rifle and the theft of a four-shilling tin of meat – led to the forfeiture of pay, de-rating and several lengthy periods of incarceration, on one occasion at Parkhurst. In addition, when he was transferred to a machine-gun company he was prevented from going back to the Western Front in May 1917 as he was found to be underage, even though his date of birth at attestation was given as 13 November 1896 and by that time he should have been aged 20! Simpson survived and was demobilised in February 1919, doubtless to reflect in later years on a particularly eventful war.

Monday, 4 September 1916 – Hood Battalion, Bois de Noulette
I spent from 10.00am till midday and from 3.00pm till 5.00pm taking the band practice. We practised a selection from Gounod's *Faust*, the 'Turkish Patrol' (Michaelis), Schubert's 'Serenade', Joyce's waltz 'Salome', a somewhat Schubertian march called 'Punchinello' (Rimmer) and Elgar's 'Pomp & Circumstance', march No. 4.

At about 4.15pm, by which time several officers and men had

collected to hear us, I ceased practice and made then play through all the above things, except 'Punchinello', preceded by Elgar's 'Pomp & Circumstance' No. 1. The CO is wrapped up in the band and is scouring all the neighbouring units for additional players.

Tuesday, 5 September 1916 – Hood Battalion, Bois de Noulette

I have a nice mare, but a canter makes her extremely restless and it is an hour or more afterwards before she settles down to walk. I wrote more letters before lunch.

At 10.00am I took band practice and practised a selection of Sullivan. Most of his tunes seem to me to possess individually and some of them are really good.

Wednesday, 6 September 1916 – Hood Battalion, Souchez I sub-sector, B Company in 'Sunken Road'

Some weeks ago I received a letter from Mrs Cornish asking for the confirmation of some dates relating to Charles Lister's career [for a book on Lister] and this morning was the first opportunity I found of answering her letter. B Company relieved a company of the Drakes in Souchez I sub-sector about 11.00pm.

In the afternoon a dear little kitten about five weeks old caught my attention near the company galley and one of the servants told me it was a present from 'one of the band' to B Company. I accordingly carried it up to Sunken Road in a straw bottle protector. It was very persistent in trying to get out. Three platoons of B Company are in Sunken Road and the officers, Hilton, Dunn, and Collins are with me in a nice dugout with plenty of light. It is an old German dugout and the wall paper and remains of linoleum are still there to remind one of its origin.

While Kelly was always considered to be an eccentric character, his behaviour was starting to become even more noticeably odd to the men of the Hood Battalion. His diary reveals that his natural interest in nature and animals began to develop into an increasing obsession with cats and kittens – Sub

Lieutenant John Bentham observed that Kelly was 'intensely keen' on the animals. 'We never had less than four or five cats in the line with us, and when we went out to rest each platoon officer had to take one in a sandbag.'

Bentham also refers to Kelly loathing having dirty hands, so insisted on wearing gloves, as well as brushing his teeth at least 12 times a day: 'His constant calling to his batman for fresh water to clean his teeth got on everyone's nerves'. What Bentham described as 'very eccentric' would today be diagnosed as symptoms of obsessive-compulsive disorder (OCD) – symptoms which increase when people are exposed to prolonged periods of physical and mental stress but which, in Kelly's case, did not prevent him from functioning as a highly efficient officer and leader.

Thursday, 7 September 1916 – Hood Battalion, Souchez I sub-sector, B Company in Sunken Road

In addition to our own kitten there is a family of four kittens and a shy mother, which inhabit the trench.

I reconnoitred a trench running out at right angles to Company Trench towards Souchez Station Guard. We eventually stumbled across a listening post and were greeted with fixed bayonets and bombs in hand. 'Fred' being the password the following words were exchanged: 'Alt! Who goes there?'

'Fred.'

Sentry (doubtfully): 'Fred what!' as though he were not quite convinced. I got to bed about 12.30pm.

Friday, 8 September 1916 – Hood Battalion, Souchez I sub-sector, B Company in Sunken Road

Another fine day – wind north-west, hence 'gas-alert'.

I was rung up by Egerton about 9.00am telling me to go and see Freyberg who had some good news for me. After speculating as to whether it was leave or the prospect of going to the Somme or something equally exciting I found that Egerton and I had got the DSO and Distinguished Service Cross (DSC) respectively. We owe our good fortune apparently to an official mistake in omitting our names from the last Dardanelles Despatch. Freyberg has apparently given them no peace and the result is honours for both of us! He does fight well for his battalion and is also extremely generous in championing his friends' interests.

Later in the day I saw both mentions in the paper, the reason assigned being 'In recognition of their services with the Royal Naval Division in the Gallipoli Peninsula.' The DSC is generally associated with acts of bravery and I have an uneasy feeling that I shall be expected to live up to the standard!

I dined in headquarters mess with Freyberg, Asquith, Egerton and Montagu. After dinner Edmondson came in to know whether we had seen several airships pass south of us in the moonlight.

**Saturday, 9 September 1916 – Hood Battalion, Souchez I
sub-sector, B Company in Sunken Road**

There was a fairly thick mist till about 10.30am and under cover of it I took a walk through the ruined village of Souchez, which is a little over 100 yards away to the south. If it had been less cold I should have felt tempted to have a bathe in a pool of the river which flows through the middle of the village.

Early in the morning after a perilous chase through a fastness of barbed wire we caught one of the shiest of the kittens and brought it in to give it milk. In the evening Dunn caught the mother of the family, who was very glad of some cheese. She would have no liberties taken, however, and treated us to some awful threats which were occasionally backed up by cuffs of her paws. One of the tamest of her kittens, who came forward to smooth over difficulties and reconcile her to a domestic life, got an awful blow in the face.

At 11.30pm I took PO [David] Weir with me and we walked first to the Souchez sugar refinery on the road to Ablain St Nazaire and from there back through Souchez and up the DuckWalk to the 'Quarry' on the slopes of Vimy Ridge. From here we returned via Souchez Station Guard, having spent about an hour out. All this open ground with the river flowing through it makes this sub-sector extremely interesting. The bare, shelled tree trunks of the wood on the other side of the river reminded me of Dorothea Mackellar's poem 'Core of my Heart, My Country' where she talks of the 'ring-barked' forests 'all tragic to the moon.'

Monday, 11 September 1916 – Hood Battalion, Souchez I sub-sector, B Company in Sunken Road

I wrote a couple of letters to [my commanding generals] about my DSC 'enclosing my cheque' as Asquith suggested! The little, wild-eyed black and white kitten actually came into our dugout of its own accord. The mother comes for her milk, but woe-betide any of her kittens who ventures too near.

Tuesday, 12 September 1916 – Hood Battalion, B Company in 'Maistre Line', Lorette Spur near Ablain St Nazaire

We were relieved by B Company, Drake Battalion (Lieutenant P P Cotton) at 9.45pm. I just managed to catch the black and white kitten before we moved off, and she was carried off in a sandbag by Collins. After we had gone as far as the Souchez refinery, I found a man had taken one of the grey kittens and I relieved him of it. I thus had two kittens to carry, the other being the little baby – [named] Noulette. The bigger kitten was terrified at the sight and noise of the transport.

We reached our trench on the right of Lorette Spur about 11.30pm just as it was beginning to drizzle. The company is mostly in dugouts in the amphitheatre that looks towards the ruined church some 350 yards from my headquarters.

Kelly found himself in a reserve trench – the Maistre Line, named after French General Paul Maistre – which scrawled its way up the southern shoulder and across the crest of the Lorette Spur and then ran down its northern flank. The 'ruined church' he mentions was all that remained of the pulverized chapel of Notre Dame de Lorette, where today stands the vast French National Cemetery and ossuary of Notre Dame de Lorette.

The Lorette Spur was deemed so significant due to the ferocity of the fighting on this sector – and because of its sweeping vistas over to Vimy Ridge and the plain of Douai beyond – that it was selected as the site of the Notre Dame de Lorette International Memorial carrying the names, in alphabetical order, of the 580,000 from all the combatant countries who died in northern France. It was inaugurated on 11 November 2014 by President Hollande of France.

A statue of General Maistre stands 400 yards from the cemetery car park, at the spot where his command post was thought to have been situated in May 1915.

Thursday, 14 September 1916 – Hood Battalion, B Company in Maistre Line, right of Lorette Spur

I had to attend the CO's defaulters [dealing with men who had evaded duty] at 10.00am and it was about 10.45am before I got to the band. We practised [the] *1812* [*Overture*] from then till 12.15pm and again from 3.00pm till 4.30pm by which time we managed to play it right through after a fashion. The tunes, I think are good, but I feel there might be more development of them.

Saturday, 16 September 1916 – Hood Battalion, B Company in Maistre Line, right of Lorette Spur

It was a nice warm day. I had meant to get through a good deal of correspondence but Freyberg dropped in about 11.00am for a talk and Egerton and Montagu about 6.00pm to persuade me to go for a stroll with them.

After dinner I went down to the headquarters mess and conducted a programme consisting of a selection from *Faust*, Joyce's waltz 'Songe d'Automne', the 'Turkish Patrol', Elger's 'Pomp & Circumstance' No. I, Joyce's 'The Vision of Salome', Tchaikovsky's *1812* and the battalion's parade ground tune 'Cave and Bay'. Most of the programme went extremely well, but there were perilous moments in *1812* at which we have not had sufficient work.

Nelson had ridden over from Hersin to dinner and Fish and Hilton were also guests. After the band had departed we sang 'Green Grow the Rushes, O!' It was a very jolly evening.

News had come through in the afternoon to the effect that we were being relieved out of this sector the following day and we were all a good deal excited by our curiosity as to where we are going. It looks as though we would follow the way of all flesh to the Somme – unless there is some other push in preparation.

It was at this time, noted Arthur Asquith, that Kelly conducted the Hood band in Tchaikovsky's 1812 Overture in Noulette Wood to the accompaniment of a bombardment by British gun batteries dug in amongst the trees.

In a letter to Asquith written in December 1916, Maisie Kelly wrote that it was her brother's 'very keen wish to play the 1812 to the sound of real guns' and Kelly himself confessed as much in a letter written on 24 September 1916 to his friend Edward Speyer, so it is surprising that he makes but a passing reference to the concert the Hood Battalion band staged in September 1916.

We have two highly reliable witnesses to the event, however. In addition to Arthur Asquith, who was at pains to mark the event in his copy of the diary to confirm it had happened, we also have Able Seaman Joe Murray's account as described in an interview with Hood Battalion historian Len Sellers before Murray's death: 'The Hood Battalion had a lovely band, and just behind the huts Kelly, a classical scholar and a wonderful musician, was conducting the band, playing Tchaikovsky's 1812 Overture. It was originally composed for the opening of a cathedral in St Petersburg; but at the last moment they thought that the guns firing would affect the stained glass and might break it. But we heard it as Tchaikovsky had wanted to hear it: all the guns were firing like hell.'

Sunday, 17 September, 1916 – Hood Battalion, Bois de la Haie [west of Carency]

The 4th [Battalion] Middlesex arrived about 9.00pm but it was about two hours later before PO [Joseph] Laybourn had reported from the centre section with his platoon. We marched to tents in Bois de la

Haie and as we marched it came on to rain and continued doing so all night.

Monday, 18 September 1916 – Hood Battalion, Hermin

It was raining and blowing when we awoke and both wind and rain increased into a blizzard for the whole of our six-or seven-mile march to Hermin. We left about 11.15am and were by way of lunching on the way. The cooks couldn't, however, get the water on the field kitchen to boil and after 40 minutes' halt we continued our march. We reached Hermin about 3.00pm; wet-through – literally. The wet had trickled down into my boots and my Burberry was little or no protection to my coat and breeches. We got an excellent omelette, however, soon after arrival and an hour or two later our kit had arrived and we could change. Wind and rain ceased about 5.00pm and it was a calm evening.

After dinner I produced the part-songs and in B Company Mess we did 'Annie Laurie', 'The Three Chafers' and 'King Charles' (Grenville Bantock). We also sang 'Green Grow the Rushes, O!' and 'The Wraggle Taggle Gypsies, O!' One of the new officers, Coombes, can read a little. He and some of the others sang a ludicrous thing á la 'My Old Man's a Fireman' – 'Sing a Song of Sixpence' to the tune of 'O Come All Ye Faithful', which I had not heard before.

There was a company commanders' meeting at 9.00pm in which the old and ever thorny question of officers' kit was brought up. Apparently a motor lorry and a few General Service (GS) wagons were quite insufficient to cope with it in yesterday's move! I can't help feeling that with all the present severity and the threats of things, the quantity will not be much reduced.

Arthur Asquith noted that Sub Lieutenant William James Coombes, an ex-school teacher, lost his left leg as the result of a wound sustained in a successful night attack on the Puisieux and River Trenches on the Somme on 3 February 1917 and afterwards became a captain in the Royal Naval Air Service.

Friday, 22 September 1916 – Hood Battalion, Hermin

It was a lovely day and our battalion manoeuvres on a beautiful piece of sloping ground to the south of Ranchicourt were one of the pleasantest experiences of the war.

We left Hermin – a delightful little village and untouched by shells – about 10.00am and after an hour's march reached the scene of the day's work. As a preliminary the company commanders were sent out on their horses to look at the ground and as it was intersected by small trenches (laid out in the scheme of the German trenches on Vimy Ridge, so we heard) we had the most delightful steeple chase over turf and stubble with jumps about every 100 yards in places.

The ground rose towards a couple of woods with an entry between to some turf beyond and from the top there was a glorious view of the Vale of Ranchicourt from Divion up to the high ground beyond Fresnicourt, six miles or so from end-to-end. It is a most lovely countryside.

Before lunch we practised advancing up the slope – about 1,000 yards in length – firstly in 'blobs' and then in four lines. In the afternoon we did some battalion drill on the high ground beyond the woods. As this was the first battalion drill which I have ever seen – much less taken part in – I was in a perpetual state of wondering what was going to happen next. B Company went all astray in the first manoeuvre we had to carry out and after that I lost all sense of shame and applied to one of my new officers – [Sub Lieutenant Lawrence] Matcham – fresh from 2nd Anson – and Levey when in difficulties.

I rode home across country with Freyberg – Asquith and Egerton riding on ahead. I dined with headquarters mess where to my horror I learned that Freyberg had determined on a test mobilisation of the battalion at short notice. The orders were given out at 10.00pm and we were supposed to pass some cross roads nearly half-a-mile away at 11.00pm. We reached the rendezvous at 11.20pm. Neither officers nor men were in the best of moods, as all kits had to be packed and loaded on to a G S wagon. A Company arrived at the rendezvous a few minutes in advance of B Company but it was half-an-hour before

C and D Companies were both present. The battalion had a short route march.

Kelly's statement – that the full battalion drill was the first he had ever seen, never mind taken part in – seems incredible given his months of trench warfare and battle experience at Gallipoli and now on the Western Front but Asquith explains it succinctly in a note accompanying the diary. 'The Drake Battalion, [in which Kelly had served initially] whilst training in Berwickshire, had been too much scattered for battalion drill to be possible and Kelly had only joined the Hood about two days before its departure for Gallipoli where, of course, battalion drill was out of the question.'

Tuesday, 26 September 1916 – Hood Battalion, Hermin
We fell in again at 9.30am and marched off as a battalion from the cross roads in [trench map square] 'F 23' to the training ground near Lubigny. The German trenches on Vimy Ridge have been cut out there – at least it is said they are a copy of them – and the battalion practised an assault of the whole system, consisting of front line, support and reserve.

Freyberg had issued elaborate and excellent type-written orders which he had thought out with considerable care. We made the same assault again after lunch to correct the morning's mistakes. About 3.30pm the companies marched home independently and I rode off with Asquith, Egerton and Montagu to try a high jump that had been erected on the top of the hill. My mare, Phyllis, has evidently not done any high jumping, but I managed to get her over it twice after a fashion and on the way back she also jumped a low rail through a gateway. Excellent news came through from the Somme – Lesbœufs, Morval, and Fregicourt being occupied.

Thursday, 28 September 1916 – Hood Battalion, Hermin
We had another brigade field day on ground near Chelers. Like yesterday the day's operations were rendered valueless by the orders being issued far too late.

At 3.00pm the battalions threw out a firing line over which an aeroplane scouted for an hour and a half – conveying its information back to brigade and battalion headquarters. Every fifth man in the front line had been issued with a Roman candle to show [observers in the aeroplane so they could] jot down the [position of the] line thus displayed – that is after it had circled over the line, emitted a series of long blasts from a claxon horn and had fired a white light. We waited in vain for these signals, though the aeroplane frequently crossed our line and after an hour-and-a-half's struggle against sleep we packed up and marched home.

Markey dined with us in D Company mess and I took down the words of a delightful song beginning 'She was poor, but she was honest' of which [Second Lieutenant Alfred] Brandt and Cockey used to sing snatches. I am always curious as to how far the men themselves are really affected by the sentiment of such songs, for example the last verse:

'It's the same the 'ole world over, It's the poor what gets the blame, While the rich man lives in clover, Don't it seem a b----y shame'. I've never heard them sing this one, but they certainly were sentimental over 'Oh, I Am but a Poor Blind Boy'.

Friday, 29 September 1916 – Hood Battalion, Hermin

We breakfasted at 6.00am and half the battalion – two platoons of each company – marched off to Hermin for the RN Divisional Field day – the first the RND has ever had I believe. It was a foggy, wet day. The Hood Battalion were in reserve in the operation which meant that all our men and officers were detailed for imaginary carrying parties. I thus spent the morning with Freyberg, Egerton and other company commanders watching the various battalions coming out in line. The operations consisted in taking a system of trenches and lasted from about 9.30am till 12.30pm. As far as I could judge they seemed to be well-planned and carried out.

Major Lough (DAQMG or some such thing) told us Greece had declared war on Bulgaria.

Sunday, 1 October 1916 – Hood Battalion, Hermin

The house is full of cats, including the three we brought from Noulette and Sunken Road. Their playing is a perpetual joy.

Monday, 2 October 1916 – Hood Battalion, Hermin

It was a wet, depressing day, but the rain was not too heavy to interfere with the company doing bayonet fighting for the greater part of the morning. The new [army] method of teaching this [with one leg forward as opposed to the navy's method of both knees bent] seems to be excellent and the men like it more than any other subject partly, perhaps, from the clever way in which it is presented as a matter for common sense and not parade discipline.

I had the NCOs in at 2.30pm and read them out some notes about the recent Somme fighting. We heard definitely that we were to go to the Somme in the afternoon and quite shortly.

There was a company commanders' meeting at 6.00pm at which Freyberg passed on the information he had got at a previous battalion commanders' meeting. According to this the authorities are confident the next push forward will be decisive, an absolute ascendency having been established over the Germans, who are said to be demoralised. I think there is more in this than the customary assurances given before one goes in to have one's head broken – but my memory goes back to 4 June [1915] and Denis Browne's charming optimism.

SOMME

OCTOBER 1916–NOVEMBER 1916

'Good hunting'

K*elly was right to treat the claims of the 'authorities' – that German morale was at rock bottom and that one more push would be 'decisive' – with cautious optimism, given the disastrous start to the campaign on 1 July 1916 and the terrific intensity of the subsequent fighting over the weeks that followed.*

The campaign itself had started with such great hopes and the events of that single day have coloured British views of the Somme ever since. Hundreds of thousands of words in scores of books, articles and films have focussed on that infamous 'First Day' and the loss – almost 20,000 dead and nearly 40,000 wounded – of so many eager Kitchener volunteers from locally raised 'Pals' battalions, who had enlisted during the summer and autumn of 1914. Yet the Battle of the Somme was to drag on for another 140 days after that dreadful start, sucking in units from almost every arm of the British Army, regulars, territorials and New Army alike, eventually consuming 419,000 British and between 437,000 and 680,000 German casualties by the time it ended in late November 1916.

Now, as the seasons shifted and slid into autumn, and with the onset of winter fast approaching, long gone were any last vestiges of the heady fervour

with which the British Army had gone into action on the morning of 1 July.
Gone were the long days of summer and the vicious fighting for the charnel
houses which were the Somme woods and the Poziéres Ridge; gone even,
were the set-piece successes which saw the storming of the village fortress of
Thiepval – a 1 July objective – on 26 September 1916, almost three months
behind schedule at a cost of thousands of lives. The days were shortening, the
rains would surely come and the tortured battlefield would soon be awash with
glutinous, grey mud.

As Kelly wrote up his diary on the evening of 4 October 1916 in a camp
behind the lines at Forceville, the Battle of the Somme was into its 96th day.
Just over three months after the high hopes of a successful breakthrough had
been swept away in a maelstrom of machine gun bullets and shell fire on 1 July
1916, the Somme had descended into a titanic struggle of grinding attrition.
A commander of conviction, the British Commander-in-Chief, Sir Douglas
Haig, remained convinced that German resolve and morale was always on the
verge of collapse, and he sought to push whatever advantages his army had
gained in three months of the most fierce fighting imaginable. The results, aside
from several major set-piece encounters, was an almost continuous and rolling
programme of smaller-scale, narrow-front infantry operations supported by
artillery and trench mortars.

Given the worsening weather, the deteriorating conditions on the ground
and the subtleties of the terrain – a hidden dip here, an obliterated parapet
there – these operations were as confusing as they must have been terrifying
for those involved. Often men fought time and time again in nerve shredding,
close-quarters encounters; doing their duty for a few yards of battered trench
and learning the brutal and bloody lessons of trench fighting in a battle which
the German Army, initially refusing to give up a metre of ground – later
admitted had sapped its strength. Those lessons learned by the British on the
Somme – lessons bought with the lives of thousands – ultimately shaped the
fighting capabilities of both the British and German armies for the remainder
of the war and would eventually make the British Army the best in the world
during the final battles of 1918.

The Battle of the Ancre Heights – which began three days before Kelly arrived at Forceville – would see a final drive into the labyrinthine depths of the German stronghold of the Schwaben Redoubt, a field fortress which had dominated the Thiepval spur on the eastern slopes of the Ancre valley and for which the Germans would make the British pay dearly – yard for bloody yard. And when that battle ran its course there would be one final effort to force the Germans out of their defences on the western bank of the River Ancre in a last gasp effort to seize the villages of Beaumont Hamel and Serre – objectives which should have fallen on the opening day – and Beaucourt-sur-Ancre in the valley floor. In doing so the British hoped to gain a tactical advantage for future operations. That final battle would begin on 13 November 1916 and would become known as the Battle of the Ancre. To the names of the illustrious army units which had already fought on the Somme the RND would now be added. It would be 'a last desperate gamble against all odds', according to Douglas Jerrold, the adjutant of the Hawke Battalion in 1916, who later wrote the war history of the RND. It would be the 'last throw of the year's campaigning', the RND representing the 'final piece' left to play.

The RND was at last entering the fray after three months of unremitting shelling, slaughter on an industrial scale and deteriorating weather. The texture of the fighting had changed, the RND had arrived and the sailors of the navy were to fight on the Somme. This would be Kelly's battlefield.

The following appeared as an extensive addendum to the typescript, handwritten by Arthur Asquith on Clovelly Court headed notepaper.

At the opening of this chapter I will quote some passages from the diary which gives an idea of Kelly's savage delight in the detection and exposure of posings and affectations of anything tinged with melodrama or smudged with sloppiness of execution. During a particularly wet time in the trenches he writes:

'On the top of the depressing conditions we found ourselves subjected to very considerable worry and discomfort. An army unit [two platoons plus bombers and two Lewis guns of the 7th Battalion Royal Fusiliers and 1st HAC] came up at 5.00pm to carry out an enterprise the object of which appeared to be to advance the line by occupying Point A [The Mound] a feature of the ground 150 yards in front of part of my front line.

'The first intimation I had that anything unusual was to take place was about 4.45pm when an offhand signaller from the [190th] Brigade arrive at my headquarters and asked whether he could dump his gear for the night as he'd come to take over the telephone. I had not finished having trouble with him before I was sent to battalion headquarters. There I learnt that this army unit was due to reach my headquarters dugout at 5.00pm and that I must withdraw my officers and garrison to make room for their men and their temporary battalion headquarters. From beginning to end our battalion had no advice of anything taking place on its sector!

'I accordingly hastened back but had hardly passed the word for my men to pack up before the garrison of the incoming unit for my headquarters dugout was upon us. On my return I had found the brigade major of the 190th Brigade [Major C F Jerram] and the second-in-command of the army unit established in my headquarters, but, oddly enough, with no provision for lighting, and if I had not been able to give them candles I don't see how they could have carried on.

'The progress of the incoming party up the trenches just happened as an instance of really poor staff work, to coincide with a raid on our left, and, in consequence, the German barrage fire on our communication trenches accounted for some six casualties. On my way down I came across an unfortunate man who, in addition to having a large piece blown out of the top of his skull, was buried in the bottom of the trench. [Later it would be confirmed that Lieutenant Arthur Scott and Lance Corporal Charles McCarthy of the 7th Royal Fusiliers had been killed and eight men had been wounded.]

'All that pertained to the operation was touched by a quaint element of melodrama, when for instance I began, "I hear you are going to take Point A?" I got the answer "Yes! Don't you envy us?" from a company commander. Again, what seemed to me some not quite natural remarks were passed by the hero of the piece, Captain "X" [Captain John Forster, 7th Royal Fusiliers], to the brigade major and vice versa:

'Brigade major: "Bad weather, I'm afraid."

'Captain "X": "Oh, it's just the weather I want."

'Brigade major: "Well, good hunting."

'Hereupon "X" left, and his exit was followed by some such remark as, "Well, if the thing can be done at all, 'X' is the man for it." Everyone agreed and there was an air of gravity as of men looking at a difficult situation, fully and squarely.

'What the party really set out to do I couldn't make out, but that there had been inadequate preparation both in thought and disposition was obvious. They filed out from the Lewis gun position. One would have thought from here they would advance along the road, but, instead, the party spent much time and labour in climbing up a steep disused trench to Point B – one of my posts, which they could have reached direct from my headquarters along the main communication trench – and, in the process, one of their men got buried so deep that he took no further part in the operations, two of our men digging him out.

'From Point B they filed out through the wire and got down into the re-entrant 25 yards or more in front. They then crossed the railway a third time and made for their objective – so I presume. What seems to have taken place is that they happened on some unexpected wire in front of the German trench, were also bombed and returned.

'Captain "X" had not, it seems, made the thorough reconnaissance he was said to have carried out a night or two back. The evidence of much of what was said and done I gleaned from two of my company officers. There was a dramatic note struck by Captain "X" who burst into my headquarters dugout saying, 'I'm very sorry, Sir, the thing's been a ghastly failure!' The colonel administered comfort by saying, "It's for you I'm sorry – I'm sure if you couldn't do it no-one else could," and the chorus murmured, "I am sorry for 'X', he'll feel it more than anything I know!"

'Except for the casualties on the way up I don't think any officers or men were lost or even wounded and the whole enterprise rather smacked of the couplet:

'The King of France with ten thousand men

'Went to Spain and came back again.'

'I was awaiting news of the operations at battalion headquarters with Freyberg and Egerton when the news came – about 10.00pm – that the party had returned without accomplishing anything and I had to take my long-suffering garrison back to my headquarters dugout.

'The colonel and second-in-command of the unit concerned and their brigade major left the sector without risking a visit to our own [battalion] headquarters where Freyberg was waiting for them. Compared with our north country men the rank and file of our visitors are like a lot of schoolgirls.'

For Kelly, mention of this incident was an unfailing source of merriment. The phrase 'good hunting' became a sort of 'family joke' in the battalion and these were in fact Kelly's parting words to Freyberg prior to the action of 13 November 1916 [the opening day of the Battle of the Ancre] in which he lost his life.

Leonard Borwick commenting on Kelly's description of this incident wrote, 'With a little less crudity of the acting one feels that Captain "X" at least might have escaped altogether. I think for Cleg it will have been, as much as anything, that the captain's technique wasn't up to requirements.'

Captain John Forster was, according to his commanding officer, quoted in The Royal Fusiliers in the Great War, *'another of those wonderful fellows who don't seem to know what fear is'. Kelly would doubtless have disapproved of Forster's penchant for blowing a hunting horn to rally his men, a feat he performed to good effect during the German spring offensive on 23 March 1918 when he covered the 7th Battalion's retirement. He died of wounds on 2 October 1918 and is buried at Sunken Road Cemetery, Boisleux–St Marc south of Arras.*

Wednesday, 4 October 1916 – Hood Battalion, Forceville No. 1 Camp

Reveille went at 1.15am and the battalion marched off at 3.10am via Frévillers, Herlin [le Vert], Bailleul [aux-Cornailles] to Ligny St Flochel, where we entrained. We reached the station after a march of about eight miles at 6.45am but did not entrain till 9.00am. It rained for an hour or so, while we were doing so.

We spent the whole day moving at a snail's pace with frequent stoppages to Acheux [en-Amiénois] – by roundabout way. We reached our destination at 8.30pm and by 10.00pm were established in an orchard close by Forceville. It was a tiring day and the majority of officers, having relied on the official time-table, which gave 1.20pm as our hour of arrival at Acheux, had not brought enough to eat.

It was curious that in approaching the greatest battle in the world's history one couldn't hear a sound of a gun – although one could see the flashes. The wind must have been accountable for the complete silence. Frisbury had secured a couple of bottles of (sweet) champagne and they were very welcome on arrival in camp. A and B Companies' officers share a hut.

Thursday, 5 October 1916 – Hood Battalion, Forceville No. 1 Camp

It was a day of rest and I didn't get up till midday. Heald arrived back from Boulogne from the Flying Corps [RFC], to await further orders. It was the first time I had seen him since [a frosty] exchange of notes, making up a coldness that existed between us since the beginning of June, and late at night, on our way home from dinner we had an opportunity of clearing things up. I walked in with him, Bailey, Bentham and Hall to Acheux – a most disappointing place from its lack of shape – at 3.50pm.

On our way back we saw some 'tanks' – our first view of them. The exaggerated accounts I had had of their size made me disappointed with them. I had heard they were 100 feet long – that they carried a six-inch gun and had a crew of 30 men. The ones we saw yesterday had two three-pounder guns, were about 35 feet long and could not have contained more than about ten men. Their height was about 9 feet but they had a framework over that upon which – so we were told – a platform or structure for machine guns is placed. The colours they were painted were certainly fine and python-like. They ran on two caterpillars which rotate the whole length of the side – not on four separate caterpillars as we had been told.

I was reading Robert Bridge's anthology *The Spirit of Man* after our return, when Phil Kershaw suddenly came in – in excellent and characteristic form. He insisted on Heald – whom I had asked to dine in our mess – and me going back to dine with him in Section 18 of the kite balloons whose mess was about two miles away down the main road. An amusing if somewhat uncomfortable conversation ensued in which Phil inveighed against the kite balloons and besought me to try and get him out into the Hoods. A chance remark brought on a discussion about Ireland in which he gave vent to a violent and impassioned outburst against England. This was really uncomfortable and Heald and I argued against him. I didn't know he was as ardent a nationalist, though Heald twitted him with having done nothing for his country – in spite of all his talk. He reminded him of [George Bernard Shaw's] *John Bull's Other Island*. He turned out a 'tender' – a sort of motor bus – for us, which I feel sure was not in order.

Philip Kershaw, who had been wounded severely in the chest during the Gallipoli campaign and had later suffered with typhoid, had transferred from the RND to the RFC – Kite Balloon Section – on 14 February 1916.

Friday, 6 October 1916 – Hood Battalion, Forceville No. 1 Camp

The company had baths at Acheux and did a little bayonet fighting by platoons in the afternoon. I took the band at 8.30pm but there were several important men – such as the euphonium player – on leave and *1812* was impossible. We learnt Elgar's 'Pomp and Circumstance' March No. 2, however, which we had not learnt before. After dinner we had part-singing – about eight of us, including two officers' servants – Lewis and [Able Seaman William] Colebrook. We know 'Annie Laurie', 'The Chafers', 'Maiden, Listen', and Vaughan Williams' 'To the Ploughboy' now and can make a shot at Granville Bantock's 'Give a Rouse'. We also sang some choruses out of the Hood books.

I went to a cinema at 5.15pm with Heald, Hall and other officers and enjoyed it a great deal. Charlie Chaplin, however, is not as funny as his great reputation would have one believe.

Saturday, 7 October 1916 – Hood Battalion, Forceville No. 1 Camp

I had a perfectly delightful day riding to Amiens with Arthur Asquith. In the middle of a wet week we found the only fine day; cloudy in places but fresh and with not too little sun. Our route lay through Varennes and Contay – a total distance of about 28 kilometres. We did both journeys, to and fro, in two hours 40 minutes and my mare, Phyllis, did wonderfully well.

It was divine, open country and in places we could canter for miles along the side of the road. We had lunch at the Hotel du Rhin – excellent food, but slow waiting, as is usual in war time – and in the afternoon we had baths and did some shopping, besides looking at the cathedral. The west end and the choir stalls are sandbagged up against artillery fire or bombs. This was only done last year, so the verger told me.

Tuesday, 10 October 1916 – Hood Battalion, Forceville No. 1 Camp

It was a fine day. I left Collins with the company and took the remainder of the officers and Heald – who is attached to us for messing – up to La Signy Farm, to show them the lie of the land in view of our forthcoming advance. We also took eight runners to familiarise them with landmarks.

After dinner we sang part-songs in a little partition of a hut at the back of the quartermaster's store. We are not very popular while we are practising and there was quite an air of an early Christian secret gathering about our meeting. We practised Elgar's 'After Many a Dusty Mile' which we had not tried before. A Hawke officer, Gold, took a bass part.

Looking due east from the protection of an observation post constructed in the cellars of La Signy Farm, Kelly's eyes would have scanned a landscape steeped in blood and tragedy.

La Signy Farm was a headquarters position located almost exactly halfway between the villages of Colincamps – behind British lines – and Serre, a village fortress which lay behind four lines of German trenches and belts of barbed wire at the northern extremity of the Somme battlefield.

The French had forced the Germans back to their present positions in a great battle in June 1915 before the British had arrived. Serre was attacked on 1 July 1916 by the Kitchener volunteers of the Pals Battalions from the towns and cities of the northern industrial heartlands of England: Accrington, Barnsley, Bradford, Durham, Leeds and Sheffield.

On that one dreadful day alone, the 31st Infantry Division, of which these proud citizen soldiers were a part, lost 1,349 killed, 2,169 wounded, 74 missing and eight prisoners – a total of 3,600. Not a single inch of ground had been gained. On the same day, just a little further south, the Germans defending the village of Beaumont Hamel and their front-line trenches, scrawling their way down the slopes into the valley of the River Ancre beyond, had repulsed further British attacks with correspondingly crippling losses.

Now, towards mid-October, these villages still stood defiant, hindering further British progress on their left flank across the hard-won Thiepval Ridge above the eastern slopes of the Ancre. As the nights drew in, Commander-in-Chief Sir Douglas Haig felt that one last push to secure Serre, Beaumont Hamel and Beaucourt-sur-Ancre in the Ancre valley itself would give them a sound tactical springboard for future operations when the better weather came again in 1917. Kelly knew that at some point soon he would be required to take part in that 'advance'.

Wednesday, 11 October 1916 – Hood Battalion, Forceville No. 1 Camp

An excellent band of the King's (Liverpool) Regiment played in Forceville from 10.30am till midday. There were about 50 players and in addition to the brass instruments there were flutes, oboes, clarinets, bassoons, horns and a xylophone. The bandmaster indulged in mannerisms which one felt were as essential to his calling as a prima donna's airs and graces are to hers – something intensely artificial yet amusing. He had a waxed moustache.

Freyberg was beside himself with excitement in the brigade head-quarters, while Colonel Wilson and I talked to the staff captain. He was very busy enquiring from the bandmaster how he should set to work to get eight clarinets, a bandmaster, etc. I took the Hood band in the afternoon. We sang some part-songs in an isolated outhouse after dinner and Frisbury came in with characteristics keenness to take part.

Thursday, 12 October 1916 – Hood Battalion, Forceville No. 1 Camp

When we got back I heard that Sketchley, GSO 2, had been killed and General Paris wounded the same day in the trenches. I am sorry about Sketchley, whom I liked personally and thought highly of in his professional capacity. A shell, so I heard later, made a direct hit on his head and broke General Paris's leg in two places.

Freyberg and the doctor (McCracken) came in after dinner and we had part-songs and choruses. It was Heald's last night with the battalion and we made merry. During dinner we had an amusing little profession of faith on the part of Hilton on the subject of swearing and a sort of Shavian attack on his uncompromising attitude by Heald.

Ivan Heald transferred to 25 Squadron of the RFC as an observer/gunner and, after one triumphant duel in the air, his Fe2b, piloted by Second Lieutenant D S Johnson, was shot down in flames and crashed in woods near Thelus, Arras on 4 December 1916. He is buried, along with Johnson, in Cabaret Rouge Cemetery, Souchez. A book of Heald's newspaper columns and letters from Gallipoli and France (Ivan Heald – Hero and Humorist) was published in 1917.

Friday, 13 October 1916 – Hood Battalion, Forceville No. 1 Camp

The company was all used up in working parties – so I rode with Asquith to Auchonvillers in order to explore the trenches in front of Beaumont Hamel. After getting to a point where we could see Thiepval and the high ground beyond the Ancre on the right, we set out along the front line, in the direction of Serre.

During about three-quarters of a mile I don't believe we saw more than 30 men and at times we began to wonder whether the men hadn't been withdrawn for a bombardment. The support trenches seem to be equally lightly held. Our intention of keeping to the front line was frustrated by a part of it having recently been blown in and we were obliged to retrace our steps some 300 yards and make our way to the rear, to a piece of dead ground called 'White City'. To do this we have to descend a tunnel which led down under the parapet and then led back for several hundred yards. It seemed to be the only communication from the rear to that part of the front line. We ate some sandwiches at White City and then made our way back to Auchonvillers by a communication trench called 'Sixth Avenue'.

Asquith was very much himself in asking a host of questions of the men he met in the trenches. They have evidently been told they must give no information to strangers and were mostly on the defensive.

I was sorry to miss Sketchley's funeral, which took place in Forceville at 3.00pm.

I dined with Alister Kirby in his mess at Varennes. He is on the staff of General de Rougemont, but the latter was not there as he is acting as GOC 63rd RND until the new General Chute (or Short?) arrives.

On the afternoon of 12 October 1916, Major Sketchley had been accompanying General Paris on a visit to the line when a German shell landed 400 yards along Sixth Avenue communication trench north of the village of Auchonvillers. The explosion broke the general's leg, with fragments hitting him in the head and arm and fatally fracturing the skull of his trusted staff officer. Sketchley's head wound was so severe that he died the same day in the 148th (1st Royal

Naval) Field Ambulance in Forceville. He still lies in Forceville Communal Cemetery and Extension.

Kelly had heard that General Paris's leg had been broken in two places and his injuries were such that they later resulted in its amputation. He and Asquith must have passed the exact spot when they traversed the same trench the following day. There would be a brief interregnum before a new commanding general, appointed by the army, could take over. In the meantime that role was filled first by artilleryman Brigadier General Cecil de Rougement and then, for one day only on 16 October, Brigadier General Charles Trotman of the RND who had stood in for General Paris on several occasions previously.

Kelly and Alister Kirby shared many things in common: both had attended Eton, both were members of Leander Club in Henley-on-Thames and both were Olympic rowing gold medallists. Kirby had rowed for Oxford in the Boat Race every year from 1906 to 1909 but was only in the winning crew in 1909. He was captain of the Leander Eight which won the gold medal for Great Britain at the 1912 summer Olympics in Stockholm. On the outbreak of the First World War Kirby was commissioned into the 1/5 (City of London) Battalion (The London Rifle Brigade) and had various staff jobs. He died of illness in March 1917 and is buried at Mazargues War Cemetery, Marseilles, France.

With Kirby being on the staff of the temporary CO of Kelly's RND, for the time being too they shared a commanding officer, but Kelly knew a permanent replacement for General Paris was on the way. He was not quite sure of the new general's surname or indeed how to spell it, but he would come to know it only too well soon enough. With General Paris – a Royal Marine through and through – gone the army grasped the opportunity to install a true 'army' man in his place in an effort to curb the independent spirit of the sailors of the RND and in so doing bend the unit to the army's will. The 'new broom' selected to sweep away the nautical customs so beloved of men like Kelly and instil some good, old-fashioned army 'spit 'n' polish' into what was seen as an undisciplined, unruly and untidy mob, was Major General Cameron 'Tiger' Shute. Shute – a veteran of the Sudan in the late 1880s – was certainly no Archibald Paris. He had no affinity with and *therefore no love or sentimentality for the RND and, as events turned out, the feeling grew to be entirely mutual.*

Shute, officially appointed on 17 October 1916, was particularly critical of what he saw as the lax trench management of the RND; kit strewn about willy-nilly and rifles plastered with mud. During a snap inspection of the Hood trenches held by Kelly's B Company one day in late October 1916, Sub Lieutenant John Bentham recorded that Shute picked up a mud-bespattered rifle and declaimed loudly that such neglect was disgraceful and was typical of the low standards of the RND while a 'white-faced anxious looking Kelly' hovered in the background. Kelly's blushes were spared by Sub Lieutenant Hall who chimed in to say that it had been salvaged the previous night and was awaiting return to a dump for cleaning. His quick wit saved the day: Shute congratulated Hall on his zeal while, according to Bentham, 'Kelly nearly had a fit and our CO [Freyberg] grinned, well knowing or guessing the real truth.'

It was also said that Shute was extremely critical of the layout and construction of the RND latrines, fearing that poor field hygiene in atrocious conditions could lead to outbreaks of dysentery. Following another particularly critical inspection of the trenches by their new general, A P Herbert of the Hawke Battalion penned a poem which encapsulated the feelings of most men – officers and ratings alike – of the RND towards General Cameron Deane Shute:

> *The general inspecting the trenches*
> *Exclaimed with a horrified shout*
> *'I refuse to command a division*
> *Which leaves its excreta about.'*
>
> *But nobody took any notice*
> *No-one was prepared to refute,*
> *That the presence of shit was congenial*
> *Compared to the presence of Shute.*

And certain responsible critics
Made haste to reply to his words
Observing that his staff advisers
Consisted entirely of turds.

For shit may be shot at odd corners
And paper supplied there to suit,
But a shit would be shot without mourners
If someone shot that shit Shute.

Monday, 16 October 1916 – Hood Battalion, Ancre I sector, Hamel

Reveille went at 3.30am and the battalion moved off at 5.30am. Asquith took the company commanders and company sergeant majors on in advance and guides took us to our various parts of the line.

B Company is on the right and holds posts with sentry groups dotted about in the marshy ground on the [River] Ancre, half-way between Hamel and St Pierre Divion. Their names are 'Bastion', 'Picturedrome' – both on slightly higher ground a few yards to the west of the railway – 'Lancashire', 'Crow's Nest' and 'Corner Post' to the east of the railway; and 'Bridge Post' and 'Mill Post' – the former only held at night – just by the Ancre.

On the high ground 200 yards or so to the west, I have a platoon in 'Sloane Street' in a portion of the trench which is less blown about than most of the trenches thereabouts. My company headquarters is in 'Kentish Caves', a system of excavations in the side of a mound like a railway embankment. Across the river is Thiepval Wood and the high ground on which both sides send a great many shells.

The position is rather like the Souchez I sector, the Ancre and the Souchez rivers flanking the positions in a similar way and the high ground beyond in this case corresponding to Vimy Ridge in the other. This is, if anything, more beautiful and interesting than Souchez. There are about 350 yards of low-lying wooded ground between me and the rising ground on the further side of the Ancre and the river has two channels – so it seems from my night wanderings to the Mill Post – and supplies the water for numberless pretty pools. The German line is about 350 yards in front of Bastion Post.

The battalion is covering a front of some 1,500 yards. Battalion headquarters are back behind a ridge this side of Hamel. The relief was complete about 11.00am.

We were to have two guides sent us to relieve the Mill Post – a red house in a yard with a shell-proof shelter inside it – after dark, but as these had not put in an appearance by 9.00pm I took out the reliefs and brought in the corporal and his party of the 11th Royal Sussex – the battalion we had relieved. After having made a complete tour of my line I turned in at 11.00pm.

We were shelled during the night, one of my men, [Able Seaman George] Miller on Corner Post, being killed while I was posting the Mill House Post, 200 yards to the right. Also while I was patrolling along 'Peche Street' from Sloane Street to the front line with Bentham and an NCO or two, we had some heavy shell bursts near us. It rained during the remainder of the night. I have Sub Lieutenants Bentham, Dunn and Matcham up with me – the remainder of my officers being left in Forceville.

Tuesday, 17 October 1916 – Hood Battalion, Ancre I sector, north-east of Hamel

We were shelled pretty heavily throughout the day and the neighbourhood of my headquarters was not healthy. About 4.00pm the Germans, who had been observed leaving their support trench up the hill beyond the Ancre, attacked on the top of the ridge in two waves, but were unsuccessful. I missed seeing the attack.

I spent a busy day – a large part of it being spent at battalion headquarters at company commanders' meetings, etc. Freyberg is very wisely trying to forecast our part in the forthcoming attack and is making all preparations to meet difficulties in advance.

Just as we were beginning dinner Bentham came in with the

information that the [Royal Engineers'] Dump near Corner Post was on fire. I at once sent for water tins and went there with him, Dunn and [CPO Taylor]. It was not as bad as I feared. A sandbag or two of SAA [small arms ammunition] was smouldering – with occasional cartridge explosions, so Bentham said, though none occurred when I was there; but, in amongst them were a number of Mills bombs [grenades]. I poured a couple of tins of water on and then left orders for two more to be emptied on to make sure. The remainder of the ammunition and bombs were a few yards away. A shell had apparently set the sandbags smouldering.

I visited the Mill Post and my other posts with Freyberg and [Sub Lieutenant William] Arblaster, the Scout Officer, between 12 midnight and 1.00am in pouring rain.

Wednesday, 18 October 1916 – Hood Battalion, Ancre I sector, north-east of Hamel

There was a company commanders' meeting at 10.00am at which information of the Boche lines in front of us, culled from the experience of some officers who had come out of the last advance alive, was imparted to us. We are being relieved of half our sector on the left and it looks as though the battalion frontage will be my frontage of posts and 100 yards or so to the left.

We are in that stage of preparation for big operations in which counter-orders come several times a day. It is exciting and amusing. I spent the afternoon concerting a night patrol with Montagu, (D Company) to search the ground in front of us and examine the German wire, 200 yards in front of Bastion Post and we took great pains to point out the lie of the ground to the officers and NCOs concerned. At the same time General Philips went up to Bastion Post to observe and later Colonel Wilson and some Hawke officers came up.

At 5.30pm I was summoned to battalion headquarters and told our patrol was washed out. In its place a large party was to go out and dig a new line about 60 yards from the Boche wire – a second and third line being added later – as an assembly point for the attack. To most of us this seems like giving away our intentions and another advantage lies in the whole new line being in enfilade from the German lines and strong-points to the right.

I spent an hour and a half after dinner reading the notes as to enemy dispositions dugouts, mg [machine gun] positions, etc. It was not reassuring reading. I made the rounds with Dunn about 11.45pm. My 34 men in Sloane Street were relieved by C Company about 10.00pm. There was pretty heavy shelling from 9.30pm on.

Thursday, 19 October 1916 – Hood Battalion, Ancre I sector, B Company in Kentish Caves and outposts

During lunch some tank officers looked in. Colonel [St George] Smith of the Dublins [10th Battalion, Royal Dublin Fusiliers] and some of his officers came in after lunch and I showed them round the posts until I was sent for to headquarters.

Frisbury has sent in my name, Dunn's and CPO Taylor's for mention for putting out the fire in the RE Dump the night before last. Our intentions were excellent and full of courage but the extent of the fire was not such as to call forth much heroism. I remonstrated but was told the report had already gone.

There was a company commanders' meeting about 4.45pm. A dozen of Christopher's Port and a pie from Amiens arrived after breakfast and cheered us up.

The trenches are very wet, though they are nowhere – at least those I frequent – more than 9 inches deep in water. In taking out a sentry to the advanced 'Night Listening Post' on the left of Bastion Post the spirit seized me to explore the ground in front and carry out the object of the cancelled patrols of the night before. I found the party, which had been sent out at midnight, digging within about 30 or 40 yards of the German wires. I had heard them making a noise like the building of a city from Bastion Post, but the Boche, who had been strafing the empty ground earlier in the evening, seemed to be unaware of their proximity.

I had some difficulty in finding the Night Listening Post from which I had emerged; I had in the meantime made a thorough reconnaissance of the green bank on a 100 yards front and I got in over the wire about 50 yards to the left in the unoccupied part of the line which has been so knocked about by shell fire.

On the way back to my headquarters I explored what I took to be a trench marked 'Foch Street' on the left of 'Burel Avenue' about 60 yards behind Bastion Post. My object was to find trenches in which men could be massed overnight for the impending attacks. I went along it for about 100 yards at which point it became too much damaged for use. A very close shell and the instinctive certainty of others to follow made me beat a hasty retreat into Kentish Caves. The second burst at the entrance into which I had just turned. The sector had been shelled pretty heavily earlier in the evening but from midnight till 3.00am things had been quieter.

Friday, 20 October 1916 – Hood Battalion, billets in Englebelmer
Harmsworth, the Hawke company commander, arrived shortly after 9.00am and I gave him information about the sector his company was relieving a few hours later. We were relieved at midday and got to Englebelmer about 2.00pm. I found Phyllis, my mare, waiting for me at Mesnil and I rode on in advance to find our billets.

Just as I was leaving Kentish Caves about half-a-dozen German aeroplanes appeared to our north and performed a number of evolutions, which gave me the impression that they wished us to think them very fine fellows. There was only one Allied machine up at the same time and it had perforce to be somewhat circumspect, but it hung about in the offing until more of ours arrived like vultures out of the blue and then the visitors disappeared. Their planes glisten and look much cleaner than ours.

Soon after we were installed at our billet in Englebelmer a balloon drifted over from the German lines at a great height and travelling at a great pace with the strong wind. We had the satisfaction of seeing it attacked by several of our planes and come down. Presently a second balloon came over but this one was left unattacked. Someone suggested they might contain pamphlets intended for the French population and that they had no-one in the car.

There were two delightful blue-grey kittens in Kentish Caves and a large blue-grey cat that frequented Corner Post and Mill House Post.

Lieutenant, The Honourable Vere Sidney Tudor Harmsworth of the Hawke, was the son of newspaper proprietor Harold Harmsworth, later 1st Viscount Rothermere. He had served in Gallipoli and was killed on 13 November 1916.

Sunday, 22 October 1916 – Hood Battalion, working party in no man's land

I had to take a digging party of about 200 men to work on the assaulting trenches that are being dug in front of Bastion Post. During the final halt in Roberts Trench when I was sending the men out in parties of 25 or so, each with an officer, to be put to work – a good many rum-jars or minnies – I am not sure which – began to come over.

Monday, 23 October 1916 – Hood Battalion, Mesnil

We lost our way down the communication trenches in the early morning. We knocked off work at 4.15am – and arrived back at Mesnil in separate parties about 6.00am.

I had a fairly busy day hearing, receiving and digesting orders as to our dispositions in the impending attack. There was a company commanders' meeting at 8.15pm at which I was incapable of keeping awake and after half a dozen times at which Frisbury caught me winking he, very kindly, told me I had better go to bed. There was a tense bombardment at 6.00am.

Tuesday, 24 October 1916 – Hood Battalion, Mesnil

It was a dull, wet day and, late in the afternoon, I heard that Y Day had been postponed one day – the day after tomorrow instead of tomorrow.

I was very thankful as we are behind hand with our arrangements in B Company.

I spent the whole day reading and detailing orders. There was a company commanders' meeting at 2.00pm.

The Boche sent over some gas shells in the morning, some of which fell near B Company galley. Several men were slightly gassed and later in the day it transpired that the CO and some of our men who had been up to the trenches on a working party had got a dose of gas from shells. Some of the men were sick and the others felt queer. I wrote my diary up to date after dinner.

Kelly was now getting used to rotating in and out of the trenches and outposts on the Ancre I sector in front of the village of Hamel on the west bank of the River Ancre.

His reference to Y Day, written in a village just under a mile and a half behind the line, is revealing. During the planning for an attack the day of the assault was always written as Z Day, with the three days leading up to it designated W, X and Y, the reason being that attacks were often liable to multiple postponements – as Kelly's entries testify – and inserting the names of days would have entailed much re-writing and reprinting of orders, possibly resulting in confusion. The noting of Y Day is a clear indication that he knew his involvement in a forthcoming attack was inevitable. Nevertheless, he still found time in the trenches to work on his 'Elegy to Rupert Brooke' and a piano sonata whilst he waited for word of the impending assault.

Wednesday, 25 October 1916 – Mesnil, in my billets
Bentham and I set out at 8.00am to try and get a view from the high ground on the opposite side of the river, of the railway bank at the side of the German trenches which we are shortly going to assault. There is reported to be a deep dugout with entrances in this bank and I was anxious to locate them if I could.

We walked across the river just above Authuille and then took the road up to Thiepval intending to make for the 'Crucifix', which is marked on the map, but is not in existence, so I hear. Two officers we met on the way told us, however, that we should see nothing there, so we turned to the left and walked through Thiepval Wood – or, rather, the appalling wilderness of tree-stumps and lacerated earth which was once a wood – to the northern edge where we got an excellent view of both the bank and the trenches over which we are to advance.

We came back straight down the river and crossed it by 'Northern Causeway', some planks laid on what appeared to have once been a road or railway (now submerged). They were shelling Mesnil with biggish shells most of the morning – at intervals of about three minutes – and as we came down the river two shells pitched in the water and made a lovely fountain. The river marsh ground looks lovely in spite of the desolation and there are a number of moor hens in it.

I spent an hour or more after lunch lecturing my two Lewis gun teams on the forthcoming operations and their part in them. It rained all the afternoon and the attack was again postponed. We are living in great discomfort, though the cellar in which we sleep is safe and not as uncomfortable as the not-rain-proof ground floor room where we eat and sit.

Thursday, 26 October 1916 – Hood Battalion, Mesnil

We heard that Sub Lieutenant Davidson, a Canadian who joined the Hoods in January 1916, was missing and that PO Colquhoun, whom he had taken out on patrol with him, had come in with his arm almost blown off.

There was to have been a raid by the Hood tonight which Davidson and Chapman were to have taken. Davidson had gone out to reconnoitre and according to what I heard that Colonel Wilson had said, he vowed he was going to bring in a prisoner. It seems very uncertain as to what actually occurred. Colquhoun apparently said they had got into the German trench and had been bombed. The Fifth Army is carrying out raids all along its front but the Hood raid has been washed out. It strikes me as a dangerous policy on the eve of a big attack in which all ranks have been instructed in the details and objectives.

I set out with Montagu, [Sub Lieutenant William] Bolus, and one of my Lewis gunners at 10.30am with the intention of getting to a part of the recently-captured ground across the river from where we could see Beaucourt and the line of our forthcoming advance there. We walked up the hollow behind Thiepval Wood until we got on to the high ground north of it. From here we walked over the shell holes till we got into the front line and were rewarded with an excellent view of our objective.

The land up there is an indescribable scene of desolation. For acres and acres (as far as one could see) there was no sign of vegetable life, just a sea of lacerated earth, with here and there the traces of a former trench system. The presence of these former communications was confirmed by the corpses – some of them horribly mangled and with glazed eyes, others trodden almost out of sight in the mud. Though I was quite callous – as everyone appears to be at the front – I was haunted by the sense of terrible tragedy – the triumph of death and destruction over life. Why is it, however, that such a terrible scene as this does not touch such depths within one as a phrase by a great poet about such things? Art goes deeper than reality: perhaps because in reality one is one's own artist and does not see the full significance of the facts.

There were no trenches in the sense of an excavation or breastwork giving protection – just tracks from shell hole to shell hole. The ground was newly won and no-one knew the way about – if such a thing could be known of a wilderness which had no features. We must have been near the celebrated Schwaben Redoubt. I cut my finger rather badly on a jagged piece of shell case, but luckily found a tube of iodine in my pocket. I had a bath in the afternoon and rubbed my feet and legs with whale oil, which has been issued as a protection against the cold and wet. Hilton had gone back to Hédauville when I returned.

Sub Lieutenant George Thorold Davidson was from Toronto in Canada. Bizarrely, even though evacuation preparations were well under way, he had sailed from Alexandria for Gallipoli on Boxing Day 1915 and joined the Hood on the day Kelly and the battalion left the peninsula. Posted as 'missing' on 26 October 1916, his name appeared on an official German list forwarded through the Red Cross in April 1917 stating that he had died on 26 October 'whilst prisoner of war'.

PO Alexander Colquhoun, his patrol partner that night, had been severely wounded in the face and right shoulder by a German bomb and after crawling back to the Hood trenches was evacuated to hospital in England; first at Frensham Hill and then the Royal Naval Hospital Haslar in Gosport, Hampshire. He never served again, being discharged as 'unserviceable' in April 1918 due to the severity of his wounds.

Friday, 27 October 1916 – Hood Battalion, Mesnil

It was a dull cold and windy day with occasional showers of rain. In B Company we spent the morning experimenting, with Leading Seaman John Robinson in full marching order less haversack, as to the best way of attaching a pick first and then a shovel. In the afternoon, with the platoon commanders, I went into the question of the allocation of Mills bombs, buckets of twelve bombs, picks and shovels, wire-cutters, phosphorous [P] bombs and brassards for P bombers to the different platoons – quite an effort of organisation was required.

After dinner I wrote a harp part for my 'Elegy in Memoriam Rupert Brooke' and made a copy of it. I had not a score and had to write the numbers of bar rests from memory. Y Day has again been postponed.

Wednesday, 1 November 1916 – Hood Battalion, in huts at Puchevillers

Although the weather's far from dry, Freyberg thinks the attack may come off within the next ten days – or not at all. In either case he thinks we shall be taken back some way behind the line for the winter, with a view of training us for the spring offensive.

The task of the Hood Battalion during the coming battle – operating on the extreme right flank of the RND's attack – would be to break through the first three lines of German trenches, clear and consolidate them and press on to capture three more lines of trenches, eventually taking the village of Beaucourt-sur-Ancre, located hard by the parallel curves of the road and railway line sweeping out to the north-east along the valley floor.

In command of B Company, Kelly would lead the Hood's right flank, hugging the line of the road and railway just yards from the flooded valley floor and clearing German strongpoints and dugouts in the embankments above the road. In this he would be assisted by a protection party of one company of 1st/1st HAC fighting along the railway to his right. It was an extremely difficult task but Kelly and the men of the Hood were confident of success.

Friday, 3 November 1916 – Hood Battalion, Puchevillers

I spent the day in bed until 6.00pm, when I got up to attend a company commanders' meeting.

Freyberg had just been to a meeting at which the order had reached him from General Philips that the naval salute in the division was to give way to the military salute and that beards were to cease. I have always feared that my beard would sooner or later be called into question, but I don't mean to give in without a struggle! Both Colonel Wilson and Freyberg said they didn't feel they could pass on the order.

I read about half of A P Herbert's *Half-Hours at Helles*, and found the verse excellent reading. He is assistant adjutant in the Hawke Battalion. The brigade was inspected by General Shute in the morning and he expressed himself as being very agreeably surprised by its excellence – somewhat of a contrast to his recent memorandum on its lack of discipline.

Saturday, 4 November 1916 – Hood Battalion, Englebelmer

We made a start at 9.15am and marched some 13 miles to Englebelmer via Toutencourt, Varennes and Hédauville. It was fine but the roads were very muddy. I was acting as second-in-command at the rear of the column – that is, behind the 1st Line transport – and had a lively time preventing lorries and other cars from passing us on the march. A Red Cross ambulance with a Canadian ASC officer sitting by the driver tried to rush by, but I managed to get my mare in front of him and with the column on the right of the road he was helpless and had to fall in behind.

We reached Engelbelmer about 3.15pm. I drafted a letter to Boosey & Co. for Freyberg, asking for the usual strength of bands, at 6.00pm. He is anxious to have a really good band of about 36 players with a good percentage of woodwind. Our present band is *hors de combat* by reason of recent casualties.

Monday, 6 November 1916 – Hood Battalion, Ancre I sector, B Company in Kentish Caves and outposts

I spent from midnight to 2.00am going round the line. It was not raining.

We were told at the meeting earlier in the day that today was W Day and that the attack would probably come off, whatever the weather. I accordingly went up to the trenches prepared for [storing] the bags and left my diary behind – though I wrote some of it in a pocket book for subsequent inclusion when I should get my kit again.

Tuesday, 7 November 1916 – Hood Battalion, Ancre I sector, B Company in Kentish Caves and outposts

It was a dull day with a south-west wind and heavy rain which put the trenches in an unspeakable condition – the water in some places being a foot-and-a-half deep and the mud such as to tear one's gumboots (thigh) off one's feet.

Wednesday, 8 November 1916 – Hood Battalion, Ancre I sector, B Company in Kentish Caves and outposts

I found that General Shute had been round my part of the line and Hall was full of the way he had flourished a copy of my [trench] defence scheme in his face and talked his head off about the conditions and needs of the sector. The general had sent back Nicholson – his ADC – to ask Hall's name and as a corroboration of Hall's story the following paragraphs appeared the following day in the 63rd Division [report] No. G.936/34/1:

'1. The Divisional Commander this afternoon visited the right flank of the Divisional Sector including Kentish Caves.

'2. He noticed a large number of various articles which should be valued, especially near "Shank Hill Road", "Devil's Staircase" and "Lancashire Post". A very intelligent young officer of the Hood Battalion whom he met [Hall] said that he had the matter in hand but there did not seem to be enough men at his disposal to thoroughly carry out this work and a special party should be sent down for the purpose at an early opportunity. Speaking generally the Divisional Commander is very pleased with all he saw on this flank today.'

Hall said he was sure it was the defence scheme – which he happened to have on him – and the picket state, which I had made him prepare, showing the number of sentries on his posts, their reliefs, the hours of work and the number of hours in which they were available for work such as trench improvement or salvage, [that had impressed the general]. I had also insisted on his shaving in the morning and had in fact prepared for the general about as well as could have been done.

Thursday, 9 November 1916 – Hood Battalion, Ancre I sector, B Company in Kentish Caves

Another day in trenches like the preceding ones. In the afternoon, a GSO 3 from another army, a supercilious little fool of about 25, came to see me about the desirability of keeping in touch with the unit across the river [Ancre] and at 10.30pm Freyberg came up to go out there with me to reconnoitre the ground.

After returning, I walked up the road from Corner Post with him and Egerton on the no man's land, where the new assembly trenches have been dug, before returning to go round my sector. The sentries at Lancashire Post had seen a Boche patrol the night before – in the same place as one which had been observed the night before that from Picturedrome Post when the HAC were filing out.

Friday, 10 November 1916 – Hood Battalion, Mesnil

There was an intensive bombardment on our part in the early morning and we did not stand-to-arms.

B Company [Hawke Battalion] under Lieutenant Harmsworth relieved us at 11.30am and we went to Mesnil. It was a bright, sunny day. I was very sleepy at dinner and went to bed soon after.

Saturday, 11 November 1916 – Hood Battalion, Mesnil

It was a dull, misty, still day and the sun did not appear. I walked to Martinsart for a good hot bath at 10.30am.

We had parade at midday and 3.00pm. Early in the afternoon, I tested some fuses of P bombs and we set alight to two P bombs in a trench at the back of our billets on the other side of the road. They emitted a great deal of smoke. There was an officers' meeting at headquarters at 6.00pm. Fish dined with us.

It appears to be X Day.

Sunday, 12 November 1916 – Hood Battalion

POSTSCRIPT TO THE ORIGINAL TYPESCRIPT

BY LIEUTENANT COLONEL BERNARD FREYBERG VC
OFFICER COMMANDING THE HOOD BATTALION
JULY 1915–APRIL 1917

O nly those who have taken part in a large offensive (similar to the one carried out by the Fifth Army on 13 November 1916) can understand the excitement and anxiety in the minds of every responsible officer, in the date Kelly's diary ends so abruptly with the entry:

Sunday, 12 November 1916 – Hood Battalion

That he was interrupted and was never able to finish is obvious. Kelly, who was most systematic about his life, had probably just settled down to write of his tiring day of inspections, finishing up perhaps with that most precious of all entries – the record of the thoughts and feelings of the fighting soldier.

It has now fallen to my lot to fill up the hiatus that exists between his last detailed entry, dated 11 November 1916, and dawn on 13 November 1916, when he was killed, gallantly leading his men on the slopes in front of Beaucourt.

On 12 November Kelly's company were billeted in Mesnil, and his headquarters were situated in a small cellar; the house, as indeed was the whole town, had been knocked down by shell fire, and it was in this cave, only a few feet square that he, with his company officers cooked, ate and slept, the staircase serving the dual role of chimney and entrance.

Mesnil being in the middle of our gun line, artillery pieces of all calibres were wheel-to-wheel all round us. The general scheme of the offensive included a hurricane bombardment at dawn every morning for a week before the attack was to take place, so that reveille on the 12th was unnecessary. When the bombardment opened all those who weren't already about crept from their holes in the ground and stood in the misty darkness watching the fury of the scene all round.

The mass of field guns were situated forward of our position and their regular drumming sound showed us they were shooting a practice barrage. The long range pieces were mostly behind us and periodically 60-pounders and 6-inch, high velocity guns deafened us with their vicious reports, throwing their shrieking projectiles just clear of our heads. We all stood with watches in our hands, for the time it took the German gunners to answer our bombardment was the factor which determined how quickly the assembled troops must clear no man's land.

Kelly's last day was spent inspecting his company battle arrangements. The rifles, gas masks, iron rations, water bottles and ammunition of all ranks had to be carefully examined, Lewis guns to be checked and the necessary drums of ammunition filled, while the special battle stores, such as Mills and smoke bombs, wire cutters, aeroplane flares, Very lights, SOS signals and carrier pigeons had to be issued to the correct people. Company commanders [like Kelly] lectured to all ranks who were taking part in the attack and then examined the non-commissioned officers to make certain that they understood the main features of the scheme. As we were close to the line and under enemy observation this could only be done by platoons, and necessitated the company commander giving four distinct lectures.

In addition to all this detail work, the men had to be paid early to give them the chance of buying cigarettes and the little luxuries they liked so much, such as sardines, fancy biscuits and chocolate, to supplement their excellently nutritious, but otherwise unattractive battle rations.

POSTSCRIPT TO THE ORIGINAL TYPESCRIPT

All this part of the work of a company commander, Kelly attended to, with that meticulous accuracy and conscientiousness which were so well known to all of us who had come in contact with him as a soldier. The examination of his non-commissioned officers and platoon commanders he did most carefully, no detail being too small, and it kept him going until about 3.00pm, which was about the time I think he started to write his interrupted entry, with less than an hour before the approach march commenced.

At 3.00pm I sent for all company commanders, as there was a difficulty over filling the men's water bottles, the pipeline from Englebelmer having been cut by shell fire. At 3.30pm we commenced our approach march; the first part of the journey to Hamel we negotiated by communication trench in the daylight, but forward of this village we moved after dark, marching to our places in the assembly area, across the open, by a taped route.

Kelly's B Company was on the right next to the river and they were shelled as they marched into position. The Hood Battalion assembled on the left of the River Ancre on a front of 300 yards, our foremost troops being within 200 yards of the enemy front line. We formed up in four distinct waves of about a man to every two yards. Immediately behind our battalion were two others – the Drake and the 1st Honourable Artillery Company – assembled upon the same plan, so that in all there were 12 waves, one behind the other, on a piece of ground 300 yards wide and not more than 100 yards deep. In front of each wave were four subaltern officers whose duty it was to direct all movement during the battle and to re-organise the salvage whenever the opportunity allowed.

The Fifth Army was attacking upon a front of eight miles, so that assembled for four miles on either side of us a similar number of men were lying. The attack, which was delivered in considerable force, was divided into three distinct phases. Our part, the first, was to double forward, getting as close as possible to our barrage as soon as it opened, ready to rush in and dispute the possession of the enemy trenches every time our artillery lengthened their range.

All 12 waves on our sector were lying in the open, but they had orders to get into the recently-dug assembly trenches in event of hostile artillery fire. At the last minute and without any warning, a bearer sub-division of a field ambulance, a light trench mortar battery and a large detachment of pioneers and engineers arrived, making the assembly area look like a crowded thoroughfare, until everyone settled down for the night. It seemed impossible that the enemy would not see the commotion.

After assembling, the orders were for the men to put on greatcoats and sleep, while Kelly posted a strong Lewis gun patrol to cover our front, and prevent enemy patrols from discovering us in position. Only one officer and man per company were to remain awake.

It was not very cold, and the moon was in its second quarter. The assembly was complete by 9.00pm and from then on until 5.45am next morning, when we launched the attack, we were in a most dangerous and vulnerable position. Had we been shelled we should have suffered terrible casualties, and would most probably have been too disorganised to go forward at the appointed time.

At midnight I went across to speak to Kelly. I had to step over men the whole way. It was unnaturally quiet and the men all seemed to be sleeping, but closer inspection showed them to be awake, lying with their heads on their arms, peering out into the night. One or two spoke, but the bulk seemed to be in another world. I asked some of them next night, as we lay in the shell holes in front of Beaucourt, what they had been thinking about. They all said their thoughts had been of the future – not one thought of the past.

Kelly was in very high spirits, certain, as he always was, that the war would be over in the spring, and he came back to my headquarters in a shell hole for 'brigade time', which was to come through to us at midnight [to synchronise watches].

There had been some enemy shelling, but not on our sector, otherwise the night had passed in complete silence. At 5.15am there was a slight stir all along the line, the ghost-like sound of thousands of invisible men sitting up and taking off their great-coats, and in spite of all warnings to the contrary, there came the slight mellow note of the wooden entrenching tool handle rattling against the bayonet scabbard. Then came the unmistakable smell of tea, and we knew for many it would be the last meal.

At 5.30am with only 15 minutes to go, I went across quickly to see if everything was in order. Kelly's patrol in front was in trouble; some bombs were thrown and it retaliated as it withdrew.

On the extreme right, overlooking the River Ancre, (with only a minute or two before the attack was launched) I had my last talk with Kelly. We had been daily companions for the last two years, and he, Asquith, Egerton and I were the sole survivors of the battalion which left Avonmouth for Gallipoli at the commencement of 1915. I wanted to wish him 'God speed', but somehow it seemed too theatrical; instead we talked rather awkwardly and synchronised our watches.

At 5.45am all the assaulting troops fixed bayonets. They muffled the bayonet catch and ring and the rifle muzzle in their great-coats to strangle the metallic click as the two engaged. Everything was now ready, save the opening and closing of the bolt as they stood up, to transfer a round from the charged magazine to the chamber.

The officers stood counting the minutes to zero, looking at their luminous watches, and at 5.45am to the second the whole sky in rear was suddenly lit up by hundreds of flashes, and the guns had fired. Our 12 waves were now running hard to get clear of the enemy counter-barrage, which we knew would fall on our assembly area in eight minutes.

When the attack started it was pitch dark and, in addition, the 'Scotch mist', the smoke and fumes from the bursting shells didn't improve the visibility, while any illumination from the shower of enemy lights and the flashes from shell bursts was minimised by the thickness of the atmosphere. Some of our men were hit by our own shells, which they had risked to make certain of getting [to] the [German] trenches and dugouts before the enemy could recover from our bombardment. Some of our own guns were shooting short into the attacking infantry, especially on the right, and we were frightened for B Company. Everywhere was confusion – we were nearly choked by the acrid stink of cordite, while in the luminous mist all we could see were lines of hurrying figures, whose arms, rigidly holding their rifles, gave them a wooden appearance.

Our task in the battle was to capture the front-line system, and as we advanced north-east by compass, we passed the burning entrances of dugouts, which showed that the phosphorus bombs were taking effect. These dugouts were elaborate two-storeyed affairs, with electric light and in one case, a lift. It was in rushing a strongpoint at the entrance to one of these, that Kelly was killed. Owing to our heavy casualties it was never known really how it all happened, but it appears that someone on Kelly's left had missed a dugout entrance from which the enemy were starting to shoot.

The situation was critical. Unless the strongpoint was captured at once, enemy machine guns would pop up everywhere; hesitation would have endangered the success of the whole attack on our front. Kelly, being an experienced soldier, knew this quite as well as he must have known the risk he was taking, when with the few men he had hastily gathered, he rushed the machine gun. A few of the men reached the position, but Kelly with most of them was killed at the moment of victory. It was but one of several similar incidents which made our success that day possible.

At 6.05am we had completed the capture of our objective. The losses in the attack were enormous. Of the 25 officers and 535 other ranks who had crossed no man's land 20 minutes earlier, but 4 officers and 250 men answered the roll-call on the captured objective.

And in return for these losses, barring some prisoners and a few enemy dead, we could only point to a strip of pock-marked, muddy ground 300 yards wide and 800 deep. But Kelly and others of our best men did not give their lives in vain, for that night these few square yards of ours were the most precious on the Western Front. They enabled the Fifth Army to exploit northward and they were the sole avenue of approach by which reinforcements could be hurried during darkness to our weak line in front of Beaucourt. Had the enemy been able to close this hole between themselves and the river, the history of the Battle of the Ancre, and perhaps of the Somme itself, would have to be re-written.

AFTERWORD

The Hood's medical officer, William McCracken, found Frederick Kelly 'shot through the back of the head just opposite a dugout in German 3rd line'. He later wrote to Arthur Asquith saying that he 'felt like crying' at the sight of the dead and the plight of the seriously wounded.

Cardy Montagu, himself badly wounded but a survivor, reported that 'poor Cleg was killed right at the beginning. He was so enthusiastic about the whole thing and told me the night before he was really glad to be in it'. Montagu reported that Kelly, setting an example at the head of his men, had led an attack on a bombing post and that the Germans had 'showed fight'. According to his adoring sister Maisie, it was Kelly's wish that he might die in such a fashion. Certainly on the eve of battle, it appears to have been his expectation.

Kelly's fellow B Company officer John Bentham described the night of 12/13 November 1916 as one of 'feverish excitement' as the men made ready for battle and wrote home in case of 'accidents'. Big holes had been dug at the rear which the officers were told were burial pits being made ready for those who would be killed. Kelly had made a speech after which he and his platoon officers had exchanged cheques for £5 as a 'grim sort of joke', the idea being that those who survived cashed the cheques of those who were killed. According to Bentham, 'Kelly seemed insistent that he would not survive'.

Kelly was dead but the Battle of the Ancre was far from over. The inspirational figure of Bernard Freyberg, always visible, always leading from the front, had galvanised the remnants of the Hood and Drake Battalions and urged them on to take further objectives that day – earning a well-deserved VC in the process – but it took the best part of another day of hard fighting and heavy losses to finally subdue the village of Beaucourt.

The battle itself ended on 18 November 1916 but the final death toll for the November campaign bore witness to the enormous cost to the RND – 100 officers and 1,600 men killed and some 2,500 wounded. Kelly had died in the last big set-piece battle of the Battle of the Somme and his unfinished piano sonata, which he was working on right up to the last few days of his life and which ends very abruptly, jarringly, unnervingly in mid-phrase on an unresolved chord, serves as an epitaph for him and for all those of the RND – for all those of all nations – who perished before their time.

According to Arthur Asquith's contribution to his obituary in the *Eton Chronicle*, the 'highly strung' Kelly had died as he had lived; warm-heartedly loyal to his friends yet intolerant of insincerity, pretentiousness and bad manners.

Unlike many men of the Hood whose remains were never found, Kelly's body was at least recovered and was buried west of the railway in the Ancre valley and close to the centre of the village of Hamel. It remains a mystery why, given that the nearest CWGC cemetery at Hamel is just 350 yards from his original burial place, his body was disinterred and moved to Martinsart Military Cemetery more than a mile away. Kelly's final resting place is a peaceful spot today and, for a CWGC cemetery, very unusual – his headstone is not of the more usual white Portland stone or the marble now being used but of red

Corsehill or Locharbriggs sandstone. Back in England, his heartbroken sister Maisie commissioned sculptor Eric Gill to design a calvary which still stands today close to his home in Bisham. This distinctive memorial commemorates him and others of the village who gave their lives in the war.

In December 2012 Kelly's medals – his Distinguished Service Cross, still in its Garrard & Co. case, 1914–15 Star, British War and Victory medals with an oak leaf clasp signifying his mention in despatches, together with a London Olympics 1908 commemorative medallion – went under the hammer at auction and were sold for £6,500. These are tangible reminders of Frederick Septimus Kelly the warrior.

And of course there is his music, which continues to grow in popularity today, particularly in Australia the land of his birth. Within Kelly's lifetime, Frank Bridge conducted his 'Elegy' at a Memorial Concert for Rupert Brooke held at Rugby School on 28 March 1916, although without the important part for harp which Kelly added at the end of October 1916, shortly before his death. Bridge repeated it – this time complete with the harp part – at the Wigmore Hall, London on 2 May 1919 at a memorial concert for Kelly himself. Attended by family and friends, Jelly d'Arányi was disappointed at not being invited to play his violin sonata. Two years later Donald Tovey, another composer, conductor and writer whom Kelly knew well, conducted it at the Usher Hall, Edinburgh, on 19 February 1921.

Despite the widespread acclaim which greeted his 'Elegy', Kelly's music gradually slipped into obscurity for much of the twentieth century and would have done so entirely were it not for several recordings made of the 'Elegy'. But thanks to enthusiasts in Australia, led most notably by the music scholar and former director of the Canberra International Music Festival, Chris Latham, his body of work has re-entered the public's consciousness in both Australia and in Britain.

On 17 August 2014, as part of a special concert commemorating the centenary outbreak of the First World War during the BBC's Proms Season, Kelly's 'Elegy' was performed by the BBC Scottish Symphony

Orchestra at the Royal Albert Hall in London. But perhaps the most poignant performance of all was that by the National Symphony Orchestra during the 2012 Henley Festival. There, on the banks of the Thames, just a few feet away from Kelly's greatest triumph as an oarsman in 1908, his 'Elegy' was performed to acclaim. On that summer's evening almost a century after the piece had been written, there was no place more appropriate to hear the 'Elegy' written for Brooke and remember two of the great and enduring achievements of this most remarkable of 'temporary military gentlemen': his rowing and his music. As Kelly's friend and flatmate Leonard Borwick observed, the 'Elegy' was 'no mere expression of personal grief or loss, but, a symbol, rather, of the continuity of life, giving thoughts of Eternity – and as such, for all who knew or loved "Cleg" Kelly, his own most fitting and perfect memorial.'

ACKNOWLEDGEMENTS

I t seemed a good idea at the time. Towards the end of a blisteringly hot day criss-crossing the peninsula in May 2012, Graham hit on the idea that we should take a dip in the Aegean off what was, in 1915, known as X Beach to do one final session of recording. We had travelled to Gallipoli with Steve Williams, the British rower who had won Olympic gold in 2004 and 2008 in Athens and Beijing to follow in the footsteps of Frederick Septimus Kelly for a radio documentary on his life to coincide with the London 2012 Olympics.

We had spent all day recording at some of the locations which we knew, from his war diary, would have been well-known to Kelly during his service on the peninsular with the Hood Battalion of the RND from late April 1915 to early January 1916; W Beach or Lancashire Landing, the RND dugouts near Skew Bridge Cemetery, the sites of the White and Brown Houses just off the Krithia Road and his final position overlooking the deep Kereves Dere Ravine. At each spot, as we uncovered more of Kelly's story and peeled back more and more layers of his character we began to be drawn into the story of a man who, like Steve Williams, had achieved the sporting pinnacle of Olympic gold more than a century earlier.

We knew from his diary that Frederick Kelly had swum off X Beach several times and Graham was keen for Steve to do the same and to record his reflections. We were dry and dusty; the water was warm and inviting so we duly donned trunks and waded in, talked, splashed around a little and recorded the audio but we had not reckoned on the jet black sea urchins lurking on the rocks below. Emerging in some pain several minutes later with bleeding feet Jon stopped counting at 25 urchin spines firmly embedded in toes, soles and heels. The Gallipoli Peninsula had claimed another casualty almost 97 years to the week after Frederick Kelly had been wounded in action – ironically in the right heel – during fighting south of the village of Krithia on 4 June 1915.

The following month we travelled to France to complete the recording of the documentary. Our exploration of his desire to continue composing his music, in the context of his war experience on the very sites on the Somme where he wrote some of his final phrases, enabled us to gain a deeper understanding of Kelly's complex personality. The documentary has succeeded in bringing the life and music of Frederick Kelly to the attention of a wider audience with its transmission on both local and national BBC radio but neither of us realised that when we first set out on our journey to tell the story of this remarkable man – a journey which ended at his grave near the village of Martinsart – that it would eventually lead to the publication of his personal experience of war exactly 100 years after he first set foot on the Gallipoli Peninsula.

Our grateful thanks then are due to Christopher Page, ex-naval officer and expert on the RND at war and the acclaimed biographer of Arthur Asquith, who first alerted us to the existence of the diary in typescript during our research for the documentary and to Arthur Asquith's grandson, John Rous for his kind permission in allowing us to edit and publish it in addition to using his grandfather's original preface. If it were not for Arthur Asquith's foresight and tenacity in reading, typing and initiating an early edit of the diaries – and more importantly keeping a copy of them in the Asquith family – then there would simply be no book today. As the custodian of the Asquith typescript John Rous has been an enthusiastic supporter of the project from the very beginning and his help and encouragement are truly appreciated.

In particular we must thank members of Frederick's Kelly's extended family, particularly his great-niece Carol Jones in Australia who has given her wholehearted support to our desire to bring his words to a wider readership from the start. She gave freely of her time in a busy schedule to meet Graham in Oxford during a trip to England and she and her husband Terry, who were touched when they eventually heard our documentary 'Down Under', granted us permission – as did Carol's relative Janine Arundel – to use their great-uncle's words. It was Carol who put us in touch with Kevin Gordon in the USA, the owner of the originals of John Singer Sargent's sketches of Kelly and his sister Maisie, and we are grateful to Kevin for his warm-hearted assistance in allowing us to reproduce them.

Although we knew immediately what a remarkable and unique document Kelly's war diary was we also knew that to bring Kelly to life – both on radio and now in the pages of his diary – we needed the wholehearted support, help, advice, and encouragement of a great many people with a deep knowledge of and expertise in their particular field. One cannot get much better then, than a double Olympic gold medallist to help tell the story of a fellow Olympian and we could not have chosen a better person to 'present' the documentary. Not only did Steve Williams throw himself into our project his was an intelligent, articulate voice when he began to tread the fields of battle in Kelly's shoes. He also agreed to commit his thoughts to a foreword to this book. Thank you Steve, for your support and companionship, even when Jon threatened to run away with both your gold medals at Istanbul airport!

Len Sellers is a recognised expert and author on the RND in general and the Hood Battalion in particular. His book on the Hood and his

RND magazines are required reading for anyone interested in the sailors who fought on land. Len has been an enormous source of help and encouragement. Thank you Len.

We should also like to record our gratitude to the following – in no particular order – who, during the course of our research, provided valuable assistance either in the loan of or permission to use documents, maps and photographs or commented on early draft sections: Dr Robert Treharne Jones – Press, Publicity and Marketing Officer at Leander Club, Henley-on-Thames and the 'the voice of rowing'; Chris Latham – former Director of the Canberra International Music Festival and expert on Kelly's wartime compositions; Dr Thérèse Radic of the University of Melbourne – author of *Race Against Time*, Kelly's earlier diaries; Duncan McClarty – Editor of BBC Radio Berkshire who supported the original documentary; Mike Read – broadcaster and biographer of Rupert Brooke; the staff of the River and Rowing Museum at Henley-on-Thames who were always patient and helpful in answering our queries; George Newlands of maritime books specialists McLaren Books of Helensburgh, Scotland and Mélanie Mahé.

Our thanks also go to Peter Hart – author of marvellous books on both Gallipoli and the Somme who read draft extracts of certain sections. Peter has been known to lay the blame for any errors on those of his friends who read early drafts of his work so Peter, if anything is wrong with the sections you read it's all down to you!

Our agent David Luxton has once again worked his magic to ensure that we were able to get Kelly's voice heard. He is that rare thing in a literary agent; a history graduate and a sports fan, whose interests almost exactly match our own. What more could an author ask? His calm advice and constant encouragement are greatly appreciated.

At Blink Publishing, Acquisitions and Rights Director Clare Tillyer initially recognised the potential in Kelly's diary and Joel Simons, our editor, has acted as a trusted point of reference, assuming the all-important and invaluable role as sounding board and 'critical friend' with huge reserves of patience. Thanks also to Lucian Randall, our copyeditor, and to our publicist Lizzie Dorney-Kingdom whose energy on our behalf was admirable.

At home, our wives and children – Jon's wife Heather and daughter Georgia, and Graham's wife Ursula and children Maisie (who, despite what some might think, was not named after Cleg's sister) and Archie (who was not named after anti-aircraft fire) – have continued to indulge our several trips to Turkey and France and our anti-social working habits. We could not do what we do without them and thank them for their constant encouragement, their seemingly limitless patience, understanding and uplifting cups of tea and biscuits which restored the spirit at exactly the moment when the body was ready to give up.

If anyone else who has been kind enough to help us in any way has been missed out, please be assured that this has not been intentional. To those so affected please accept our sincere apologies.

In all instances every effort has been made to seek appropriate permissions where necessary but if, inadvertently, these have been overlooked then we or the publishers should be pleased to hear from copyright holders. If any errors or omissions remain, then they are entirely due to oversights on our part.

Last, but not least, we owe an enormous debt of gratitude to Frederick Kelly. If he had not had the drive, the strength or the perseverance to pick up his pen almost every day to confide his thoughts to his diary – often amid the most terrifying, desensitising and dehumanising conditions imaginable – then this book would not have been possible. To Frederick Kelly then: Olympic hero, noted composer and a true leader of men.

INDEX